T0200847

HIGH-PERFORMANCE HETEROGENEOUS COMPUTING

WILEY SERIES ON PARALLEL AND DISTRIBUTED COMPUTING

Series Editor: Albert Y. Zomaya

Parallel and Distributed Simulation Systems / Richard Fujimoto

Mobile Processing in Distributed and Open Environments / Peter Sapaty

Introduction to Parallel Algorithms / C. Xavier and S. S. Iyengar

Solutions to Parallel and Distributed Computing Problems: Lessons from Biological Sciences / Albert Y. Zomaya, Fikret Ercal, and Stephan Olariu (*Editors*)

Parallel and Distributed Computing: A Survey of Models, Paradigms, and Approaches / Claudia Leopold

Fundamentals of Distributed Object Systems: A CORBA Perspective / Zahir Tari and Omran Bukhres

Pipelined Processor Farms: Structured Design for Embedded Parallel Systems / Martin Fleury and Andrew Downton

Handbook of Wireless Networks and Mobile Computing / Ivan Stojmenović (*Editor*)

Internet-Based Workflow Management: Toward a Semantic Web / Dan C. Marinescu

Parallel Computing on Heterogeneous Networks / Alexey L. Lastovetsky

Performance Evaluation and Characteization of Parallel and Distributed Computing Tools / Salim Hariri and Manish Parashar

Distributed Computing: Fundamentals, Simulations and Advanced Topics, *Second Edition* / Hagit Attiya and Jennifer Welch

Smart Environments: Technology, Protocols, and Applications / Diane Cook and Sajal Das

Fundamentals of Computer Organization and Architecture / Mostafa Abd-El-Barr and Hesham El-Rewini

Advanced Computer Architecture and Parallel Processing / Hesham El-Rewini and Mostafa Abd-El-Barr

UPC: Distributed Shared Memory Programming / Tarek El-Ghazawi, William Carlson, Thomas Sterling, and Katherine Yelick

Handbook of Sensor Networks: Algorithms and Architectures / Ivan Stojmenović (*Editor*)

Parallel Metaheuristics: A New Class of Algorithms / Enrique Alba (*Editor*)

Design and Analysis of Distributed Algorithms / Nicola Santoro

Task Scheduling for Parallel Systems / Oliver Sinnen

Computing for Numerical Methods Using Visual C++ / Shaharuddin Salleh, Albert Y. Zomaya, and Sakhinah A. Bakar

Architecture-Independent Programming for Wireless Sensor Networks / Amol B. Bakshi and Viktor K. Prasanna

High-Performance Parallel Database Processing and Grid Databases / David Taniar, Clement Leung, Wenny Rahayu, and Sushant Goel

Algorithms and Protocols for Wireless and Mobile Ad Hoc Networks / Azzedine Boukerche (*Editor*)

Algorithms and Protocols for Wireless Sensor Networks / Azzedine Boukerche (*Editor*)

Optimization Techniques for Solving Complex Problems / Enrique Alba, Christian Blum, Pedro Isasi, Coromoto León, and Juan Antonio Gómez (*Editors*)

Emerging Wireless LANs, Wireless PANs, and Wireless MANs: IEEE 802.11, IEEE 802.15, IEEE 802.16 Wireless Standard Family / Yang Xiao and Yi Pan (*Editors*)

High-Performance Heterogeneous Computing / Alexey L. Lastovetsky and Jack Dongarra

HIGH-PERFORMANCE HETEROGENEOUS COMPUTING

Alexey L. Lastovetsky
University College Dublin

Jack J. Dongarra
University of Tennessee

A JOHN WILEY & SONS, INC., PUBLICATION

Library of Congress Cataloging-in-Publication Data

Lastovetsky, Alexey, 1957–
  High performance heterogeneous computing / Alexey L. Lastovetsky, Jack Dongarra.
    p. cm.—(Wiley series in parallel and distributed computing)
  Includes bibliographical references and index.
  ISBN 978-0-470-04039-3 (cloth)
1. High performance computing.   2. Heterogeneous computing.   3. Computer networks.
I. Dongarra, J. J.   II. Title.
  QA76.88.L38 2009
  004.6–dc22
                                                                    2009011754

Printed in the United States of America
10 9 8 7 6 5 4 3 2 1

CONTENTS

In recent years, the evolution and growth of the techniques and platforms commonly used for high-performance computing (HPC) in the context of different application domains have been truly astonishing. While parallel computing systems have now achieved certain maturity, thanks to high-level libraries (such as ScaLAPACK, the scalable linear algebra package) or runtime libraries (such as MPI, the message passing interface), recent advances in these technologies pose several challenging research issues. Indeed, current HPC-oriented environments are extremely complex and very difficult to manage, particularly for extreme-scale application problems.

At the very low level, latest-generation CPUs are made of multicore processors that can be general purpose or highly specialized in nature. On the other hand, several processors can be assembled into a so-called symmetrical multiprocessor (SMP), which can also have access to powerful specialized processors, namely graphics processing units (GPUs), which are now increasingly being used for programmable computing resulting from their advent in the video game industry, which significantly reduced their cost and availability. Modern HPC-oriented parallel computers are typically composed of several SMP nodes interconnected by a network. This kind of infrastructure is hierarchical and represents a first class of heterogeneous system in which the communication time between two processing units is different, depending on whether the units are on the same chip, on the same node, or not. Moreover, current hardware trends anticipate a further increase in the number of cores (in a hierarchical way) inside the chip, thus increasing the overall heterogeneity even more toward building extreme-scale systems.

At a higher level, the emergence of heterogeneous computing now allows groups of users to benefit from networks of processors that are already available in their research laboratories. This is a second type of infrastructure where both the network and the processing units are heterogeneous in nature. Specifically, the goal here is to deal with networks that interconnect a large number of heterogeneous computers that can significantly differ from one another in terms of their hardware and software architecture, including different types of CPUs operating at different clock speeds and under different design paradigms, and with different memory sizes, caching strategies, and operating systems.

At the high end, computers are increasingly interconnected together throughout wide area networks to form large-scale distributed systems with high computing capacity. Furthermore, computers located in different laboratories can collaborate in the solution of a common problem. Therefore, the current trends of HPC are clearly oriented toward extreme-scale, complex infrastructures with a great deal of intrinsic heterogeneity and many different hierarchical levels.

It is important to note that all the heterogeneity levels mentioned above are tightly linked. First, some of the nodes in computational distributed environments may be multicore SMP clusters. Second, multicore chips will soon be fully heterogeneous with special-purpose cores (e.g., multimedia, recognition, networking), and not only GPUs, mixed with general-purpose ones. Third, these different levels share many common problems such as efficient programming, scalability, and latency management.

The extreme scale of these environments comes from every level: (a) low level: number of CPUs, number of cores per processor; (b) medium level: number of nodes (e.g., with memory); (c) high level: distributed/large-scale (geographical dispersion, latency, etc.); and (d) application: extreme-scale problem size (e.g., calculation intensive and/or data intensive).

It is realistic to expect that large-scale infrastructures composed of dozens of sites, each composed of several heterogeneous computers, some having thousands of more than 16-core processors, will be available for scientists and engineers. Therefore, the knowledge on how to efficiently use, program, and scale applications on such future infrastructures is very important. While this area is wide open for research and development, it will be unfair to say that it has not been studied yet. In fact, some fundamental models and algorithms for these platforms have been proposed and analyzed. First programming tools and applications have been also designed and implemented. This book gives the state of the art in the field. It analyzes the main challenges of high-performance heterogeneous computing and presents how these challenges have been addressed so far. The ongoing academic research, development, and uses of heterogeneous parallel and distributed computing are placed in the context of scientific computing. While the book is primarily a reference for researchers and developers involved in scientific computing on heterogeneous platforms, it can also serve as a textbook for an advanced university course on high-performance heterogeneous computing.

Alexey L. Lastovetsky
Jack J. Dongarra

ACKNOWLEDGMENTS

We are thankful to Albert Zomaya for his positive attitude to the idea of this book. We would like to thank the anonymous reviewers of the original book proposal for very useful comments and suggestions. We also express our sincere gratitude to the Science Foundation Ireland. Without their support of our collaboration over last five years, this book could not be possible.

PART I

HETEROGENEOUS PLATFORMS: TAXONOMY, TYPICAL USES, AND PROGRAMMING ISSUES

In this part, we outline the existing platforms used for high-performance heterogeneous computing and the typical ways these platforms are used by their end users. We understand a platform as a hardware/software environment used to produce and execute application programs. We also outline programming issues encountered by scientific programmers when they write applications for heterogeneous platforms.

High-Performance Heterogeneous Computing, by Alexey L. Lastovetsky and Jack J. Dongarra
Copyright © 2009 John Wiley & Sons, Inc.

CHAPTER 1

Heterogeneous Platforms and Their Uses

1.1 TAXONOMY OF HETEROGENEOUS PLATFORMS

Heterogeneous platforms used for parallel and distributed computing always include

- multiple processors and
- a communication network interconnecting the processors.

Distributed memory multiprocessor systems can be heterogeneous in many ways. At the same time, there is only one way for such a system to be homogeneous, namely:

- All processors in the system have to be identical and interconnected via a homogeneous communication network, that is, a network providing communication links of the same latency and bandwidth between any pair of processors.
- The same system software (operating system, compilers, libraries, etc.) should be used to generate and execute application programs.

This definition, however, is not complete. One more important restriction has to be satisfied: The system has to be dedicated; that is, at any time it can execute only one application, thus providing all its resources to this application. We will later see how the violation of this restriction can make the system heterogeneous. In practice, the property of dedication can be implemented not only by providing the whole physical system to a single application but also by partitioning the system into logically independent subsystems and providing the nonintersecting partitions to different applications.

High-Performance Heterogeneous Computing, by Alexey L. Lastovetsky and Jack J. Dongarra
Copyright © 2009 John Wiley & Sons, Inc.

Homogeneous distributed memory multiprocessor systems are designed for high-performance parallel computing and are typically used to run a relatively small number of similar parallel applications.

The property of homogeneity is easy to break and may be quite expensive to keep. Any distributed memory multiprocessor system will become heterogeneous if it allows several independent users to simultaneously run their applications on the same set of processors. The point is that, in this case, different identical processors may have different workloads, and hence demonstrate different performances for different runs of the same application depending on external computations and communications.

Clusters of commodity processors are seen as cheap alternatives to very expensive vendor homogeneous distributed memory multiprocessor systems. However, they have many hidden costs required to maintain their homogeneity. First, they cannot be used as multitasking computer systems, allowing several independent users to simultaneously run their applications on the same set of processors. Such a usage immediately makes them heterogeneous because of the dynamic change of the performance of each particular processor. Second, to maintain the homogeneity over time, a full replacement of the system would be required, which can be quite expensive.

Thus, distributed memory multiprocessor systems are naturally heterogeneous, and the property of heterogeneity is an intrinsic property of the overwhelming majority of such systems.

In addition to platforms, which are heterogeneous by nature, one interesting trend is heterogeneous hardware designed by vendors for high-performance computing. The said heterogeneous design is mainly motivated by applications and will be briefly outlined in the next section.

Now we would like to classify the platforms in the increasing order of heterogeneity and complexity and briefly characterize each heterogeneous system. The classes are

- vendor-designed heterogeneous systems,
- heterogeneous clusters,
- local networks of computers (LNCs),
- organizational global networks of computers, and
- general-purpose global networks of computers.

1.2 VENDOR-DESIGNED HETEROGENEOUS SYSTEMS

Heterogeneous computing has seen renewed attention with such examples as the general programming of graphical processing units (GPUs), the Clear Speed (ClearSpeed, 2008, Bristol, UK) Single Instruction Multiple Data (SIMD) attached accelerator, and the IBM (Armonk, NY) Cell architecture (Gschwind *et al.*, 2006).

There has been a marked increase in interest in heterogeneous computing for high performance. Spawned in part by the significant performances demonstrated by special-purpose devices such as GPUs, the idea of finding ways to leverage these industry investments for more general-purpose technical computing has become enticing, with a number of projects mostly in the academia as well as some work in national laboratories. However, the move toward heterogeneous computing is driven by more than the perceived opportunity of "low-hanging fruit." Cray Inc. has described a strategy based on their XT3 system (Vetter *et al.*, 2006), derived from Sandia National Laboratories' Red Storm. Such future systems using an AMD Opteron-based and mesh-interconnected Massively Parallel Processing (MPP) structure will provide the means to support accelerators such as a possible future vector-based processor, or even possibly Field Programmable Gate Arrays (FPGA) devices. The start-up company ClearSpeed has gained much interest in their attached array processor using a custom SIMD processing chip that plugs in to the PCI-X slot of otherwise conventional motherboards. For compute-intensive applications, the possibilities of a one to two order of magnitude performance increase with as little as a 10-W power consumption increase is very attractive.

Perhaps the most exciting advance has been the long-awaited Cell architecture from the partnership of IBM, Sony, and Toshiba (Fig. 1.1). Cell combines the attributes of both multicore and heterogeneous computing. Designed, at least in part, as the breakthrough component to revolutionize the gaming industry in the body of the Sony Playstation 3, both IBM and much of the community look to this part as a major leap in delivered performance. Cell

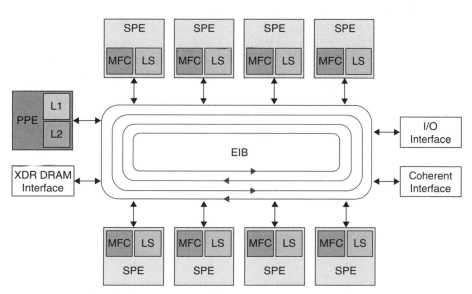

Figure 1.1. The IBM Cell, a heterogeneous multicore processor, incorporates one power processing element (PPE) and eight synergistic processing elements (SPEs). (Figure courtesy of Mercury Computer Systems, Inc.)

incorporates nine cores, one general-purpose PowerPC architecture and eight special-purpose "synergistic processing element (SPE)" processors that emphasize 32-bit arithmetic, with a peak performance of 204 gigaflop/s in 32-bit arithmetic per chip at 3.2 GHz.

Heterogeneous computing, like multicore structures, offer possible new opportunities in performance and power efficiency but impose significant, perhaps even daunting, challenges to application users and software designers. Partitioning the work among parallel processors has proven hard enough, but having to qualify such partitioning by the nature of the work performed and employing multi-instruction set architecture (ISA) environments aggravates the problem substantially. While the promise may be great, so are the problems that have to be resolved. This year has seen initial efforts to address these obstacles and garner the possible performance wins. Teaming between Intel and ClearSpeed is just one example of new and concerted efforts to accomplish this. Recent work at the University of Tennessee applying an iterative refinement technique has demonstrated that 64-bit accuracy can achieve eight times the performance of the normal 64-bit mode of the Cell architecture by exploiting the 32-bit SPEs (Buttari *et al.*, 2007).

Japan has undertaken an ambitious program: the "Kei-soku" project to deploy a 10-petaflops scale system for initial operation by 2011. While the planning for this initiative is still ongoing and the exact structure of the system is under study, key activities are being pursued with a new national High Performance Computing (HPC) Institute being established at RIKEN (2008). Technology elements being studied include various aspects of interconnect technologies, both wire and optical, as well as low-power device technologies, some of which are targeted to a 0.045-μm feature size. NEC, Fujitsu, and Hitachi are providing strong industrial support with academic partners, including University of Tokyo, Tokyo Institute of Technology, University of Tsukuba, and Keio University among others. The actual design is far from certain, but there are some indications that a heterogeneous system structure is receiving strong consideration, integrating both scalar and vector processing components, possibly with the addition of special-purpose accelerators such as the MD-Grape (Fukushige *et al.*, 1996). With a possible budget equivalent to over US\$1 billion (just under 1 billion euros) and a power consumption of 36 MW (including cooling), this would be the most ambitious computing project yet pursued by the Asian community, and it is providing strong leadership toward inaugurating the Petaflops Age (1–1000 petaflops).

1.3 HETEROGENEOUS CLUSTERS

A heterogeneous cluster (Fig. 1.2) is a dedicated system designed mainly for high-performance parallel computing, which is obtained from the classical homogeneous cluster architecture by relaxing one of its three key properties, thus leading to the situation wherein:

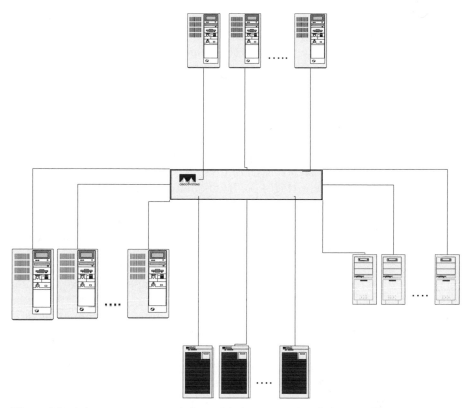

Figure 1.2. A heterogeneous switch-enabled computational cluster with processors of different architectures.

- Processors in the cluster may not be identical.
- The communication network may have a regular but heterogeneous structure. For example, it can consist of a number of faster communication segments interconnected by relatively slow links. Such a structure can be obtained by connecting several homogeneous clusters in a single multicluster.
- The cluster may be a multitasking computer system, allowing several independent users to simultaneously run their applications on the same set of processors (but still dedicated to high-performance parallel computing). As we have discussed, this, in particular, makes the performance characteristics of the processors dynamic and nonidentical.

The heterogeneity of the processors can take different forms. The processors can be of different architectures. They may be of the same architecture but of different models. They may be of the same architecture and model but running different operating systems. They may be of the same architecture and model and running the same operating system but configured differently or using different basic softwares to produce executables (compilers, runtime libraries, etc.). All the differences in the systems' hardware and software can have an impact on the performance and other characteristics of the processors.

In terms of parallel programming, the most demanding is a multitasking heterogeneous cluster made up of processors of different architectures interconnected via a heterogeneous communication network.

1.4 LOCAL NETWORK OF COMPUTERS (LNC)

In the general case, an LNC consists of diverse computers interconnected via mixed network equipment (Fig. 1.3). By its nature, LNCs are multiuser and multitasking computer systems. Therefore, just like highly heterogeneous clusters, LNCs consist of processors of different architectures, which can dynamically change their performance characteristics, interconnected via a heterogeneous communication network.

Unlike heterogeneous clusters, which are parallel architectures designed mainly for high-performance computing, LNCs are general-purpose computer systems typically associated with individual organizations. This affects the heterogeneity of this platform in several ways. First, the communication network of a typical LNC is not regular and balanced as in heterogeneous clusters. The topology and structure of the communication network in such an LNC are determined by many different factors, among which high-performance computing is far from being a primary one if considered at

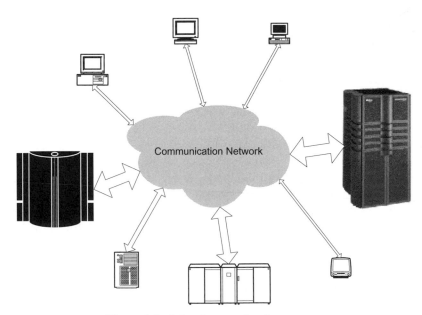

Figure 1.3. A local network of computers.

all. The primary factors include the structure of the organization, the tasks that are solved on the computers of the LNC, the security requirements, the construction restrictions, the budget limitations, and the qualification of technical personnel, etc. An additional important factor is that the communication network is constantly being developed rather than fixed once and for all. The development is normally occasional and incremental; therefore, the structure of the communication network reflects the evolution of the organization rather than its current snapshot. All the factors make the communication network of the LNC extremely heterogeneous and irregular. Some communication links in this network may be of very low latency and/or low bandwidth.

Second, different computers may have different functions in the LNC. Some computers can be relatively isolated. Some computers may provide services to other computers of the LNC. Some computers provide services to both local and external computers. These result to different computers having different levels of integration into the network. The heavier the integration, the more dynamic and stochastic the workload of the computer is, and the less predictable its performance characteristics are. Another aspect of this functional heterogeneity is that a heavy server is normally configured differently compared with ordinary computers. In particular, a server is typically configured to avoid paging, and hence to avoid any dramatic drop in performance with the growth of requests to be served. At the same time, this results in the abnormal termination of any application that tries to allocate more memory than what fits into the main memory of the computer, leading to the loss of continuity of its characteristics.

Third, in general-purpose LNCs, different components are not as strongly integrated and controlled as in heterogeneous clusters. LNCs are much less centralized computer systems than heterogeneous clusters. They consist of relatively autonomous computers, each of which may be used and administered independently by its users. As a result, their configuration is much more dynamic than that of heterogeneous clusters. Computers in the LNC can come and go just because their users switch them on and off or reboot them.

1.5   GLOBAL NETWORK OF COMPUTERS (GNC)

Unlike an LNC, all components of which are situated locally, a GNC includes computers that are geographically distributed (Fig. 1.4). There are three main types of GNCs, which we briefly present in the increasing order of their heterogeneity.

The first type of GNC is a dedicated system for high-performance computing that consists of several interconnected homogeneous distributed memory multiprocessor systems or/and heterogeneous clusters. Apart from the geographical distribution of its components, such a computer system is similar to heterogeneous clusters.

The second type of GNC is an organizational network. Such a network comprises geographically distributed computer resources of some individual

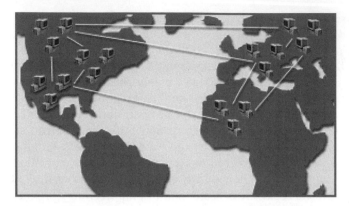

Figure 1.4. A global network of computers.

organization. The organizational network can be seen as a geographically extended LNC. It is typically managed by a strong team of hardware and software experts. Its levels of integration, centralization, and uniformity are often even higher than that of LNCs. Therefore, apart from the geographical distribution of their components, organizational networks of computers are quite similar to LNCs.

Finally, the third type of GNC is a general-purpose GNC. Such a network consists of individual computers interconnected via the Internet. Each of the computers is managed independently. This is the most heterogeneous, irregular, loosely integrated, and dynamic type of heterogeneous network.

1.6 GRID-BASED SYSTEMS

Grid computing received a lot of attention and funding over the last decade, while the concepts and ideas have been around for a while (Smarr and Catlett, 1992). The definitions of Grid computing are various and rather vague (Foster, 2002; GridToday, 2004). Grid computing is declared as a new computing model aimed at the better use of many separate computers connected by a network. Thus, the platform targeted by Grid computing is a heterogeneous network of computers. Therefore, it is important to formulate our vision of Grid-based heterogeneous platforms and their relation to traditional distributed heterogeneous platforms in the context of scientific computing on such platforms.

As they are now, Grid-based systems provide a mechanism for a single log-in to a group of resources. In Grid-based systems, the user does not need to separately log in at each session to each of the resources that the user wants to access. The Grid middleware will do it for the user. It will keep a list of available resources that the user have discovered and add them to a list in the past. Upon the user's log-in to the Grid-based system, it will detect which of the resources are available now, and it will log in to all the available resources on behalf of the user. This is the main difference of Grid-based systems from traditional distributed systems, where individual access to the distributed resources is the full responsibility of the user.

A number of services can be build on top of this mechanism, thus forming a Grid operating environment. There are different models of the operating environment supported by different Grid middlewares such as Globus (2008) and Unicore (2008). From the scientific computing point of view, it is important to note that as soon as the user has logged in to all distributed resources, then there is no difference between a traditional heterogeneous distributed system and a Grid-based heterogeneous distributed system.

1.7 OTHER HETEROGENEOUS PLATFORMS

Of course, our list of heterogeneous distributed memory multiprocessor systems is not comprehensive. We only outlined systems that are most relevant for scientific computing. Some other examples of heterogeneous sets of interconnected processing deviccs are

- mobile telecommunication systems with different types of processors, from ones embedded into mobile phones to central computers processing calls, and
- embedded control multiprocessor systems (cars, airplanes, spaceships, household, etc.).

1.8 TYPICAL USES OF HETEROGENEOUS PLATFORMS

In this section, we outline how heterogeneous networks of computers are typically used by their end users. In general, heterogeneous networks are used traditionally, for parallel computing, or for distributed computing.

1.8.1 Traditional Use

The traditional use means that the network of computers is used just as an extension of the user's computer. This computer can be serial or parallel. The application to be run is a traditional application, that is, one that can be executed on the user's computer. The code of the application and input data are provided by the user. The only difference from the fully traditional execution of the application is that it can be executed not only on the user's computer but also on any other relevant computer of the network. The decision where to execute one or other applications is made by the operating environment and is mainly aimed at the better utilization of available computing resources (e.g., at higher throughput of the network of computers as a whole multiuser computer system). Faster execution of each individual application is not the main goal of the operating environment, but it can be achieved for some applications as a side effect of its scheduling policy. This use of the heterogeneous network assumes that the application, and hence the software, is portable and can be run on another computing resource. This assumption may not be true for some applications.

1.8.2 Parallel Computing

A heterogeneous network of computers can be used for parallel computing. The network is used as a parallel computer system in order to accelerate the solution of a single problem. In this case, the user provides a dedicated parallel application written to efficiently solve the problem on the heterogeneous network of computers. High performance is the main goal of this type of use. As in the case of traditional use, the user provides both the (source) code of the application and input data. In the general case, when all computers of the network are of a different architecture, the source code is sent to the computers, where it is locally compiled. All the computers are supposed to provide all libraries necessary to produce local executables.

1.8.3 Distributed Computing

A heterogeneous network of computers can be also used for distributed computing. In the case of parallel computing, the application can be executed on the user's computer or on any other single computer of the network. The only reason to involve more than one computer is to accelerate the execution of the application. Unlike parallel computing, distributed computing deals with situations wherein the application cannot be executed on the user's computer because not all components of the application are available on this computer. One such situation is when some components of the code of the application cannot be provided by the user and are only available on remote computers. There are various reasons behind this: the user's computer may not have the resources to execute such a code component; the efforts and amount of resources needed to install the code component on the user's computer are too significant compared with the frequency of its execution; this code may be not available for installation; or it may make sense to execute this code only on the remote processor (say, associated with an ATM machine), etc.

Another situation is when some components of input data for this application cannot be provided by the user and reside on remote storage devices. For example, the size of the data may be too big for the disk storage of the user's computer, the data for the application are provided by some external party (remote scientific device, remote data base, remote application, and so on), or the executable file may not be compatible with the machine architecture.

The most complex is the situation when both some components of the code of the application and some components of its input data are not available on the user's computer.

CHAPTER 2

Programming Issues

Programming for heterogeneous networks of computers is a difficult task. Among others, performance, fault tolerance, and arithmetic heterogeneity are perhaps the most important and challenging issues of heterogeneous parallel and distributed programming.

Performance is one of the primary issues of parallel programming for any parallel architecture, but it becomes particularly challenging for programming for parallel heterogeneous networks. Performance is also one of the primary issues of high-performance distributed computing.

Fault tolerance has always been one of the primary issues of distributed computing. Interestingly, this has not been the case for parallel applications running on traditional homogeneous parallel architectures. The probability of unexpected resource failures in a centralized dedicated parallel computer system was quite small because the system had a relatively small number of processors. This only becomes an issue for modern large-scale parallel systems counting tens of thousands of processors with different interconnection schemes. At the same time, this probability reaches quite high figures for common networks of computers of even a relatively small size. First, any individual computer in such a network may be switched off or rebooted unexpectedly for other users in the network. The same may happen with any other resource in the network. Second, not all elements of the common network of computers are equally reliable. These factors make fault tolerance a desirable feature for parallel applications intended to run on common networks of computers; and the longer the execution time of the application is, the more critical the feature becomes.

Arithmetic heterogeneity has never been an issue of parallel programming for traditional homogeneous parallel architectures. All arithmetic data types are uniformly represented in all processors of such a system, and their transfer between the processors does not change their value. In heterogeneous platforms, the same arithmetic data type may have different representations in different processors. In addition, arithmetic values may change in the heterogeneous communication network during transfer even between processors

High-Performance Heterogeneous Computing, by Alexey L. Lastovetsky and Jack J. Dongarra
Copyright © 2009 John Wiley & Sons, Inc.

with the same data representation. Thus, arithmetic heterogeneity is a new parallel programming issue specific to heterogeneous parallel computing. The finer the granularity of the parallel application is and the more communications its execution involves, the more frequently arithmetic values from different processors are mixed in computations, and hence the more serious this issue becomes. At the same time, if the problem and the method of solution is not ill conditioned, then arithmetic heterogeneity is not a serious issue for distributed computing.

In this chapter, we analyze these three issues with respect to parallel and distributed programming for heterogeneous networks of computers.

2.1 PERFORMANCE

In this section, we outline the performance issues of scientific programming for heterogeneous platforms and discuss how different aspects of heterogeneity contribute their specific challenges to the problem of achieving top performance on such platforms. We start with the very basic implications from the heterogeneity of processors. Then, we analyze how memory heterogeneity, memory constraints, heterogeneity of integration of the processors into the network, and unbalance between the performance of the processors and the performance of the communication network further complicate the performance issue. Finally, we look at the performance-related challenges posed by the heterogeneity of communication networks.

An immediate implication from the heterogeneity of processors in a network of computers is that the processors run at different speeds. A good parallel application for a homogeneous distributed memory multiprocessor system tries to evenly distribute computations over available processors. This very distribution ensures the maximal speedup on the system consisting of identical processors. If the processors run at different speeds, faster processors will quickly perform their part of the computations and begin waiting for slower processors at points of synchronization and data transfer. Therefore, the total time of computations will be determined by the time elapsed on the slowest processor. In other words, when executing parallel applications, which evenly distribute computations among available processors, a set of heterogeneous processors will demonstrate the same performance as a set of identical processors equivalent to the slowest processor in the heterogeneous set.

Therefore, a good parallel application for the heterogeneous platform must distribute computations unevenly taking into account the difference in processor speed. The faster the processor is, the more computations it must perform. Ideally, in the case of independent parallel computations (that is, computations on parallel processors without synchronization or data transfer), the volume of computations performed by a processor should be proportional to its speed.

Distribution of computations over the processors in proportion to their spced assumes that the programmers know at least the relative speeds of the processor in the form of positive constants. The performance of the corresponding application will strongly depend on the accuracy of estimation of the relative speed. If this estimation is not accurate enough, the load of the processors will be unbalanced, resulting in poorer execution performance. Unfortunately, the problem of accurate estimation of the relative speed of processors is not as easy as it may look. Of course, if we consider two processors, which only differ in clock rate, it is not a problem to accurately estimate their relative speed. We can use a single test code to measure their relative speed, and the relative speed will be the same for any application. This approach may also work if the processors used in computations have very similar architectural characteristics.

However, if we consider processors of very different architectures, the situation changes drastically. Everything in the processors may be different: the set of instructions, the number of instruction execution units, the number of registers, the structure of memory hierarchy, the size of each memory level, and so on. Therefore, the processors may demonstrate different relative speeds for different applications. Moreover, processors of the same architecture but of different models or configurations may also demonstrate different relative speeds on different applications. Even different applications of the same narrow class may be executed by two different processors at significantly different relative speeds.

Thus, the relative speeds of heterogeneous processors are application specific, which makes the problem of their accurate estimation nontrivial. The test code used to measure the relative speed should be carefully designed for each particular application.

Another complication of the problem comes up if the heterogeneous platform allows for multitasking, wherein several independent users can simultaneously run their applications on the same set of processors. In this case, the relative speed of the processors can dynamically change depending on the external load.

The accuracy of estimation of the relative speed of the processors not only depends on how representative is the test code used to obtain the relative speed or how frequently this estimation is performed during the execution of the application. Some objective factors do not allow us to estimate the speed of some processors accurately enough. One of these factors is the level of integration of the processor into the network. As we have discussed in Chapter 1, in general-purpose local and global networks integrated into the Internet, most computers and their operating systems periodically run some routine processes interacting with the Internet, and some computers act as servers for other computers. This results in constant unpredictable fluctuations in the workload of processors in such a network. This changing transient load will cause fluctuations in the speed of processors, in that the speed of the processor will vary when measured at different times while executing the same task. We would like to stress that this additional challenge is specific to general-purpose local and global heterogeneous networks. Heterogeneous clusters dedicated to high-performance computing are much more regular and predictable in this respect.

So far, we implicitly assumed that the relative speed of processors being application specific does not depend on the size of the computational task solved by the processors. This assumption is quite realistic if the code executed by the processors fully fits into the main memory. However, as soon as the restriction is relaxed, it may not be realistic anymore. The point is that beginning from some problem size, a task of the same size will still fit into the main memory of some processors and will stop fitting into the main memory of others, causing the paging and visible degradation of the speed of these processors. This means that their relative speed will start significantly changing in favor of nonpaging processors as soon as the problem size exceeds the critical value. Moreover, even if two processors of different architectures have almost the same size of main memory, they may employ different paging algorithms, resulting in different levels of speed degradation for a task of the same size, which again leads to the change of their relative speed as the problem size exceeds the threshold causing the paging. Thus, memory heterogeneity and paging effects significantly complicate the problem of accurate estimation of the relative speed of heterogeneous processors. Estimations obtained in the absence of paging may be inaccurate when the paging occurs and vice versa.

Yet another additional challenge is also related to memory and specific to general-purpose networks of computers. It occurs when the network includes computers that are configured to avoid paging. This is typical of computers used as a main server. If the computational task allocated to such a computer does not fit into the main memory, it will crash. In this case, the problem of optimal distribution of computations over the processors of the network becomes more difficult, having the additional restriction on the maximal size of tasks to be assigned to some processors.

One more factor that has a significant impact on the optimal distribution of computations over heterogeneous processors has not been taken into account so far. This factor is the communication network interconnecting the processors, even if the network is homogeneous. This factor can only be neglected if the contribution of communication operations in the total execution time of the application is negligibly small compared with that of computations. Communication networks in heterogeneous platforms are typically not as well balanced with the number and speed of the processors as those in dedicated homogeneous high-performance multiprocessor systems. Therefore, it is much more likely that the cost of communication for some applications will not compensate the gains due to parallelization if all available processors are involved in its execution. In this case, the problem of optimal distribution of computations over the processors becomes much more complex as the space of possible solutions will significantly increase, including distributions not only over all available processors but also over subsets of processors.

For distributed memory platforms with homogeneous communication networks providing parallel communication links of the same performance between each pair of processors, the problem of minimizing the communication cost of the application can typically be reduced to the problem of minimizing the total volume of communications. The heterogeneity of the communication network changes the situation, making the problem of minimizing the communication cost much more difficult. Indeed, a larger amount of data communicated through faster links only may lead to less overall communication cost than a smaller amount of data communicated through all the links, both fast and slow. Even if each communication link in such a heterogeneous platform is characterized just by one number, the corresponding optimization problem will have to deal with up to p^2 additional parameters, where p is the number of processors.

The heterogeneity of the communication network also makes the optimal distribution of computations, minimizing the overall computation/communication cost, much more of a challenging task. For example, even in the case of homogeneous processors interconnected by a heterogeneous network, such an optimal distribution can be uneven. Additional challenges are brought by possible dynamic changes of the performance characteristics of the communication links due to multitasking or integration into the Internet.

2.2 FAULT TOLERANCE

In this section, we outline the fault tolerance issues of scientific programming for heterogeneous platforms and discuss how different aspects of heterogeneity add their specific challenges to the problem of tolerating failures on such platforms. The ideas that follow in this section can be applied to both heterogeneous and homogeneous processing.

The unquenchable desire of scientists to run ever larger simulations and analyze ever larger data sets is fueling a relentless escalation in the size of supercomputing clusters from hundreds to thousands, to even tens of thousands of processors. Unfortunately, the struggle to design systems that can scale up in this way also exposes the current limits of our understanding of how to efficiently translate such increases in computing resources into corresponding increases in scientific productivity. One increasingly urgent part of this knowledge gap lies in the critical area of *reliability and fault tolerance*.

Even when making generous assumptions on the reliability of a single processor, it is clear that as the processor count in high-end clusters and heterogeneous systems grows into the tens of thousands, the mean time to failure (MTTF) will drop from hundreds of days to a few hours, or less. The type of 100,000-processor machines projected in the next few years can expect to experience processor failure almost daily, perhaps hourly. Although today's architectures are robust enough to incur process failures without suffering complete system failure, at this scale and failure rate, the only technique available to application developers for providing fault tolerance within the current parallel programming model—checkpoint/restart—has performance and conceptual limitations that make it inadequate for the future needs of the communities that will use these systems.

After a brief decline in popularity, distributed memory machines containing large numbers of processors have returned to fulfill the promise of delivering high performance to scientific applications. While it would be most convenient for application scientists to simply port their message passing interface (MPI) codes to these machines, perhaps instrument them with a global checkpointing system, and then sit back and enjoy the performance improvements, there are several features of these machines and their typical operating environments that render this impossible:

- *Large Numbers of Processors Mean More Failures.* Builders of distributed machines are targeting them to have tens, or even hundreds, of thousands of processors (e.g., the Blue Gene [IBM] has 128,000 processors). While that represents a great potential of computing power, it also represents a great potential increase in the system failure rate. Given independent failures, if the failure rate of one processor is X, then the rate of failure of the first processor in an N processor system is NX. Thus, if the single processor rate of failure is one per year, the rate of processor failure in a system of 128,000 processors is one per 6 hours! Clearly, failures must be accounted for in the programming system.
- *Message-Passing Systems Must Tolerate Single-Processor Failures.* As a by-product of the previous point, the programming environment of such systems must be able to identify and tolerate single-processor failures. Historically, MPI systems crash upon processor failures, requiring applications to utilize global checkpointing and restart to tolerate them. However, such high failure rates imply that global checkpointing approaches are too inefficient.
- *Limited Bandwidth to Shared, Stable Storage.* High-performance machines pay a great deal of attention to providing high-performance storage capabilities. However, with so many processors and hierarchies of networks, access to shared storage will necessarily be a bottleneck. Although at peak input/output (I/O) performance the needs of global checkpointing may be supported, such checkpointing will seriously conflict with both messaging and regular I/O of the application program.

Fault tolerance techniques can usually be divided into three big branches and some hybrid techniques. The first branch is *messaging logging*. In this branch, there are three subbranches: *pessimistic messaging logging, optimistic messaging logging*, and *casual messaging logging*. The second branch is *checkpointing and rollback recovery*. There are also three subbranches in this branch: *network disk-based checkpointing and rollback recovery, diskless checkpointing and rollback recovery*, and *local disk-based checkpointing and rollback recovery*. The third branch is *algorithm-based fault tolerance*.

There has been much work on fault tolerance techniques for high-performance computing. These efforts come in basically four categories and can be adapted to heterogeneous computing.

1. *System-Level Checkpoint/Message Logging:* Most fault tolerance schemes in the literature belong to this category. The idea of this approach is to incorporate fault tolerance into the system level so that the application can be recovered automatically without any efforts from the application programmer. The most important advantage of this approach is its transparency. However, due to lack of knowledge about the semantics of the application, the system typically backs up all the processes and logs all messages, thus often introducing a huge amount of fault tolerance overhead.

2. *Compiler-Based Fault Tolerance Approach:* The idea of this approach is to exploit the knowledge of the compiler to insert the checkpoint at the best place and to exclude irrelevant memory areas to reduce the size of the checkpoint. This approach is also transparent. However, due to the inability of the compiler to determine the state of the communication channels at the time of the checkpoint, this approach is difficult to use in parallel/distributed applications that communicate through message passing.

3. *User-Level Checkpoint Libraries:* The idea of this approach is to provide some checkpoint libraries to the programmer and let the programmer decide where, when, and what to checkpoint. The disadvantage of this approach is its nontransparency. However, due to the involvement of the programmer in the checkpoint, the size of the checkpoint can be reduced considerably, and hence the fault tolerance overhead can also be reduced considerably.

4. *Algorithmic Fault Tolerance Approach:* The idea of this approach is to leverage the knowledge of algorithms to reduce the fault tolerance overhead to the minimum. In this approach, the programmer has to decide not only where, when, and what to checkpoint but also how to do the checkpoint, and hence the programmer must have deep knowledge about the application. However, if this approach can be incorporated into widely used application libraries such as ScaLAPACK and PETSc, then it is possible to reduce both the involvement of the application programmer and the overhead of the fault tolerance to a minimum.

2.3   ARITHMETIC HETEROGENEITY

There are special challenges associated with writing reliable numerical software on systems containing heterogeneous platforms, that is, processors that may do floating-point arithmetic differently. This includes not just machines with completely different floating-point formats and semantics, such as Cray vector computers running *Cray arithmetic* versus workstations running IEEE-standard floating-point arithmetic, but even supposedly identical machines running with different compilers, or even just different compiler options or runtime environments.

The basic problem occurs when making *data dependent branches* on different platforms. The flow of an algorithm is usually data dependent, and therefore slight variations in the data may lead to different processors executing completely different sections of code.

Now we attempt a definition of an arithmetically heterogeneous platform. The three main issues determining the classification are the hardware, the communication layer, and the software (operating system, compiler, compiler options). Any differences in these areas can potentially affect the behavior of the application. Specifically, the following conditions must be satisfied before a platform can be considered *arithmetically homogeneous*:

1. The hardware of each processor guarantees the same storage representation and the same results for operations on floating-point numbers.
2. If a floating-point number is communicated between processors, the communication layer guarantees the exact transmittal of the floating-point value.
3. The software (operating system, compiler, compiler options) on each processor also guarantees the same storage representation and the same results for operations on floating-point numbers.

We regard an *arithmetically homogeneous machine* as one, which satisfies condition 1. An *arithmetically homogeneous network* is a collection of homogeneous machines, which additionally satisfies condition 2. Finally, an *arithmetically homogeneous platform* is a homogeneous network, which satisfies condition 3. We can then make the obvious definition that an *arithmetically heterogeneous platform* is one that is not homogeneous. The requirements for an arithmetically homogeneous platform are quite stringent and are frequently not met in networks of workstations, or in PCs, even when each computer in the network is the same model.

Some areas of distinction are obvious, such as a difference in the architecture of two machines or the type of communication layer implemented. Some hardware and software issues, however, can potentially affect the behavior of the application and be difficult to diagnose. For example, the determination of machine parameters such as machine precision, overflow, and underflow, the implementation of complex arithmetic such as complex division, or the handling of NaNs and subnormal numbers could differ. Some of these subtleties may only become apparent when the arithmetic operations occur on the edge of the range of representable numbers.

The difficult question that remains unanswered for scientific programmers is: When can we *guarantee* that heterogeneous computing is safe? There is also the question of just how much additional programming effort should we expend to gain additional robustness.

Machine parameters such as the relative machine precision, the underflow and overflow thresholds, and the smallest value, which can be safely reciprocated, are frequently used in numerical linear algebra computations, as well as in many other numerical computations. Without due care, variations in these values between processors can cause problems, such as those mentioned above. Many such problems can be eliminated by using the *largest* machine precision among all participating processors.

The IEEE standard for binary floating-point arithmetic (IEEE, 1985) specifies how machines conforming to the standard should represent floating-point values. We refer to machines conforming to this standard as *IEEE machines*.[1] Thus, when we communicate floating-point numbers between IEEE machines, we might hope that each processor has the same value. This is a reasonable hope and will often be realized. For example, external data representation (XDR) (SunSoft, 1993), uses the IEEE representation for floating-point numbers, and therefore a message-passing system that uses XDR will communicate floating-point numbers without change.[2] Parallel Virtual Machine (PVM) is an example of a system that uses XDR. MPI suggests the use of XDR but does not mandate its use (Snir *et al.*, 1996). Unless we have additional information about the implementation, we cannot assume that floating-point numbers will be communicated without change on IEEE machines when using MPI. Note that there is also an IEEE standard concerned with standardizing data formats to aid data conversion between processors (IEEE, 1994).

Rigorous testing of the ScaLAPACK package, particularly for floating-point values close to the edge of representable numbers, exposed additional dangers that must be avoided in floating-point arithmetic (Demmel *et al.*, 2007). For example, it is a sad reflection that some compilers still do not implement complex arithmetic carefully. In particular, unscaled complex division still occurs on certain architectures, leading to unnecessary overflow.[3] To handle this difficulty, ScaLAPACK, as LAPACK, restricts the range of representable numbers by a call to routine PDLABAD (in double precision), the equivalent of the LAPACK routine DLABAD, which replaces the smallest and largest representable numbers by their respective square roots in order to give protection from underflow or overflow on machines that do not take the care to scale on operations such as complex division. PDLABAD calls DLABAD locally on each process and then communicates the minimum and maximum values, respectively. Arguably, there should be separate routines for real and complex arithmetic, but there is a hope that the need for DLABAD will eventually disappear.

This is particularly irritating if one machine in a network is causing us to impose unnecessary restrictions on all the machines in the network, but without such a restriction, catastrophic results can occur during computations near the overflow or underflow thresholds.

Another problem encountered during the testing is in the way that subnormal (denormalized) numbers are handled on certain (near) IEEE

---

[1] It should be noted that there is also a radix independent standard (IEEE, 1987).
[2] It is not clear whether or not this can be assumed for subnormal (denormalized) numbers.
[3] At the time of testing ScaLAPACK version 1.2, the HP9000 exhibited this behavior.

architectures. By default, some architectures flush subnormal numbers to zero.[4] Thus, if the computation involves numbers near underflow and a subnormal number is communicated to such a machine, the computational results may be invalid and the subsequent behavior unpredictable. Often such machines have a compiler switch to allow the handling of subnormal numbers, but it can be nonobvious and we cannot guarantee that users will use such a switch.

This behavior occurred during the heterogeneous testing of the linear least squares routines when the input test matrix was a full-rank matrix scaled near underflow. During the course of the computation, a subnormal number was communicated, then this value was unrecognized on receipt, and a floating-point exception was flagged. The execution on the processor was killed, subsequently causing the execution on the other processors to hang. A solution would be to replace subnormal numbers either with zero, or with the nearest normal number, but we are somewhat reluctant to implement this solution as ScaLAPACK does not seem to be the correct software level at which to address the problem.

The suggestions made so far certainly do not solve all of the problems. We are still left with major concerns for problems associated with varying floating-point representations and arithmetic operations between different processors, different compilers, and different compiler options.

We tried to illustrate some of the potential difficulties concerned with floating-point computations on heterogeneous platforms. Some of these difficulties are straightforward to address, while others require considerably more thought. All of them require some additional level of defensive programming to ensure the usual standards of reliability that users have come to expect from packages such as LAPACK and ScaLAPACK.

We have presented reasonably straightforward solutions to the problems associated with floating-point machine parameters and global values, and we have discussed the use of a controlling process to solve some of the difficulties of algorithmic integrity. This can probably be used to solve most of these problems. Although in some cases, this might be at the expense of considerable additional overhead, usually in terms of additional communication, which is also imposed on an arithmetically homogeneous network unless we have separate code for the homogeneous case. Unless we can devise a satisfactory test for arithmetic homogeneity, and hence have separate paths within the code, a separate code would defeat the aim of portability.

A topic that we have not discussed is that of the additional testing necessary to give confidence in heterogeneous platforms. The testing strategies that are needed are similar to those already employed in reputable software packages such as LAPACK, but it may be very hard to produce actual test examples that would detect incorrect implementations of the algorithms because, as we have seen, the failures are likely to be very sensitive to the computing environment and, in addition, may be nondeterministic.

---

[4] The DEC Alpha, at the time of writing, is an example.

PART II

PERFORMANCE MODELS OF HETEROGENEOUS PLATFORMS AND DESIGN OF HETEROGENEOUS ALGORITHMS

In this part, we present the state of the art in two related fields—modeling the performance of heterogeneous platforms for high-performance computing and design and analysis of heterogeneous algorithms with the models.

CHAPTER 3

Distribution of Computations with Constant Performance Models of Heterogeneous Processors

3.1 SIMPLEST CONSTANT PERFORMANCE MODEL OF HETEROGENEOUS PROCESSORS AND OPTIMAL DISTRIBUTION OF INDEPENDENT UNITS OF COMPUTATION WITH THIS MODEL

Heterogeneity of processors is one of the main sources of performance programming issues. As we have seen in Chapter 2, the immediate and most important performance-related implication from the heterogeneity of processors is that the processors run at different speeds. The simplest performance model, capturing this feature and abstracting from the others, sees a heterogeneous network of computers as a set of interconnected processors, each of which is characterized by a single positive constant representing its speed. Two important parameters of the model include

- p, the number of the processors, and
- $S = \{s_1, s_2, \ldots, s_p\}$, the speeds of the processors.

The speed of the processors can be either *absolute* or *relative*. The absolute speed of the processors is understood as the number of computational units performed by the processor per one time unit. The relative speed of the processor can be obtained by the normalization of its absolute speed so that $\Sigma_{i=1}^{p} s_i = 1$. Some researchers also use the reciprocal of the speed, which they call the execution time of the processor. For example, if s_i is the absolute speed of processor P_i, then $t_i = \dfrac{1}{s_i}$ will be the execution time of this processor giving the number of time units needed to perform one unit of computation on processor P_i.

High-Performance Heterogeneous Computing, by Alexey L. Lastovetsky and Jack J. Dongarra
Copyright © 2009 John Wiley & Sons, Inc.

The performance model presented above does not have parameters describing the communication network. Nonetheless, as we will later see, even in the framework of such a simple model, the communication cost of parallel algorithms can be taken into account.

Now we consider a simple but fundamental optimization problem with this model—the problem of optimal distribution of independent equal units of computation over a set of heterogeneous processors. The solution of this problem is used as a basic building block in solutions of more complicated optimization problems.

The problem can be formulated as follows. Given n independent units of computations, each of equal size (i.e., each requiring the same amount of work), how can we assign these units to p $(p < n)$ physical processors P_1, P_2, ..., P_p of respective speeds $s_1, s_2, ..., s_p$ so that the workload is best balanced? Here, the speed s_i of processor P_i is understood as the number of units of computation performed by processor P_i per one time unit.

Then, how do we distribute the computational units to processors? The intuition says that the load of P_i should be proportional to s_i. As the loads (i.e., the numbers of units of computation) on each processor must be integers, we use the following two-step algorithm to solve the problem. Let n_i denote the number of units of computation allocated to processor P_i. Then, the overall execution time obtained with allocation $(n_1, n_2, ..., n_p)$ is given by $\max_i \frac{n_i}{s_i}$. The optimal solution will minimize the overall execution time (without taking into account communication).

Algorithm 3.1 (Beaumont *et al.*, 2001a). Optimal distribution for n independent units of computation over p processors of speeds $s_1, s_2, ..., s_p$:

- **Step 1: Initialization.** Approximate the n_i so that $\frac{n_i}{s_i} \approx const$ and $n_1 + n_2 + ... + n_p \le n$. Namely, we let $n_i = \left\lfloor \frac{s_i}{\Sigma_{i=1}^{p} s_i} \times n \right\rfloor$ for $1 \le i \le p$.

- **Step 2: Refining.** Iteratively increment some n_i until $n_1 + n_2 + ... + n_p = n$ as follows:

while $(n_1 + n_2 + ... + n_p < n)$ {
  find $k \in \{1, ..., p\}$ such that $\frac{n_k + 1}{s_k} = \min_{i=1}^{p} \frac{n_i + 1}{s_i}$;
  $n_k = n_k + 1$;
}

Proposition 3.1 (Beaumont *et al.*, 2001a). Algorithm 3.1 gives the optimal distribution.

See Appendix A for proof.

Proposition 3.2. The complexity of Algorithm 3.1 is $O(p^2)$.

Proof. The complexity of the initialization step is $O(p)$. The complexity of one iteration of the refining is $O(p)$. After the initialization step, $n_1 + n_2 + \ldots + n_p \geq n - p$. Therefore, there will be at most p iterations of the refining. Hence, the overall complexity of the algorithm will be $O(p^2)$. *End of proof.*

Proposition 3.3 (Beaumont *et al.*, 2001a). The complexity of Algorithm 3.1 can be reduced down to $O(p \times \log p)$ using *ad hoc* data structures.

The algorithm is widely used as a basic building block in the design of many heterogeneous parallel and distributed algorithms. One simple example is the following parallel algorithm of multiplication of two dense square $n \times n$ matrices, $C = A \times B$, on p heterogeneous processors:

- First, we partition matrices A and C identically into p horizontal slices such that there will be one-to-one mapping between these slices and the processors. Each processor will store its slices of matrices A and C and the whole matrix B as shown in Figure 3.1 for $p = 3$.
- All processors compute their C slices in parallel such that each element c_{ij} in C is computed as $c_{ij} = \sum_{k=0}^{n-1} a_{ik} \times b_{kj}$.

The key step of this algorithm is the partitioning of matrices A and C. An optimal partitioning will minimize the execution time of the algorithm. Let one unit of computation be the multiplication of one row of matrix A by matrix B, producing one row of the resulting matrix C. The size of this unit of computation does not depend on which rows of matrices A and C are involved in the computation. The computational unit will always include n^2 multiplications

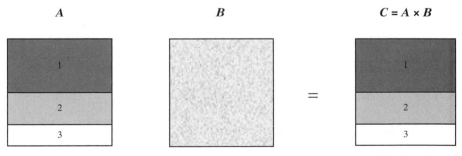

Figure 3.1. Matrix operation $C = A \times B$ with $n \times n$ matrices A, B, and C. Matrices A and C are horizontally sliced such that the number of elements in the slice is proportional to the speed of the processor.

and $n \times (n - 1)$ additions. Processor P_i will perform n_i such computation units, where n_i is the number of rows in the slice assigned to this processor, $\Sigma_{i=1}^{p} n_i = n$. Thus, the problem of optimal partitioning of matrices A and C is reduced to the problem of optimal distribution of n independent computational units of equal size over p heterogeneous processors of the respective speeds $s_1, \ldots, s_p$, where s_i is the number of rows of matrix C computed by processor P_i per one time unit. Therefore, we can apply Algorithm 3.1 to solve the partitioning problem.

Note. That straightforward application of Algorithm 3.1 has one disadvantage. In the above example, the size of the computational unit is an increasing function of n. Therefore, the absolute speed of the same processor, measured in computational units per one time unit, will be decreasing with the increase of n, and the application programmer will have to obtain this speed for each particular n used in different runs of the application. At the same time, very often, the relative speed of the processors does not depend on n for quite a wide range of values. Hence, the application programmer could obtain the relative speeds once for some particular n and use the same speeds for other values of n. Actually, nothing prevents us from using relative speeds in this case, in particular, and in Algorithm 3.1, in general. Indeed, minimization of $\dfrac{n_i + 1}{s_i}$ at the refining step of this algorithm will also minimize $\dfrac{n_i + 1}{s_i / \sum_{i=1}^{p} s_i}$, as $\Sigma_{i=1}^{p} s_i$ does not depend on i. Therefore, Algorithm 3.1 will return an optimal distribution of computational units, independent on whether we use absolute or relative speeds.

If we reflect on the above application of Algorithm 3.1, we can also make the following observation. If n is big enough and if $p \ll n$, then many straightforward algorithms of refining the distribution obtained after the initialization step will return an approximate solution, which is very close to optimal and satisfactory in practice. For example, the refining could be done by incrementing n_i in a round-robin fashion. Such algorithms return *asymptotically optimal* solutions: The larger the matrix size, the closer the solutions to the optimal ones. One obvious advantage of using modifications of Algorithm 3.1 returning not the exact but the approximate, asymptotically optimal distributions is that the complexity of the distribution algorithms can be reduced to $O(p)$.

To be specific, we have to formalize somehow the notion of an approximate optimal distribution. For example, we can define it as any distribution $n_i \left(\Sigma_{i=1}^{p} n_i = n \right)$ that satisfies the inequality $\left\lfloor \dfrac{s_i}{\sum_{i=1}^{p} s_i} \times n \right\rfloor \leq n_i \leq \left\lfloor \dfrac{s_i}{\sum_{i=1}^{p} s_i} \times n \right\rfloor + 1$.

This definition is not perfect because for some combinations of p, n, and s_i, the exact optimal distribution may not satisfy the inequality. Nevertheless, this definition allows us to mathematically formulate the problem of the approximate optimal distribution of independent equal units of computation over a set of heterogeneous processors as follows. Given n independent units of computations, each of equal size, distribute these units of work over $p(p \ll n)$ physical processors $P_1, P_2, ..., P_p$ of respective speeds $s_1, s_2, ..., s_p$ so that

- The number of computational units n_i assigned to processor P_i shall be approximately proportional to its speed, namely,

$$\left\lfloor \frac{s_i}{\sum_{i=1}^{p} s_i} \times n \right\rfloor \le n_i \le \left\lfloor \frac{s_i}{\sum_{i=1}^{p} s_i} \times n \right\rfloor + 1$$

- $\sum_{i=1}^{p} n_i = n$

3.2 DATA DISTRIBUTION PROBLEMS WITH CONSTANT PERFORMANCE MODELS OF HETEROGENEOUS PROCESSORS

In the previous section, the problem of distribution of units of computations in proportion to the speed of heterogeneous processors during multiplication of two dense square matrices was first reduced to the problem of partitioning a matrix and, in the end, to the problem of partitioning a set. This is typical in the design of heterogeneous parallel algorithms when the problem of distribution of computations in proportion to the speed of processors is reduced to the problem of partitioning some mathematical objects such as sets, matrices, graphs, and so on.

In a generic form, a typical partitioning problem with a constant performance model of heterogeneous processors can be formulated as follows:

- Given a set of p processors $P_1, P_2, ..., P_p$, the speed of each of which is characterized by a positive constant, s_i
- Partition a mathematical object of the size n (the number of elements in a set or matrix, or the number of nodes in a graph) into p subobjects of the same type (a set into subsets, a matrix into submatrices, a graph into subgraphs, etc.) so that
  - There is one-to-one mapping between the partitions and the processors
  - The size n_i of each partition is approximately proportional to the speed of the processor owing the partition, $\dfrac{n_i}{s_i} \approx const$
    - That is, it is assumed that the volume of computation is proportional to the size of the mathematical object
    - The notion of approximate proportionality is supposed to be defined for each particular problem; if it is not defined, it means that any partitioning consists of partitions, the sizes of which are approximately proportional to the speeds of the processors owing the partitions

- ◦ The partitioning satisfies some additional restrictions on the relationship between the partitions
  - ▪ For example, the submatrices of the matrix may be required to form a two-dimensional $r \times q$ arrangement, where r and q may be either given constants or the parameters of the problem, the optimal value of which should be also found
- ◦ The partitioning minimizes some functional(s), which is(are) used to estimate each partitioning
  - ▪ For example, it minimizes the sum of the perimeters of the rectangles representing the submatrices (intuitively, this functional estimates the volume of communications for some parallel algorithms)

The problem of optimal distribution of independent equal computational units presented in Section 3.1 can be formulated as the following instantiation of the generic partitioning problem:

- Given a set of p processors $P_1, P_2, \ldots, P_p$, the speed of each of which is characterized by a positive constant, s_i
- Partition a set of n elements into p subsets so that
  - ◦ There is one-to-one mapping between the partitions and the processors
  - ◦ The number of elements n_i in each partition is approximately proportional to s_i, the speed of the processor owing the partition, so that

$$\left\lfloor \frac{s_i}{\sum_{i=1}^{p} s_i} \times n \right\rfloor \le n_i \le \left\lfloor \frac{s_i}{\sum_{i=1}^{p} s_i} \times n \right\rfloor + p$$

  - ◦ The partitioning minimizes $\max_i \dfrac{n_i}{s_i}$

Another important set partitioning problem is formulated as follows:

- Given a set of p processors $P_1, P_2, \ldots, P_p$, the speed of each of which is characterized by a positive constant, s_i
- Given a set of n unequal elements, the weight of each of which is characterized by a positive constant
- Partition the set into p subsets so that
  - ◦ There is one-to-one mapping between the partitions and the processors
  - ◦ The total weight of each partition, w_i, is approximately proportional to s_i, the speed of the processor owing the partition
  - ◦ The partitioning minimizes $\max_i \dfrac{w_i}{s_i}$

Solution of the latter set partitioning problem would contribute to the solution of the problem of optimal mapping or scheduling tasks on heterogeneous platforms. Unfortunately, this set partitioning problem is known to be NP-complete (Ibarra and Kim, 1977; Garey and Johnson, 1979), which means that an efficient algorithm solving this problem is not likely to exist. Therefore, efficient algorithms giving suboptimal solutions are a practical approach to the problem. Design of suboptimal algorithms for scheduling tasks in heterogeneous platforms is an active research area that has attracted significant attention from the research community. Main applications of the algorithms are in scheduling components of operating environments for heterogeneous platforms rather than in the design and implementation of parallel algorithms for high-performance heterogeneous computing, which is the primary focus of this book. A good survey of this area can be found elsewhere (Kwok and Ahmad, 1999).

3.3 PARTITIONING WELL-ORDERED SETS WITH CONSTANT PERFORMANCE MODELS OF HETEROGENEOUS PROCESSORS

The problem of optimal distribution of computations over heterogeneous processors can be reduced to a problem of partitioning a well-ordered set for various heterogeneous parallel algorithms. Different algorithms may result in different formulations of the problem.

We know of a problem of partitioning a well-ordered set that has been formulated and solved so far. This partitioning problem occurs during the design of parallel algorithms of dense matrix factorization on heterogeneous processors with constant relative speeds. The heterogeneous parallel algorithms are obtained by modification of their prototypes designed for homogeneous processors. The modification is in the distribution of the matrix over the processors and aimed at the optimal distribution of computations during the factorization.

Let us consider how the problem of LU factorization of a dense matrix on a heterogeneous platform can be reduced to the problem of partitioning a well-ordered set with a constant performance model of heterogeneous processors. First, we briefly introduce a parallel algorithm of LU factorization on homogeneous multiprocessors, which is used as a prototype for heterogeneous modifications.

One step of the algorithm of LU factorization of a dense $(n \times b) \times (n \times b)$ matrix A is shown in Figure 3.2, where n is the number of blocks of size $b \times b$, optimal values of b depending on the memory hierarchy and on the communication-to-computation ratio of the target multiprocessor (Choi $et\ al.$, 1996a).

The LU factorization applies a sequence of transformations to form $A = P \times L \times U$, where A, L, and U are dense $(n \times b) \times (n \times b)$ matrices. P is a permutation matrix, which is stored in a vector of size $n \times b$, L is a unit lower triangular (lower triangular with 1's on the main diagonal), and U is an upper triangular.

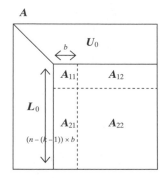
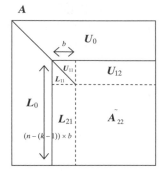

Figure 3.2. One step of the LU factorization algorithm of a dense matrix A of size $(n \times b) \times (n \times b)$.

At the k-th step of the computation ($k = 1,2,\ldots$), it is assumed that the $m \times m$ submatrix of $A^{(k)}(m = ((n - (k - 1)) \times b)$ is to be partitioned as follows:

$$\begin{pmatrix} A_{11} & A_{12} \\ A_{21} & A_{22} \end{pmatrix} = P \begin{pmatrix} L_{11} & 0 \\ L_{21} & L_{22} \end{pmatrix} \begin{pmatrix} U_{11} & U_{12} \\ 0 & U_{22} \end{pmatrix}$$

$$= P \begin{pmatrix} L_{11}U_{11} & L_{11}U_{12} \\ L_{21}U_{11} & L_{21}U_{12} + L_{22}U_{22} \end{pmatrix}$$

where the block A_{11} is $b \times b$, A_{12} is $b \times (m - b)$, A_{21} is $(m - b) \times b$, and A_{22} is $(m - b) \times (m - b)$. L_{11} is a unit lower triangular matrix, and U_{11} is an upper triangular matrix.

At first, a sequence of Gaussian eliminations is performed on the first $m \times b$ panel of $A^{(k)}$ (i.e., A_{11} and A_{21}). Once this is completed, the matrices L_{11}, L_{21}, and U_{11} are known, and we can rearrange the block equations as

$$U_{12} \leftarrow (L_{11})^{-1} A_{12},$$

$$\tilde{A}_{22} \leftarrow A_{22} - L_{21}U_{12} = L_{22}U_{22}.$$

The LU factorization can be done by recursively applying the steps outlined above to the $(m - b) \times (m - b)$ matrix $\tilde{A}_{22}$. Figure 3.2 shows how the column panels L_{11} and L_{21} and the row panels U_{11} and U_{12} are computed and how the trailing submatrix A_{22} is updated. In the figure, the regions L_0, U_0, L_{11}, U_{11}, L_{21}, and U_{12} represent data for which the corresponding computations are completed. Later row interchanges will be applied to L_0 and L_{21}.

Now we present a parallel algorithm that computes the above steps on a one-dimensional arrangement of p homogeneous processors. The algorithm can be summarized as follows:

1. A CYCLIC(b) distribution of columns is used to distribute the matrix A over a one-dimensional arrangement of p homogeneous processors as

A

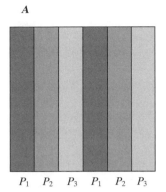

P_1 P_2 P_3 P_1 P_2 P_3

Figure 3.3. Column-oriented cyclic distribution of six column blocks on a one-dimensional array of three homogeneous processors.

shown in Figure 3.3. The cyclic distribution assigns columns of blocks with numbers $1, 2, \ldots, n$ to processors $1, 2, \ldots, p, 1, 2, \ldots, p, 1, 2, \ldots$, respectively, for a p-processor linear array ($n \gg p$), until all n columns of blocks are assigned.

2. The algorithm consists of n steps. At each step ($k = 1, 2, \ldots$)

   - The processor owning the pivot column block of the size $((n - (k - 1)) \times b) \times b$ (i.e., A_{11} and A_{21}) factors it
   - All processors apply row interchanges to the left and the right of the current column block k
   - The processor owning L_{11} broadcasts it to the rest of the processors, which convert the row panel A_{12} to U_{12}
   - The processor owning the column panel L_{21} broadcasts it to the rest of the processors
   - All the processors update their local portions of the matrix A_{22} in parallel

Because the largest fraction of the work takes place in the update of A_{22}, therefore to obtain maximum parallelism, all processors should participate in its update. Since A_{22} reduces in size as the computation progresses, a cyclic distribution is used to ensure that at any stage, A_{22} is evenly distributed over all processors, thus obtaining their balanced load.

Modifications of this algorithm for a one-dimensional arrangement of heterogeneous processors should unevenly distribute the column panels over the processors. The corresponding distribution problem can be formulated as follows. Given a dense $(n \times b) \times (n \times b)$ matrix A, how can we assign n columns of size $n \times b$ of the matrix A to $p(n > p)$ heterogeneous processors $P_1, P_2, \ldots, P_p$ of relative speeds $S = \{s_1, s_2, \ldots, s_p\}$, $\Sigma_{i=1}^{p} s_i = 1$, so that the workload at each step of the parallel LU factorization is best balanced? The relative speed s_i of processor P_i is obtained by a normalization of its (absolute) speed v_i, understood as the number of column panels updated by the processor per one time unit, $s_i = \dfrac{v_i}{\sum_{i=1}^{p} v_i}$. While v_i will increase with each next step of the LU factorization (because the height of updated column panels will decrease as the LU factorization progresses, resulting in a larger number of column panels updated by the processor per time unit), the relative speeds s_i are assumed to be constant. The optimal solution sought is the one that minimizes $\max_i \dfrac{n_i^{(k)}}{s_i}$ for each step k of the LU factorization $\left(\sum_{i=1}^{p} n_i^{(k)} = n^{(k)}\right)$, where $n^{(k)}$ is the total number of column panels updated at step k, and $n_i^{(k)}$ denotes the number of column panels allocated to processor P_i.

The motivation behind that formulation is the following. Strictly speaking, the optimal solution should minimize the total execution time of the LU factorization, which is given by $\sum_{k=1}^{n} \max_{i=1}^{p} \dfrac{n_i^{(k)}}{v_i^{(k)}}$, where $v_i^{(k)}$ is the speed of processor P_i at step k of the LU factorization and $n_i^{(k)}$ is the number of column panels updated by processor P_i at this step. However, if a solution minimizes $\max_{i=1}^{p} \dfrac{n_i^{(k)}}{v_i^{(k)}}$ for each k, it will also minimize $\sum_{k=1}^{n} \max_{i=1}^{p} \dfrac{n_i^{(k)}}{v_i^{(k)}}$. Because

$$\max_{i=1}^{p} \frac{n_i^{(k)}}{v_i^{(k)}} = \max_{i=1}^{p} \frac{n_i^{(k)}}{s_i \times \sum_{i=1}^{p} v_i^{(k)}} = \frac{1}{\sum_{i=1}^{p} v_i^{(k)}} \times \max_{i=1}^{p} \frac{n_i^{(k)}}{s_i},$$

then for any given k the problem of minimizing $\max_{i=1}^{p} \dfrac{n_i^{(k)}}{v_i^{(k)}}$ will be equivalent to the problem of minimizing $\max_{i=1}^{p} \dfrac{n_i^{(k)}}{s_i}$. Therefore, if there exists an allocation that minimizes $\max_{i=1}^{p} \dfrac{n_i^{(k)}}{s_i}$ for each step k of the LU factorization, then this allocation will be globally optimal, minimizing $\sum_{k=1}^{n} \max_{i=1}^{p} \dfrac{n_i^{(k)}}{v_i^{(k)}}$. We will see that such an allocation always exists.

If we see the n column panels of the matrix A as a well-ordered set of n elements, the above problem of optimal distribution of column panels will be equivalent to the following problem of partitioning a well-ordered set:

- Given a set of p processors $P_1, P_2, \ldots, P_p$, the speed of each of which is characterized by a positive constant, $s_i \left(\sum_{i=1}^{p} s_i = 1 \right)$
- Partition a well-ordered set $A = \{a_1, \ldots, a_n\}$ of n elements $(n > p)$ into p well-ordered subsets $A_1, \ldots, A_p$ so that
  ◦ There is one-to-one mapping between the partitions and the processors

∘ For any $k = 1, \dots, n$, the partitioning minimizes $\max_i \dfrac{n_i^{(k)}}{s_i}$, where $n_i^{(k)}$ is the number of elements left in partition A_i after deletion of the first k elements $a_1, \dots, a_k$ of the set A from partitions $A_1, \dots, A_p$

Proposition 3.4. The solution of the problem of partitioning a well-ordered set always exists.

Proof. In Boulet *et al.* (1999) and Lastovetsky and Reddy (2007a), algorithms that partition a well-ordered set A of n elements $(n > p)$ into p well-ordered subsets $A_1, \dots, A_p$ are designed, and it is proved that these algorithms always return an optimal solution (i.e., the one that minimizes all the k functionals). Details of the proof for one of the algorithms can be found in this book (the proof of Proposition 3.5). *End of proof.*

Two algorithms solving this partitioning problem have been designed so far—the Dynamic Programming (DP) algorithm (Boulet *et al.*, 1999; Beaumont *et al.*, 2001a) and the Reverse algorithm (Lastovetsky and Reddy, 2007a).

The DP Algorithm. Dynamic programming is used to distribute elements of the set over the processors. The inputs to the algorithm are p, the number of heterogeneous processors in the one-dimensional arrangement, n, the number of elements in the set A, and $S = \{s_1, s_2, \dots, s_p\}$ $(\Sigma_{i=1}^{p} s_i = 1)$, the relative speeds of the processors. The outputs are c, an integer array of size p, the i-th element of which contains the number of elements assigned to processor i, and d, an integer array of size n, the i-th element of which contains the processor to which the element a_i is assigned. The algorithm can be summarized as follows:

```
(c₁,…,cₚ)=(0,…,0);
(d₁,…,dₙ)=(0,…,0);
for(k=1; k≤n; k=k+1) {
        Cost_min=∞;
        for(i=1; i≤p; i=i+1) {
                Cost=(cᵢ+1)/sᵢ;
                if (Cost < Cost_min) { Cost_min=Cost; j=i;}
        }
        d_{n-k+1}=j;
        cⱼ=cⱼ+1;
}
```

The complexity of the DP algorithm is $O(p \times n)$. The algorithm returns the optimal allocation of the elements to the heterogeneous processors (Boulet *et al.*, 1999). The fact that the DP algorithm always returns an optimal solution is not trivial. Indeed, at each iteration of the algorithm, the next element of the set is allocated to one of the processors, namely, to a processor, minimizing the cost of the allocation. At the same time, there may be several processors with the same, minimal cost of allocation. The algorithm randomly selects one of them. It is not obvious that allocation of the element to any of these processors will result in a globally optimal allocation, but for this particular partitioning problem, this has been proved (Boulet *et al.*, 1999).

The Reverse Algorithm. This algorithm generates the optimal distribution $\left(n_1^{(k)}, \ldots, n_p^{(k)}\right)$ of the elements a_k, ..., a_n of the set $A = \{a_1, \ldots, a_n\}$ over p heterogeneous processors for each $k = 1, \ldots, n$ $\left(\Sigma_{i=1}^p n_i^{(k)} = n - k + 1\right)$ and then allocates the elements to the processors by comparing these distributions. In other words, the algorithm extracts the optimal allocation of the elements from a sequence of optimal distributions of the elements for successive subsets $A^{(k)} = \{a_k, \ldots, a_n\}$. The inputs to the algorithm are p, the number of heterogeneous processors in the one-dimensional arrangement, n, the number of elements in the set A, and $S = \{s_1, s_2, \ldots, s_p\}\left(\Sigma_{i=1}^p s_i = 1\right)$, the relative speeds of the processors. The output is d, an integer array of size n, the i-th element of which contains the processor to which the element a_i is assigned. The algorithm can be summarized as follows:

```
( d₁ , ... , dₙ ) = ( 0 , ... , 0 ) ;
w=0;
( n₁ , ... , nₚ ) =HSP(p,  n,  S) ;
for  (k=1;  k<n;  k=k+1)  {
     ( n'₁ , ... , n'ₚ )=  HSP(p,  n-k,  S) ;
     if  (w==0)
     then if  (( ∃! j∈ [1,p] ) (nⱼ== n'ⱼ +1)∧( ∀ i≠j) (nᵢ== n'ᵢ ))
              then  {dₖ=j;   (n₁ , ... , nₚ) = ( n'₁ , ... , n'ₚ ) ; }
              else  w=1;
     else if  (( ∃i∈ [1,p] ) (nᵢ< n'ᵢ ))
              then  w=w+1;
              else  {
                for  (i=1;  i≤p;  i=i+1)
                    for  (Δ=nᵢ- n'ᵢ ;  Δ≠0;  Δ=Δ-1,  w=w-1)
                        dₖ₋w=i;
                ( n₁ , ... , nₚ ) = ( n'₁ , ... , n'ₚ ) ;
                w=0;
                   }
     }
if  (( ∃i∈ [1,p] ) (nᵢ==1))
then  dₙ=i;
```

Here, HSP(*p*,*n*,*S*) (HSP stands for heterogeneous set partitioning) returns the optimal distribution of *n* elements over *p* heterogeneous processors of relative speeds $S = \{s_1, s_2, \ldots, s_p\}$ by applying Algorithm 3.1 for the optimal

TABLE 3.1 Reverse Algorithm with Three Processors, P_1, P_2, P_3

Step of the algorithm (k)	Distributions at step k			Allocation made
	P_1	P_2	P_3	
	6	2	2	
1	5	2	2	P_1
2	4	2	2	P_1
3	3	2	2	P_1
4	1	3	2	No allocation
5	1	3	1	No allocation
6	1	2	1	P_1, P_1, P_3
7	1	1	1	P_2
8	0	1	1	P_1
9	0	0	1	P_2
10				P_3

distribution of independent units of computations from Section 3.1. Thus, first we find the optimal distributions of elements for $A^{(1)}$ and $A^{(2)}$. If the distributions differ only for one processor, then we assign a_1 to this processor. The reason is that this assignment guarantees a transfer from the best workload balance for $A^{(1)}$ to the best workload balance for $A^{(2)}$. If the distributions differ for more than one processor, we postpone the allocation of a_1 and find the optimal distribution for $A^{(3)}$ and compare it with the distribution for $A^{(1)}$. If the number of elements distributed to each processor for $A^{(3)}$ does not exceed that for $A^{(1)}$, we allocate a_1 and a_2 so that the distribution for each next subset is obtained from the distribution for the immediate previous subset by the addition of one more element to one of the processors. If not, we delay the allocation of the first two elements and find the optimal distribution for $A^{(4)}$, and so on.

In Table 3.1, we demonstrate the algorithm for $n = 10$. The first column represents the step k of the algorithm. The second column shows the distributions obtained during each step by the HSP. The entry "allocation made" denotes the rank of the processor to which element a_k is assigned. At steps $k = 4$ and $k = 5$, the algorithm does not make any assignments. At $k = 6$, processor P_1 is allocated elements a_4 and a_5, and processor P_2 is allocated element a_6. The output d in this case would be $(P_1P_1P_1P_1P_1P_3P_2P_1P_2P_3)$.

Proposition 3.5 (Lastovetsky and Reddy, 2007a). The Reverse algorithm returns the optimal allocation.

See Appendix A for proof.

Proposition 3.6. (Lastovetsky and Reddy, 2007a). The complexity of the Reverse algorithm is $O(p \times n \times \log_2 p)$.

Proof. At each iteration of this algorithm, we apply the HSP, which is of complexity $O(p \times \log_2 p)$ (see Section 3.1). Testing the condition $(\exists! j \in [1, p])(n_j = n'_j + 1) \wedge (\forall i \neq j)(n_i = n'_i)$ is of complexity $O(p)$. Testing the condition $(\exists\, i \in [1, p])(n_i < n_i')$ is also of complexity $O(p)$. Finally, the total number of iterations of the inner loop of the nest of loops

```
for (i=1; i≤p; i=i+1)
    for (Δ=n_i−n_i'; Δ≠0; Δ=Δ−1, w=w−1)
        d_{k−w}=i;
```

cannot exceed the total number of allocations of elements, n. Thus, the overall complexity of the algorithm is upper bounded by $n \times O(p \times \log_2 p) + n \times O(p) + n \times O(p) + p \times n \times O(1) = O(p \times n \times \log_2 p)$. *End of proof of Proposition 3.6.*

The complexity of the Reverse algorithm is a bit worse than the complexity of the DP algorithm. At the same time, as we will see in the next chapter, the Reverse algorithm is better suitable for further extensions to more complicated, nonconstant performance models of heterogeneous processors.

Other algorithms of partitioning well-ordered sets, such as the one presented in Barbosa, Tavares, and Padilha (2000), do not guarantee the return of an optimal solution. The efficiency of the DP and Reverse algorithms is high enough so that there is no need for more efficient algorithms at the expense of the optimality of the returning solutions.

3.4 PARTITIONING MATRICES WITH CONSTANT PERFORMANCE MODELS OF HETEROGENEOUS PROCESSORS

Matrices are probably the most widely used mathematical objects in scientific computing. Therefore, no wonder that the studies of data partitioning problems mainly deal with partitioning matrices. We have seen that in many cases, the problem of optimal distribution of computations over a one-dimensional arrangement of heterogeneous processors can be reduced to the mathematical problem of partitioning a set or a well-ordered set, even if the original problem is dealing with matrices but reduced to the problem of partitioning a matrix in one dimension.

In this section, we consider matrix-partitioning problems that do not impose the additional restriction of partitioning the matrix in one dimension. The partitioning problems occur, in particular, during the design of many parallel algorithms for the solution of linear algebra problems on heterogeneous platforms.

One such problem is matrix multiplication. Matrix multiplication is a very simple but important linear algebra kernel. It also serves as a prototype for many other scientific kernels. Parallel algorithms for matrix multiplication on heterogeneous platforms have been well studied over the last decade. A typical heterogeneous matrix multiplication algorithm is designed as a modification of a well-known algorithm for matrix multiplication on homogeneous distributed memory multiprocessors. Most often, the two-dimensional block cyclic algorithm implemented in the ScaLAPACK library is used as a basis for the heterogeneous modifications. Therefore, at first, we briefly describe this basic algorithm.

The algorithm implements the matrix operation $C = A \times B$ on a two-dimensional $p \times q$ processor grid, where A and B are dense matrices. For simplicity, we assume that A and B are square $n \times n$ matrices. Then, the algorithm can be summarized as follows:

- Each element in A, B, and C is a square $r \times r$ block, and the unit of computation is the updating of one block, that is, a matrix multiplication of size r. For simplicity, we assume that n is a multiple of r.
- The blocks are scattered in a cyclic fashion along both dimensions of the $p \times q$ processor grid, so that for all $i, j \in \left\{1, \ldots, \dfrac{n}{r}\right\}$ blocks a_{ij}, b_{ij}, c_{ij} will be mapped to processor P_{IJ} so that $I = (i-1) \bmod p + 1$ and $J = (j-1) \bmod q + 1$. For simplicity, we assume that p and q divide $\dfrac{n}{r}$.

  ○ Figure 3.4 illustrates the distribution from the matrix point of view. The matrix is now partitioned into $\dfrac{n^2}{r^2 \times p \times q}$ equal rectangles, so that each row contains $\dfrac{n}{r \times q}$ rectangles, and each column contains $\dfrac{n}{r \times p}$ rectangles. All the rectangles, which are also known as *generalized blocks*, are identically partitioned into $p \times q$ equal $r \times r$ blocks, so that each row contains q blocks and each column contains p blocks. There is one-to-one mapping between these blocks and the processors. Thus, all the $\dfrac{n^2}{r^2 \times p \times q}$ rectangles of blocks are identically distributed over the $p \times q$ processor grid in a two-dimensional block fashion.

- The algorithm consists of $\dfrac{n}{r}$ steps. At each step k

  ○ A column of blocks (the pivot column) of matrix A is communicated (broadcast) horizontally (see Fig. 3.5).
    - The pivot column $a_{\bullet k}$ is owned by the column of processors $\{P_{iK}\}_{i=1}^{p}$, where $K = (k-1) \bmod q + 1$.
    - Each processor P_{iK} (for all $i \in \{1, \ldots, m\}$) horizontally broadcasts its part of the pivot column $a_{\bullet k}$ to processors $P_{i\bullet}$.
  ○ A row of blocks (the pivot row) of matrix B is communicated (broadcast) vertically (see Fig. 3.5).
    - The pivot row $b_{k\bullet}$ is owned by the row of processors $\{P_{Ki}\}_{i=1}^{m}$, where $K = (k-1) \bmod p + 1$.

	1	2	3	4	5	6	7	8	9	10	11	12	13	14	15	16	17	18	19	20	21	22	23	24
1	P_{11}	P_{12}	P_{13}	P_{14}	P_{11}	P_{12}	P_{13}	P_{14}	P_{11}	P_{12}	P_{13}	P_{14}	P_{11}	P_{12}	P_{13}	P_{14}	P_{11}	P_{12}	P_{13}	P_{14}	P_{11}	P_{12}	P_{13}	P_{14}
2	P_{21}	P_{22}	P_{23}	P_{24}	P_{21}	P_{22}	P_{23}	P_{24}	P_{21}	P_{22}	P_{23}	P_{24}	P_{21}	P_{22}	P_{23}	P_{24}	P_{21}	P_{22}	P_{23}	P_{24}	P_{21}	P_{22}	P_{23}	P_{24}
3	P_{31}	P_{32}	P_{33}	P_{34}	P_{31}	P_{32}	P_{33}	P_{34}	P_{31}	P_{32}	P_{33}	P_{34}	P_{31}	P_{32}	P_{33}	P_{34}	P_{31}	P_{32}	P_{33}	P_{34}	P_{31}	P_{32}	P_{33}	P_{34}
4	P_{11}	P_{12}	P_{13}	P_{14}	P_{11}	P_{12}	P_{13}	P_{14}	P_{11}	P_{12}	P_{13}	P_{14}	P_{11}	P_{12}	P_{13}	P_{14}	P_{11}	P_{12}	P_{13}	P_{14}	P_{11}	P_{12}	P_{13}	P_{14}
5	P_{21}	P_{22}	P_{23}	P_{24}	P_{21}	P_{22}	P_{23}	P_{24}	P_{21}	P_{22}	P_{23}	P_{24}	P_{21}	P_{22}	P_{23}	P_{24}	P_{21}	P_{22}	P_{23}	P_{24}	P_{21}	P_{22}	P_{23}	P_{24}
6	P_{31}	P_{32}	P_{33}	P_{34}	P_{31}	P_{32}	P_{33}	P_{34}	P_{31}	P_{32}	P_{33}	P_{34}	P_{31}	P_{32}	P_{33}	P_{34}	P_{31}	P_{32}	P_{33}	P_{34}	P_{31}	P_{32}	P_{33}	P_{34}
7	P_{11}	P_{12}	P_{13}	P_{14}	P_{11}	P_{12}	P_{13}	P_{14}	P_{11}	P_{12}	P_{13}	P_{14}	P_{11}	P_{12}	P_{13}	P_{14}	P_{11}	P_{12}	P_{13}	P_{13}	P_{11}	P_{12}	P_{13}	P_{14}
8	P_{21}	P_{22}	P_{23}	P_{24}	P_{21}	P_{22}	P_{23}	P_{24}	P_{21}	P_{22}	P_{23}	P_{24}	P_{21}	P_{22}	P_{23}	P_{24}	P_{21}	P_{22}	P_{23}	P_{24}	P_{21}	P_{22}	P_{23}	P_{24}
9	P_{31}	P_{32}	P_{33}	P_{34}	P_{31}	P_{32}	P_{33}	P_{34}	P_{31}	P_{32}	P_{33}	P_{34}	P_{31}	P_{32}	P_{33}	P_{34}	P_{31}	P_{32}	P_{33}	P_{34}	P_{31}	P_{32}	P_{33}	P_{34}
10	P_{11}	P_{12}	P_{13}	P_{14}	P_{11}	P_{12}	P_{13}	P_{14}	P_{11}	P_{12}	P_{13}	P_{14}	P_{11}	P_{12}	P_{13}	P_{14}	P_{11}	P_{12}	P_{13}	P_{14}	P_{11}	P_{12}	P_{13}	P_{14}
11	P_{21}	P_{22}	P_{23}	P_{24}	P_{21}	P_{22}	P_{23}	P_{24}	P_{21}	P_{22}	P_{23}	P_{24}	P_{21}	P_{22}	P_{23}	P_{24}	P_{21}	P_{22}	P_{23}	P_{24}	P_{21}	P_{22}	P_{23}	P_{24}
12	P_{31}	P_{32}	P_{33}	P_{34}	P_{31}	P_{32}	P_{33}	P_{34}	P_{31}	P_{32}	P_{33}	P_{34}	P_{31}	P_{32}	P_{33}	P_{34}	P_{31}	P_{32}	P_{33}	P_{34}	P_{31}	P_{32}	P_{33}	P_{34}
13	P_{11}	P_{12}	P_{13}	P_{14}	P_{11}	P_{12}	P_{13}	P_{14}	P_{11}	P_{12}	P_{13}	P_{14}	P_{11}	P_{12}	P_{13}	P_{14}	P_{11}	P_{12}	P_{13}	P_{14}	P_{11}	P_{12}	P_{13}	P_{14}
14	P_{21}	P_{22}	P_{23}	P_{24}	P_{21}	P_{22}	P_{23}	P_{24}	P_{21}	P_{22}	P_{23}	P_{24}	P_{21}	P_{22}	P_{23}	P_{24}	P_{21}	P_{22}	P_{23}	P_{24}	P_{21}	P_{22}	P_{23}	P_{24}
15	P_{31}	P_{32}	P_{33}	P_{34}	P_{31}	P_{32}	P_{33}	P_{34}	P_{31}	P_{32}	P_{33}	P_{34}	P_{31}	P_{32}	P_{33}	P_{34}	P_{31}	P_{32}	P_{33}	P_{34}	P_{31}	P_{32}	P_{33}	P_{34}
16	P_{11}	P_{12}	P_{13}	P_{14}	P_{11}	P_{12}	P_{13}	P_{14}	P_{11}	P_{12}	P_{13}	P_{14}	P_{11}	P_{12}	P_{13}	P_{14}	P_{11}	P_{12}	P_{13}	P_{14}	P_{11}	P_{12}	P_{13}	P_{14}
17	P_{21}	P_{22}	P_{23}	P_{24}	P_{21}	P_{22}	P_{23}	P_{24}	P_{21}	P_{22}	P_{23}	P_{24}	P_{21}	P_{22}	P_{23}	P_{24}	P_{21}	P_{22}	P_{23}	P_{24}	P_{21}	P_{22}	P_{23}	P_{24}
18	P_{31}	P_{32}	P_{33}	P_{34}	P_{31}	P_{32}	P_{33}	P_{34}	P_{31}	P_{32}	P_{33}	P_{34}	P_{31}	P_{32}	P_{33}	P_{34}	P_{31}	P_{32}	P_{33}	P_{34}	P_{31}	P_{32}	P_{33}	P_{34}
19	P_{11}	P_{12}	P_{13}	P_{14}	P_{11}	P_{12}	P_{13}	P_{14}	P_{11}	P_{12}	P_{13}	P_{14}	P_{11}	P_{12}	P_{13}	P_{14}	P_{11}	P_{12}	P_{13}	P_{14}	P_{11}	P_{12}	P_{13}	P_{14}
20	P_{21}	P_{22}	P_{23}	P_{24}	P_{21}	P_{22}	P_{23}	P_{24}	P_{21}	P_{22}	P_{23}	P_{24}	P_{21}	P_{22}	P_{23}	P_{24}	P_{21}	P_{22}	P_{23}	P_{24}	P_{21}	P_{22}	P_{23}	P_{24}
21	P_{31}	P_{32}	P_{33}	P_{34}	P_{31}	P_{32}	P_{33}	P_{34}	P_{31}	P_{32}	P_{33}	P_{34}	P_{31}	P_{32}	P_{33}	P_{34}	P_{31}	P_{32}	P_{33}	P_{34}	P_{31}	P_{32}	P_{33}	P_{34}
22	P_{11}	P_{12}	P_{13}	P_{14}	P_{11}	P_{12}	P_{13}	P_{14}	P_{11}	P_{12}	P_{13}	P_{14}	P_{11}	P_{12}	P_{13}	P_{14}	P_{11}	P_{12}	P_{13}	P_{14}	P_{11}	P_{12}	P_{13}	P_{14}
23	P_{21}	P_{22}	P_{23}	P_{24}	P_{21}	P_{22}	P_{23}	P_{24}	P_{21}	P_{22}	P_{23}	P_{24}	P_{21}	P_{22}	P_{23}	P_{24}	P_{21}	P_{22}	P_{23}	P_{24}	P_{21}	P_{22}	P_{23}	P_{24}
24	P_{31}	P_{32}	P_{33}	P_{34}	P_{31}	P_{32}	P_{33}	P_{34}	P_{31}	P_{32}	P_{33}	P_{34}	P_{31}	P_{32}	P_{33}	P_{34}	P_{31}	P_{32}	P_{33}	P_{34}	P_{31}	P_{32}	P_{33}	P_{34}

Figure 3.4. Block cyclic distribution of a matrix with 24×24 blocks over a 3×4 processor grid. The numbers on the left and on the top of the matrix represent indices of a row of blocks and a column of blocks, respectively. The labeled squares represent blocks of elements, and the label indicates at which location in the processor grid the block is stored—all blocks labeled with the same name are stored in the same processor. Each shaded and unshaded area represents different generalized blocks.

- Each processor P_{Kj} (for all $j \in \{1, ..., m\}$) vertically broadcasts its part of the pivot row $b_{k\bullet}$ to processors $P_{\bullet j}$.
  - Each processor updates each block in its C rectangle with one block from the pivot column and one block from the pivot row, so that each block c_{ij} $\left(i, j \in \left\{1, ..., \dfrac{n}{r}\right\}\right)$ of matrix C will be updated, $c_{ij} = c_{ij} + a_{ik} \times b_{kj}$ (see Fig. 3.5).

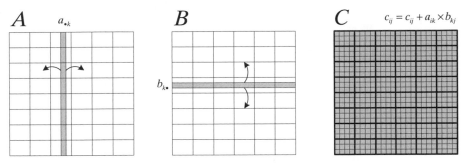

Figure 3.5. One step of the algorithm of parallel matrix–matrix multiplication based on two-dimensional block cyclic distribution of matrices A, B, and C. First, the pivot column $a_{\bullet k}$ of $r \times r$ blocks of matrix A (shown shaded gray) is broadcast horizontally, and the pivot row $b_{k \bullet}$ of $r \times r$ blocks of matrix B (shown shaded gray) is broadcast vertically. Then, each $r \times r$ block c_{ij} of matrix C (also shown shaded gray) is updated, $c_{ij} = c_{ij} + a_{ik} \times b_{kj}$.

○ Thus, after $\dfrac{n}{r}$ steps of the algorithm, each block c_{ij} of matrix C will be

$$c_{ij} = \sum_{k=1}^{\frac{n}{r}} a_{ik} \times b_{kj}, \text{ that is, } C = A \times B.$$

A number of features of this algorithm are particularly important from the point of view of its modifications for heterogeneous platforms:

- Assuming that $p \times r$ and $q \times r$ divide n, the matrices are identically partitioned into rectangular *generalized blocks* of the size $(p \times r) \times (q \times r)$ (see Fig. 3.4). Each generalized block is partitioned into $r \times r$ blocks. The blocks form a two-dimensional $p \times q$ grid, and there is one-to-one mapping between this grid of blocks and the $p \times q$ processor grid.
- At each step of the algorithm, each processor, which does not own the pivot row and column of $r \times r$ blocks, receives horizontally $\dfrac{n}{p} \times r$ elements of matrix A and vertically $\dfrac{n}{q} \times r$ elements of matrix B. Thus, the amount of data received by the processor will be $\left(\dfrac{n}{p} + \dfrac{n}{q} \right) \times r$, that is, proportional to $\left(\dfrac{n}{p} + \dfrac{n}{q} \right)$, the half-perimeter of the rectangular area allocated to this processor (see Fig. 3.6).

Modifications of the algorithm for heterogeneous platforms typically use the following general design (Kalinov and Lastovetsky, 2001):

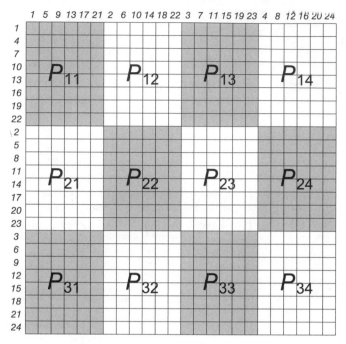

Figure 3.6. Block cyclic distribution of a matrix with 24×24 blocks over a 3×4 processor grid from a processor point of view. Each processor owns 8×6 blocks.

- Matrices **A**, **B**, and **C** are identically partitioned into equal rectangular generalized blocks
- The generalized blocks are identically partitioned into rectangles so that
  - There is a one-to-one mapping between the rectangles and the processors
  - The area of each rectangle is (approximately) proportional to the speed of the processor that has the rectangle (see Fig. 3.7).
- Then, the algorithm follows the steps of its homogeneous prototype; namely, at each step
  - The pivot column of $r \times r$ blocks of matrix **A** is broadcast horizontally
  - The pivot row of $r \times r$ blocks of matrix **B** is broadcast vertically
  - Each processor updates each block in its **C** partition with one block from the pivot column and one block from the pivot row

The motivation behind the partitioning of the generalized blocks in proportion to the speed of the processors is as follows. At each step of the algorithm, the amount of computations needed to update one $r \times r$ block of matrix **C** is the same for all the blocks. Therefore, the load of the processors will be perfectly balanced if the number of blocks updated by each processor is

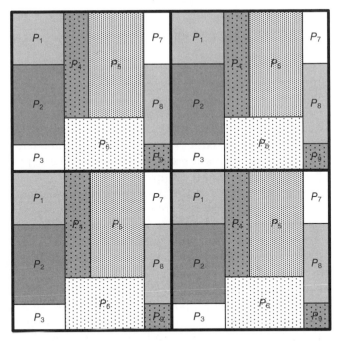

Figure 3.7. Data partitioning for parallel matrix multiplication on nine heterogeneous processors. A matrix is partitioned into four equal generalized blocks, each identically partitioned into nine rectangles. The area of each rectangle is proportional to the speed of the processor owing it.

proportional to its speed. The total number of blocks updated by the processor is equal to the number of blocks allocated to this processor in each generalized block multiplied by the total number of generalized blocks. The number of blocks in a partition of the generalized block is equal to the area of the partition measured in $r \times r$ blocks. Thus, if the area of each partition is proportional to the speed of the processor owing it, then the load of the processors will be perfectly balanced.

The general design of heterogeneous matrix multiplication algorithms introduces two new groups of algorithmic parameters:

- the size $l \times m$ of a generalized block, and
- for each processor, the size and the location of the rectangular partition of the generalized block allocated to the processor.

Correspondingly, two new optimization problems should be addressed, namely, finding the optimal size of a generalized block and finding the optimal partitioning of the generalized block.

The size of a generalized block ranges from $(p \times r) \times (q \times r)$ to $n \times n$. The parameter controls two conflicting aspects of the heterogeneous algorithm:

- the accuracy of load balancing, and
- the level of potential parallelism in the execution of successive steps of the algorithm.

The larger the value of this parameter, the larger is the total number of $r \times r$ blocks in a generalized block, and hence, the more accurately this number can be partitioned in a proportion given by positive real numbers. Therefore, the larger the value of this parameter, the better balanced the load of the processors is. On the other hand, the larger the value of this parameter, the stronger the dependence between successive steps of the parallel algorithm is, which hinders the parallel execution of the steps.

Consider two extreme cases. If the parameter is equal to $n \times n$, then the distribution will provide the best possible balance of the processors' load. At the same time, the distribution will turn into a pure two-dimensional block distribution resulting in the lowest possible level of parallel execution of successive steps of the algorithm. If the parameter is equal to $(p \times r) \times (q \times r)$, then the distribution will be identical to the homogeneous distribution, which does not bother about load balancing. At the same time, this value of the parameter will provide the highest possible level of parallel execution of successive steps of the algorithm. Thus, the optimal value of this parameter lies in between these two, resulting in a trade-off between load balancing and parallel execution of successive steps of the algorithm.

The problem of finding the optimal size of a generalized block has not received enough attention from the research community. It has not been even formulated in mathematical form yet. It is not clear if the problem can even be formulated in some form with performance models of heterogeneous platforms, including only the speeds of the processors, at all. It looks like that more detailed models, taking account of the performance of the communication network, are needed for this purpose.

Unlike the problem of optimizing the size of a generalized block, the problem of optimal partitioning of the generalized block has been well studied. So far, the studies have been interested not in an exact solution but rather in an asymptotically optimal solution, which is an approximate solution approaching the optimal one with the increase of the block size. As we have seen in Section 3.1, such relaxation of the partitioning problem makes its formulation possible not only in terms of absolute speeds of the processors but also in terms of their relative speeds. The use of relative speeds instead of absolute speeds normally simplifies the design and application of partitioning algorithms.

From the partitioning point of view, a generalized block is an integer-valued rectangular. Therefore, if we are only interested in an asymptotically optimal solution, the problem of its partitioning can be reduced to a geometrical problem of optimal partitioning of a real-valued rectangle. Indeed, given a real-valued optimal solution of the problem, its asymptotically optimal solution can be easily obtained by rounding off the real values of the optimal solution to integers.

In the most general form, the related geometrical problem has been formulated as follows (Beaumont *et al.*, 2001b):

- Given a set of p processors P_1, P_2, ..., P_p, the relative speed of each of which is characterized by a positive constant, $s_i(\Sigma_{i=1}^{p}s_i = 1)$
- Partition a unit square into p rectangles so that
  - There is one-to-one mapping between the rectangles and the processors
  - The area of the rectangle allocated to processor P_i is equal to $s_i(i \in \{1, ..., p\})$
  - The partitioning minimizes $\sum_{i=1}^{p}(w_i + h_i)$, where w_i is the width and h_i is the height of the rectangle allocated to processor $P_i(i \in \{1, ..., p\})$

Partitioning the unit square into rectangles with the area proportional to the speed of the processors is aimed at balancing the load of the processors. As a rule, there are multiple different partitionings satisfying the criterion.

Minimizing the sum of half-perimeters of the rectangles, $\sum_{i=1}^{p}(w_i + h_i)$, is aimed at minimizing the total volume of data communicated between the processors. Indeed, as we have seen, at each step of the matrix multiplication algorithm, each processor that does not own the pivot row and column receives the amount of data proportional to the half-perimeter of the rectangle it owns. Therefore, the amount of data communicated at the step between all the processors will be proportional to the sum of the half-perimeters of all rectangles, $\sum_{i=1}^{p}(w_i + h_i)$, less the sum of the heights of the rectangles owing the pivot column (which is 1 in the case of a unit square), and less the sum of the widths of the rectangles owing the pivot row (which is also 1 for a unit square). Thus, at each step, the amount of communicated data will be proportional to $\sum_{i=1}^{p}(w_i + h_i) - 2$. Because the total amount of data communicated between the processors is the same at each step of the algorithm, the total amount of data communicated during the execution of the algorithm will be also proportional to $\sum_{i=1}^{p}(w_i + h_i) - 2$. Therefore, minimization of $\sum_{i=1}^{p}(w_i + h_i) - 2$ will minimize the total volume of data communicated between the processors during the parallel matrix multiplication. Obviously, any solution minimizing $\sum_{i=1}^{p}(w_i + h_i)$ will also minimize $\sum_{i=1}^{p}(w_i + h_i) - 2$.

The use of a unit square instead of a rectangle in the formulation of the problem does not make it less general because the optimal solution of this problem for an arbitrary rectangle is obtained by straightforward scaling of the corresponding optimal solution for the unit square.

Proposition 3.7 (Beaumont *et al.*, 2001b). The general geometrical partitioning problem is NP-complete.

Note. If all communications can be performed in parallel, the communication cost will be determined by the processor sending/receiving the largest messages. A variation of the general problem, which is looking for a partitioning that minimizes $\max_{i=1}^{p}(w_i + h_i)$ rather than $\sum_{i=1}^{p}(w_i + h_i)$, would better model such a situation. That variation of the general geometrical partitioning problem has also been proved NP-complete (Beaumont *et al.*, 2001b).

The NP-completeness means that, most likely, an efficient algorithm, solving the geometrical partitioning problem in its general form, does not exist. Therefore, a number of restrictions of this problem allowing for polynomial solutions have been formulated and efficiently solved, the least restrictive of which is probably the column-based geometrical partitioning problem.

The column-based problem is obtained from the general one by imposing the additional restriction that rectangles of the partitioning make up columns, as illustrated in Figure 3.8.

The column-based geometrical partitioning problem has a polynomial solution of the complexity $O(p^3)$. The corresponding algorithm (Beaumont *et al.*, 2001b) is based on the following observations:

- There always exists an optimal column-based partitioning such that if linearly ordered columnwise, beginning from the top left corner, the rectangles of the partitioning will go in the nonincreasing order of their areas, $s_1 \geq s_2 \geq \dots \geq s_p$.

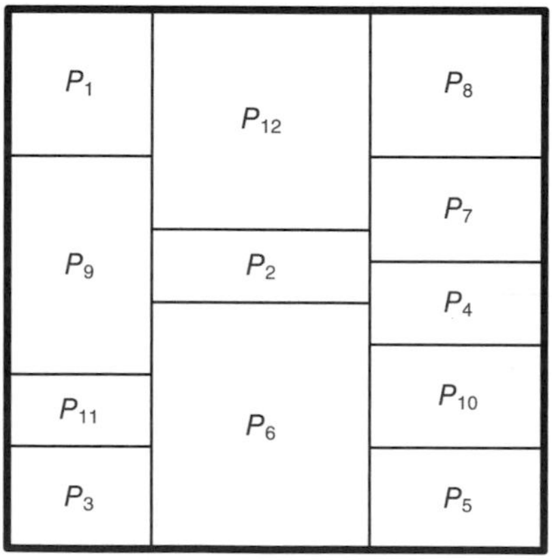

Figure 3.8. Column-based partitioning of the unit square into 12 rectangles. The rectangles of the partitioning form three columns.

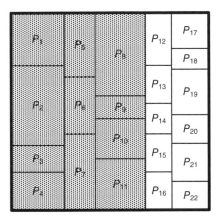

Figure 3.9. If the column-based partitioning of the unit square over processors P_1, P_2, ..., P_{22} is optimal, then the shaded rectangle will be optimally partitioned over processors P_1, P_2, ..., P_{11} by its subpartitioning.

- Let an optimal column-based partitioning, minimizing the sum of half-perimeters of the partitions, consist of c columns, each of which is made of r_i rectangles, $i \in \{1, ..., c\}$. For certainty, we assume that the i-th rectangle from the k-th column is allocated to the processor with index $\left(i + \sum_{j=1}^{k-1} r_j \right)$.

  ◦ Then, the first k columns of the partitioning ($k \in \{1, ..., c - 1\}$) will give an optimal partitioning of the rectangle, having the unit height and the width of $\sum_{i=1}^{k} w_i$ (where w_i is the width of the i-th column), over the first $q = \sum_{i=1}^{k} r_i$ processors, as illustrated in Figure 3.9.

    - Symmetrically, the last k columns of the partitioning will give an optimal partitioning of the rectangle of height 1 and width $\sum_{i=p-k+1}^{p} w_i$ over the last $q = \sum_{i=p-k+1}^{p} r_i$ processors.

  ◦ $\sum_{i=1}^{k} w_i = \sum_{j=1}^{q} s_j$, where $q = \sum_{i=1}^{k} r_i$.

    - Indeed, the area of the rectangle of height 1 and width $\sum_{i=1}^{k} w_i$ will be $1 \times \sum_{i=1}^{k} w_i = \sum_{i=1}^{k} w_i$. On the other hand, the area of this rectangle will be equal to the sum of the areas of its partitions, $\sum_{j=1}^{q} s_j$.

The algorithm can be summarized as follows.

Algorithm 3.2. Optimal column-based partitioning a unit square between p heterogeneous processors:

- First, the processors are reindexed in the nonincreasing order of their speeds, $s_1 \geq s_2 \geq \ldots \geq s_p$. The algorithm only considers partitionings, where the i-th rectangle in the linear columnwise order is mapped to processor $P_i, i \in \{1, \ldots, p\}$.
- The algorithm iteratively builds the optimal c column partitioning $\mathcal{P}(c,q)$ of a rectangle of height 1 and width $\sum_{j=1}^{q} s_j$ for all $c \in \{1, \ldots, p\}$ and $q \in \{c, \ldots, p\}$:
  - $\mathcal{P}(1,q)$ is trivial.
  - For $c > 1$, $\mathcal{P}(c,q)$ is built in two steps:
    - First, $(q - c + 1)$ candidate partitionings $\{\mathcal{P}_j(c,q)\}$ ($j \in \{1, \ldots, q - c + 1\}$) are constructed such that $\mathcal{P}_j(c,q)$ is obtained by combining the partitioning $\mathcal{P}(c - 1, q - j)$ with the straightforward partitioning of the last column (the column number c) of the width $\sum_{i=q-j+1}^{q} s_i$ into j rectangles of the corresponding areas $s_{q-j+1} \geq s_{q-j+2} \geq \ldots \geq s_q$.
    - Then, $\mathcal{P}(c,q) = \mathcal{P}_k(c,q)$ where $\mathcal{P}_k(c, q) \in \{\mathcal{P}_j(c, q)_{j=1}^{q-c+1}\}$ and minimizes the sum of the half-perimeters of the rectangles.
- The optimal column-based partitioning will be a partitioning from the set $\{\mathcal{P}(c, p)_{c=1}^{p}\}$ that minimizes the sum of half-perimeters of rectangles.

A few more restricted forms of the column-based geometrical partitioning problem have been also addressed. The pioneering result in the field was an algorithm of linear complexity solving the column-based geometrical partitioning problem under the additional assumption that the processors are already arranged into a set of processor columns (i.e., assuming that the number of columns c in the partitioning and the mapping of rectangles in each column to the processors are given). The algorithm is as follows.

Algorithm 3.3 (Kalinov and Lastovetsky, 1999a). Optimal partitioning a unit square between p heterogeneous processors arranged into c columns, each of which is made of r_j processors, $j \in \{1, \ldots, c\}$:

- Let the relative speed of the i-th processor from the j-th column, P_{ij}, be
$$s_{ij} \left(\sum_{j=1}^{c} \sum_{i=1}^{r_j} s_{ij} = 1 \right).$$

- Then, we first partition the unit square into c vertical rectangular slices such that the width of the j-th slice is $w_j = \sum_{i=1}^{r_j} s_{ij}$.
  - This partitioning makes the area of each vertical slice proportional to the sum of the speeds of the processors in the corresponding column.
- Second, each vertical slice is partitioned independently into rectangles in proportion with the speed of the processors in the corresponding processor column.

Figure 3.10 illustrates the algorithm for a 3×3 processor grid.

We can see that Algorithm 3.3 also solves a more restricted problem when the given arrangement of processors forms a two-dimensional grid.

Another restricted form, a *grid-based* geometrical partitioning problem, is obtained from the general problem by imposing the additional restriction that the heterogeneous processors owing the rectangles of the partitioning form a two-dimensional grid (as illustrated in Fig. 3.11). Equivalently, a grid-based partitioning can be defined as a partitioning of the unit square into rectangles such that there exist p and q such that any vertical line crossing the unit square will pass through exactly p rectangles and any horizontal line crossing the square will pass through exactly q rectangles.

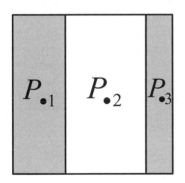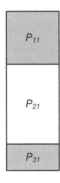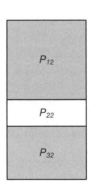

(a) Partition between processor columns   (b) Partition inside each processor column

Figure 3.10. Example of two-step partitioning of the unit square between nine heterogeneous processors arranged into a 3×3 processor grid. The relative speed of the processors is given by matrix $s = \begin{pmatrix} 0.11 & 0.25 & 0.05 \\ 0.17 & 0.09 & 0.08 \\ 0.05 & 0.17 & 0.03 \end{pmatrix}$. (a) At the first step, the unit square is partitioned in one dimension between processor columns of the 3×3 processor grid in proportion 0.33:0.51:0.16. (b) At the second step, each vertical rectangle is partitioned independently in one dimension between the processors of its column. The first rectangle will be partitioned in proportion 0.11:0.17:0.05. The second rectangle will be partitioned in proportion 0.25:0.09:0.17. The third rectangle will be partitioned in proportion 0.05:0.08:0.03.

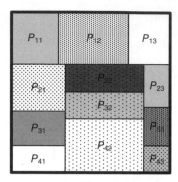

Figure 3.11. Grid-based partitioning of the unit square into 12 rectangles. The processors owing the rectangles of the partitioning form a 4×3 processor grid.

The grid-based partitioning problem has some nice properties that allow for its efficient solution.

Proposition 3.8 (Lastovetsky, 2007). Let a grid-based partitioning of the unit square between p heterogeneous processors form c columns, each of which consists of r processors, $p = r \times c$. Then, the sum of half-perimeters of the rectangles of the partitioning will be equal to $(r + c)$.

Proof. The sum of the heights of the rectangles owned by each column of processors will be equal to 1. As we have in total c columns, the sum of the heights of all rectangles of the partitioning will be equal to c. Similarly, the sum of the widths of the rectangles owned by each row of processors in the processor grid will be equal to 1. As we have in total r rows in the grid, the sum of the widths of all rectangles of the partitioning will be equal to r. Hence, the sum of the half-perimeters of all rectangles will be equal to $(r + c)$. *End of proof of Proposition 3.8.*

There are two important corollaries from Proposition 3.8:

- The shape $r \times c$ of the processor grid formed by any optimal grid-based partitioning will minimize $(r + c)$.
- The sum of the half-perimeters of the rectangles of the optimal grid-based partitioning does not depend on the mapping of the processors onto the nodes of the grid.

The grid-based geometrical partitioning problem has a polynomial solution of the complexity $O(p^{3/2})$. The corresponding algorithm is as follows.

Algorithm 3.4 (Lastovetsky, 2007). Optimal grid-based partitioning a unit square between p heterogeneous processors:

- **Step 1.** Find the optimal shape $r \times c$ of the processor grid such that $p = r \times c$ and $(r + c)$ is minimal.

- **Step 2.** Map the processors onto the nodes of the grid.
- **Step 3.** Apply Algorithm 3.3 of the optimal partitioning of the unit square to this $r \times c$ arrangement of the p heterogeneous processors.

The correctness of Algorithm 3.4 is obvious. Step 1 of the algorithm finds the optimal shape of the processor grid that minimizes the sum of the half-perimeters of any grid-based partitioning for any mapping of the processors onto the nodes of the grid. Step 3 just finds one such partitioning, the rectangles of which are proportional to the speeds of the processors. Note that the returned optimal grid-based partitioning will always be column-based due to the nature of Algorithm 3.4 (as illustrated in Fig. 3.12). Hence, the optimal grid-based partitioning can be seen as the optimal column-based partitioning under the additional restriction that all columns of the partitioning have the same number of rectangles.

Step 1 of Algorithm 3.4 can be performed by the following simple algorithm.

Algorithm 3.5. Finding r and c such that $p = r \times c$ and $(r + c)$ is minimal:

```
r = ⌊√p⌋;
while(r>1)
        if((pmodr)==0))
          goto stop;
        else
            r--;
stop:  c = p/r;
```

Proposition 3.9. Algorithm 3.5 is correct.

Proof. If p is a square number, then $r = c = \sqrt{p}$ minimizes $(r + c)$, and the algorithm works correctly in this case. Now let us assume that p is not a square

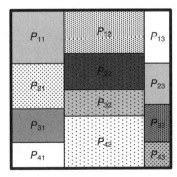

Figure 3.12. A 4×3 optimal grid-based partitioning returned by Algorithm 3.4. The rectangles of the partitioning form three columns.

number. Then, $r \neq c$. Due to symmetry, we can assume that $r < c$ without a loss of generality. We have $r + c = r + \dfrac{p}{r}$. It is easy to show that function $f(r) = r + \dfrac{p}{r}$ will be decreasing if $r < c$. Indeed, $\dfrac{df}{dr} = 1 - \dfrac{p}{r^2}$. Therefore, if $r < c$, then $r < \sqrt{p}$, and hence, $1 - \dfrac{p}{r^2} < 0$. Thus, if $0 < r_1 < c_1, 0 < r_2 < c_2, r_1 < r_2$ and $r_1 \times c_1 = r_2 \times c_2 = p$, then $r_1 + c_1 > r_2 + c_2$. Therefore, the algorithm will return the correct result if p is not a square number. *End of proof of Proposition 3.9.*

Proposition 3.10. The complexity of Algorithm 3.4 can be bounded by $O(p^{3/2})$.

Proof. The complexity of Step 1 of Algorithm 3.4 can be bounded by $O(p^{3/2})$. Indeed, we can use Algorithm 3.5 at this step. The number of iterations of the main loop of Algorithm 3.5 is no greater than $\sqrt{p}$. At each iteration, we test the condition $(p \bmod r) == 0$. A straightforward testing of this condition can be done in $\left\lceil \dfrac{p}{r} \right\rceil$ steps, each of the complexity $O(1)$ (e.g., by repeated subtraction of r from p). Therefore, the overall complexity of Algorithm 3.5 can be comfortably bounded by $O(p^{3/2})$. As we can use an arbitrary mapping of the processors onto the nodes of the $r \times c$ grid, the complexity of the Step 2 of Algorithm 3.4 can be bounded by $O(p)$. Algorithm 3.3 used in Step 3 has the complexity $O(p)$. Thus, the overall complexity of Algorithm 3.4 can be bounded by $O(p^{3/2}) + O(p) + O(p) = O(p^{3/2})$. *End of proof of Proposition 3.10.*

The grid-based partitioning problem is not the most restrictive partitioning problem that has been addressed by algorithm designers. A *Cartesian* partitioning problem is even more restrictive. The Cartesian problem can be obtained from the column-based problem by imposing the additional restriction that rectangles of the partitioning make up rows, as illustrated in Figure 3.13. A

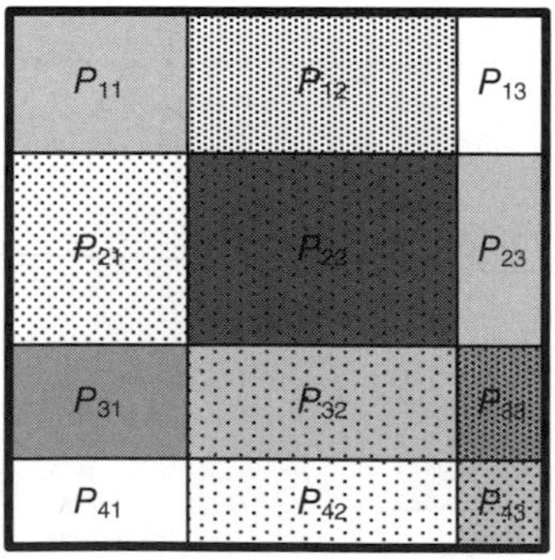

Figure 3.13. Cartesian partitioning of the unit square into 12 rectangles. The rectangles of the partitioning form a 4×3 grid. No rectangle has more than one direct neighbor in any direction (left, up, right, or down).

Cartesian partitioning can be also defined as a grid-based partitioning, rectangles of which make up both rows and columns.

Cartesian partitionings play an important role in the design of parallel heterogeneous algorithms. In particular, *scalable* heterogeneous parallel algorithms are normally based on Cartesian partitionings. The point is that in a Cartesian partitioning, no rectangle has more than one direct neighbor in any direction (left, up, right, or down), which results in scalable communication patterns for algorithms with communications only between direct neighbors. The scalability of heterogeneous parallel algorithms is considered in Chapter 6.

Despite being more restrictive than the column-based and grid-based problems, the Cartesian partitioning problem proves more difficult. The reason is that unlike optimal column-based and grid-based partitionings, an optimal Cartesian partitioning may not perfectly balance the load of processors (just because for some combinations of relative speeds, there may be no Cartesian partitioning at all perfectly balancing their load). In other words, the areas of the rectangles of the partitioning may not be proportional to the speeds of the processors. In a general form, the Cartesian partitioning problem can be formulated as follows:

- Given p processors, the speed of each of which is characterized by a given positive constant
- Find a Cartesian partitioning of a unit square such that
  ◦ There is one-to-one mapping between the rectangles of the partitioning and the processors
  ◦ The partitioning minimizes $\max_{i,j}\left\{\dfrac{h_i \times w_j}{s_{ij}}\right\}$, where h_i is the height of rectangles in the i-th row, w_j is the width of rectangles in the j-th column, and s_{ij} is the speed of the processor owing j-th rectangle in the i-th row, $i \in \{1, ..., r\}, j \in \{1, ..., c\}, p = r \times c$.

This formulation is motivated by parallel matrix algorithms requiring the same amount of computation for the calculation of each single element of the resulting matrix. The speed of a processor making the partitioning problem intuitive in the context of the matrix algorithms can be obtained as follows:

- First, the absolute speed is found by dividing the number of matrix elements of the resulting matrix computed by the processor by the computation time elapsed on the processor.
- Then, this absolute speed, expressed in numbers of matrix elements computed per time unit, is normalized by dividing by the total number of elements in the matrix.

In this case, $\dfrac{h_i \times w_j}{s_{ij}}$ will give us the computation time of the processor owing

j-th rectangle in the i-th row of the partitioning; and $\max\limits_{i,j}\left\{\dfrac{h_i \times w_j}{s_{ij}}\right\}$ will give

the total computation time, assuming the fully parallel execution of the algorithm. The cost of communication is not addressed in this formulation at all (to do it, we need additional parameters describing the communication network).

Note. The speeds s_{ij} can be further normalized such that $\sum\limits_{j}\sum\limits_{i} s_{ij} = 1$.

The Cartesian problem has not been studied in the above general form. An algorithm solving this problem has to find an optimal combination of the shape $r \times c$ of the processor grid, the mapping of the processors onto the nodes of the grid, and the sizes of rectangles allocated to the processors. However, simplified versions of the problem were studied, and the studies proved its difficulty. For example, under the additional assumption that the shape $r \times c$ of the partitioning is given, the problem proved NP-complete (Beaumont *et al.*, 2001a). Moreover, it is still unclear if there exists a polynomial algorithm solving the problem even when both the shape $r \times c$ of the grid and the mapping of the processors onto the nodes of the grid are given. The only positive result states that there exists an optimal Cartesian partitioning such that the processors will be arranged in the grid in the nonincreasing order of their speeds (in any direction—from left to right and from top to bottom) (Beaumont *et al.*, 2001a). At the same time, some efficient algorithms returning approximate solutions of the simplified versions of the Cartesian partitioning problem have been proposed (Beaumont *et al.*, 2001a; Dovolnov, Kalinov, and Klinov, 2003). They are based on the following observations (Beaumont *et al.*, 2001a):

- Let matrix $\begin{pmatrix} s_{11} & \cdots & s_{1j} & \cdots & s_{1c} \\ \vdots & & \vdots & & \vdots \\ s_{i1} & \cdots & s_{ij} & \cdots & s_{ic} \\ \vdots & & \vdots & & \vdots \\ s_{r1} & \cdots & s_{rj} & \cdots & s_{rc} \end{pmatrix}$ representing the speeds of the given

$r \times c$ arrangement of the processors be a rank-one matrix.
- Then, there exists an optimal Cartesian partitioning, which perfectly

balances the load of the processors, $\dfrac{h_i \times w_j}{s_{ij}} = const.$

Indeed, if $\begin{pmatrix} s_{11} & \cdots & s_{1j} & \cdots & s_{1c} \\ \vdots & & \vdots & & \vdots \\ s_{i1} & \cdots & s_{ij} & \cdots & s_{ic} \\ \vdots & & \vdots & & \vdots \\ s_{r1} & \cdots & s_{rj} & \cdots & s_{rc} \end{pmatrix}$ is a rank-one matrix, then

there exist $\{a_i\}_{i=1}^{r}$ and $\{b_j\}_{j=1}^{c}$ such that

$$\begin{pmatrix} s_{11} & \cdots & s_{1j} & \cdots & s_{1c} \\ \vdots & & \vdots & & \vdots \\ s_{i1} & \cdots & s_{ij} & \cdots & s_{ic} \\ \vdots & & \vdots & & \vdots \\ s_{r1} & \cdots & s_{rj} & \cdots & s_{rc} \end{pmatrix} = \begin{pmatrix} a_1 \\ \vdots \\ a_i \\ \vdots \\ a_r \end{pmatrix} \times \begin{pmatrix} b_1 & \cdots & b_j & \cdots & b_c \end{pmatrix},$$ that is, $s_{ij} = a_i \times b_j$. Let

$$h_i = \frac{\sum_j s_{ij}}{\sum_i \sum_j s_{ij}} \quad \text{and} \quad w_j = \frac{\sum_i s_{ij}}{\sum_i \sum_j s_{ij}}. \quad \text{Then,} \quad h_i = \frac{\sum_j s_{ij}}{\sum_i \sum_j s_{ij}} = \frac{a_i \times \sum_j b_j}{\sum_i a_i \times \sum_j b_j} = \frac{a_i}{\sum_i a_i}.$$

Hence, $\dfrac{h_i}{a_i} = \dfrac{1}{\sum_i a_i} = const.$ Similarly, $\dfrac{w_j}{b_j} = \dfrac{1}{\sum_j b_j} = const.$ Therefore,

$$\frac{h_i \times w_j}{s_{ij}} = \frac{h_i \times w_j}{a_i \times b_j} = \frac{h_i}{a_i} \times \frac{w_j}{b_j} = const.$$

Thus, if both the shape $r \times c$ of the processor grid and the mapping of the processors onto the nodes of the grid are given, we can use formulae

$$h_i = \frac{\sum_j s_{ij}}{\sum_i \sum_j s_{ij}} \quad \text{and} \quad w_j = \frac{\sum_i s_{ij}}{\sum_i \sum_j s_{ij}}$$ to calculate an approximate solution of the

simplified Cartesian partitioning problem (Dovolnov, Kalinov, and Klimov, 2003). This solution will be exact if the speed matrix is of rank one. In the returned partitioning, the height h_i of the rectangles in the i-th row will be proportional to the total speed of the processors in the i-th row, and the width w_j of the rectangles in the j-th column will be proportional to the total speed of the processors in the j-th column. Another efficient algorithm of calculating h_i and w_j, returning an exact solution for rank-one speed matrices, is proposed in Beaumont *et al.* (2001a).

A simple procedure returning an approximate solution of the simplified Cartesian partitioning problem when only the shape $r \times c$ of the partitioning is given has also been proposed (Beaumont *et al.*, 2001a). The procedure is as follows.

Algorithm 3.6 Finding a Cartesian partitioning of a unit square between p processors of the given shape $p = r \times c$:

- **Step 1.** Arrange the processors so that if linearly ordered row-wise, beginning from the top left corner, they will go in a nonincreasing order of their speeds.
- **Step 2.** For the processor arrangement, apply one of the above algorithms to find an approximate solution, $\{h_i\}_{i=1}^r, \{w_j\}_{j=1}^c$.
- **Step 3.** Calculate the areas $h_i \times w_j$ of the rectangles of the partitioning.
- **Step 4.** Rearrange the processors so that $\forall i, j, k, l : s_{ij} \ge s_{kl} \Leftrightarrow h_i \times w_j \ge h_k \times w_l$.

- **Step 5. If** Step 4 does not change the arrangement of the processors **then** return the current partitioning and stop the procedure **else** go to Step 2.

It is a trivial exercise to prove a property of Cartesian partitionings, similar to the property that has been formulated for grid-based partitionings in Proposition 3.8. Namely, the following proposition is true.

Proposition 3.10. Let a Cartesian partitioning of the unit square between p heterogeneous processors form c columns, each of which consists of r processors, $p = r \times c$. Then, the sum of the half-perimeters of the rectangles of the partitioning will be equal to $(r + c)$.

Thus, for Cartesian partitionings, the minimization of the communication cost, represented by the sum of the half-perimeters of the rectangles of the partitioning, does not depend on the speeds of the processors; they depend only on their total number. In other words, for Cartesian paritionings, the minimization of computation cost and the minimization of communication cost are two independent optimization problems. Any Cartesian partitioning that minimizes $(r + c)$ will optimize the communication cost. Therefore, a communicationally optimal approximate solution of the general Cartesian partitioning problem can be found by applying Algorithm 3.6 to the shape $r \times c$ returned by Algorithm 3.5.

Concluding the section on partitioning matrices with constant models of heterogeneous processors, we have to note that the geometrical partitioning problem as it was formulated in the most general form in this section is restricted to partitioning into rectangles. Thus, the general partitioning problem is itself somewhat restricted. Although there has been no formal proof of this statement yet, most researchers believe that allowing for nonrectangular partitions will not significantly improve the quality of partitioning in terms of performance but at the same time will significantly complicate solution of the partitioning problem.

This statement seems plausible, at least when the number of heterogeneous processors p is big enough. At the same time, it has been shown that if the number of heterogeneous processors is small, say two or three, then the parallel algorithms based on nonrectangular partitioning can significantly outperform their counterparts based on the rectangular one (Becker and Lastovetsky, 2006, 2007). Consider, for example, the following partitioning scheme for multiplication of two dense $N \times N$ matrices on two heterogeneous processors (Becker and Lastovetsky, 2006). As shown in Figure 3.14, the slower processor is allocated a square partition of size $q \times q$, and the faster processor receives the balance of the matrix. The value of q is calculated so that the areas of the two partitions are proportional to the speeds of the processors, thus balancing their computational load. Therefore, $q = \dfrac{N}{\sqrt{r+1}}$, where r is the ratio of processor speeds ($r > 1$).

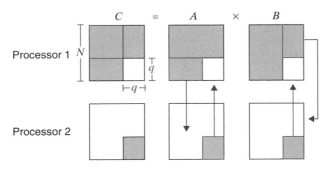

Figure 3.14. The square-corner partitioning and communication steps.

As shown in Figure 3.14, the necessary communications involve processor 1 sending two pieces of size $q \times (N - q)$ to processor 2, and processor 2 sending two pieces of size $q \times q$ to processor 1. This results in the total volume of communication equal to $2 \times N \times q$. The rectangular partitioning always results in a total volume of communication equal to N^2, regardless of the speed ratio. Trivial calculations show that if $r > 3$, then $2 \times N \times q < N^2$; that is, the square-corner total volume of communication will be less than the rectangular total volume of communication whenever the ratio of processor speeds is greater than three, and the difference between these two volumes will be quickly increasing with the increase of the speed ratio as shown in Figure 3.15.

The other advantage of this partitioning is that a large square area of matrix C can be immediately calculated by processor 1 as it does not need any data from processor 2 to perform the calculations (see Fig. 3.14), allowing the overlapping of some communications and computations.

In the case of three interconnected heterogeneous processors, the corresponding extension of the square-corner partitioning, which is shown in Figure 3.16, results in even more significant performance gains (Becker and Lastovetsky, 2007). This three-node square-corner partitioning has three partitions, the first being a square located in one corner of the matrix, the second being a square in the diagonally opposite corner, and the third being polygonal—the balance of the matrix. In a square-corner partitioning, the squares cannot overlap. This imposes the following restriction on the relative speeds of the nodes $\dfrac{s_2}{s_1} \times \dfrac{s_3}{s_1} \leq \dfrac{1}{4}$, where $s_1 + s_2 + s_3 = 1$ and s_1 is the relative speed of the node owing the balance of the matrix.

On a linear array topology, where the fastest processor is the middle node, the optimal square-corner partitioning always results in a lower total volume of communication than the optimal rectangular partitioning. The benefit of a more efficient communication schedule further reduces communication time, which in turn drives down the total execution time. On a fully connected topology, the optimal square-corner partitioning has a lower communication cost

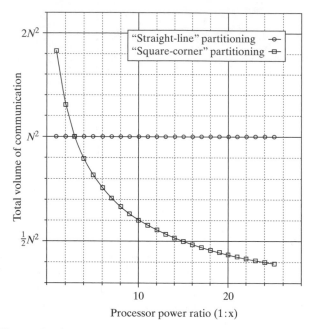

Figure 3.15. The total volume of communication for the square-corner and rectangular partitionings.

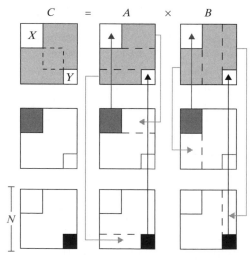

Figure 3.16. The partitions and data movements of the three node square-corner partitioning.

than the optimal rectangular partitioning for a representative range of their relative speeds.

At first glance, the case of a small number of heterogeneous processors looks rather academic and not significant in practice. Indeed, who would do parallel computing on two or three heterogeneous processors? But if we consider this configuration as a model for a small number of interconnected high-performance clusters, the practical importance of a careful study of this case becomes more evident. Such nontraditional, nonrectangular partitioning used as the top-level partitioning in hierarchical algorithms for clusters of clusters can significantly improve the performance of many applications.

CHAPTER 4

Distribution of Computations with Nonconstant Performance Models of Heterogeneous Processors

4.1 FUNCTIONAL PERFORMANCE MODEL OF HETEROGENEOUS PROCESSORS

The heterogeneous parallel and distributed algorithms considered in Chapter 3 assume that the relative speed of heterogeneous processors does not depend on the size of the computational task solved by the processors. This assumption is quite satisfactory if the code executed by the processors fully fits into the main memory. However, as soon as the restriction is relaxed, it may not be true due to paging or swapping of the application.

Two heterogeneous processors may have significantly different sizes of main memory. Therefore, beginning from some problem size, a task of the same size will still fit into the main memory of one processor and not fit into the main memory of the other, causing the paging and visible degradation of the speed of the latter. This means that the relative speed of the processors will start significantly changing in favor of the nonpaging processor as soon as the problem size exceeds the critical value.

Moreover, even if the processors have almost the same size of main memory, they may employ different paging algorithms resulting in different levels of speed degradation for a task of the same size, which again implies a change of their relative speed as the problem size exceeds the threshold causing the paging.

Thus, if we allow for paging, the assumption of the constant relative speed of heterogeneous processors, independent of the task size, will not be accurate and realistic anymore. Correspondingly, in this case, we cannot use the data partitioning algorithms presented in Chapter 3 for the optimal distribution of computations over heterogeneous processors. Indeed, in order to apply the algorithms, we have to provide them with positive constants representing the

High-Performance Heterogeneous Computing, by Alexey L. Lastovetsky and Jack J. Dongarra
Copyright © 2009 John Wiley & Sons, Inc.

speed of the processors. Whatever task size m we use to obtain the relative speeds, $s_1(m)$, ... , $s_p(m)$, it is very likely that the algorithms will return a solution $(n_1, n_2, ... , n_p)$, $\Sigma_{i=1}^{p} n_i = n$, which is far from the optimal one, that is, the solution perfectly balancing the load of the processors. The point is that the algorithms will try to achieve $\dfrac{n_i}{s_i(m)} \approx const$, which does not guarantee

$\dfrac{n_i}{s_i(n_i)} \approx const$ if $s_i(n_i)$ significantly differ from $s_i(m)$ for some $i \in \{1, ... , p\}$.

Therefore, to achieve acceptable accuracy of distribution of computations over heterogeneous processors in the possible presence of paging, more realistic performance models of heterogeneous processors are needed. In this section, we introduce one such model called the *functional* performance model (Lastovetsky and Reddy, 2007b).

Under the functional performance model, the speed of each processor is represented by a continuous function of the task size.

The speed is defined as the number of computation units performed by the processor per one time unit. The model is application specific. In particular, this means that the computation unit can be defined differently for different applications. The important requirement is that the computation unit must not vary during the execution of the application. Two examples of computation units are an arithmetical operation and the matrix update $a = a + b \times c$, where a, b, and c are $r \times r$ matrices of the fixed size r.

The task size is understood as a set of one, two, or more parameters characterizing the amount and layout of data stored and processed during the execution of the computational task. The notion of task size should not be confused with the notion of problem size, defined as the number of basic computations in the best sequential algorithm to solve the problem on a single processor (Kumar *et al.*, 1994). The number and semantics of the task size parameters are problem, or even application, specific. The important assumption is that the amount of stored data will increase with the increase of any of the task size parameters.

For example, the size of the task of multiplying two dense square $n \times n$ matrices can be represented by one parameter, n. During the computation of the task, three matrices will be stored and processed. Therefore, the total number of elements to store and process will be $3 \times n^2$. In order to compute one element of the resulting matrix, the application uses n multiplications and $(n - 1)$ additions. Hence, in total, $(2 \times n - 1) \times n^2$ arithmetical operations are needed to solve the task. If n is large enough, this number can be approximated by $2 \times n^3$. Alternatively, a combined computation unit, which is made up of one addition and one multiplication, can be used to express the volume of computation needed to multiply two large square $n \times n$ matrices. In this case, the total number of computation units will be approximately equal to n^3. Therefore, the speed of the processor demonstrated by the application when solving the task of size n can be calculated as n^3 (or $2 \times n^3$) divided by the execution time of the application. This gives us a function from the set of natural numbers representing task sizes into the set of nonnegative real numbers representing the speeds of the processor, f: $\mathbf{N} \to \mathbf{R}_+$. The functional performance model of the processor is obtained by continuous extension of function f: $\mathbf{N} \to \mathbf{R}_+$ to function g: $\mathbf{R}_+ \to \mathbf{R}_+$ (f(n) = g(n) for any n from $\mathbf{N}$).

Another example is the task of multiplying two dense rectangular $n \times k$ and $k \times m$ matrices. The size of this task is represented by three parameters, n, k, and m. The total number of matrix elements to store and process will be $(n \times k + k \times m + n \times m)$. The total number of arithmetical operations needed to solve this task is $(2 \times (k - 1)) \times n \times m$. If k is large enough, this number can be approximated by $2 \times k \times n \times m$. Alternatively, a combined computation unit made up of one addition and one multiplication can be used, resulting in the total number of computation units approximately equal to $k \times n \times m$. Therefore, the speed of the processor exposed by the application when solving the task of size (n,k,m) can be calculated as $k \times n \times m$ (or $2 \times k \times n \times m$) divided by the execution time of the application. This gives us a function f: $\mathbf{N}^3 \to \mathbf{R}_+$, mapping task sizes to the speeds of the processor. The functional performance model of the processor is obtained by a continuous extension of function f: $\mathbf{N}^3 \to \mathbf{R}_+$ to function g: $\mathbf{R}_+^3 \to \mathbf{R}_+$ (f(n,k,m) = g(n,k,m) for any (n,k,m) from $\mathbf{N}^3$).

Thus, under the functional model, the speed of the processor is represented by a continuous function of the task size. Moreover, some further assumptions are made about the shape of the function. Namely, it is assumed that along each of the task size variables, either the function is monotonically decreasing or there exists point x such that

- on the interval $[0,x]$, the function is
  - monotonically increasing,
  - concave, and
  - any straight line coming through the origin of the coordinate system intersects the graph of the function in no more than one point; and
- on the interval $[x,\infty)$, the function is monotonically decreasing.

Experiments with diverse scientific kernels and different computers show that the above assumptions are realistic and the speed of the processor can be approximated accurately enough by a function satisfying them (within the accuracy of measurements) (Lastovetsky and Twamley, 2005). Some typical shapes of the speed function are given in Figure 4.1.

Definition. We will call speed functions satisfying the formulated assumptions *canonical.*

Note. It is easy to *artificially* design a scientific kernel violating the formulated assumptions about the shape of speed function. Indeed, if in the program we

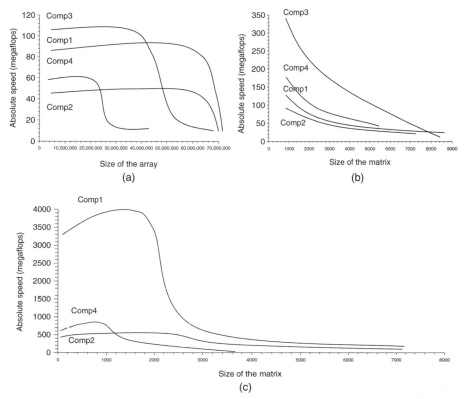

Figure 4.1. Shapes of the speed function for three different applications run on four heterogeneous processors. (a) ArrayOpsF: Arithmetic operations on three arrays of data, accessing memory in a contiguous manner, with an efficient memory referencing pattern and use of cache. (b) MatrixMult: A naive implementation of the multiplication of two dense square matrices, with the result placed in a third matrix. Memory will be accessed in a nonefficient manner. As a result, page faults start occurring for relatively small matrices, gradually increasing with the increase of the matrx size. (c) Matrix-MultATLAS: An efficient implementation of matrix multiplication utilizing the dgemm BLAS routine, optimized using ATLAS.

use naïve matrix multiplication for some matrix sizes and highly efficient ATLAS (Whaley, Petitet, and Dongarra, 2001) routine for the others, the resulting speed function will not be even continuous. We postulate that this is not the case for *naturally* designed scientific codes.

Some carefully designed codes such as ArrayOpsF (Fig. 4.1(a)) and Matrix-MultAtlas (Fig. 4.1(c)), which efficiently use memory hierarchy, demonstrate quite a sharp and distinctive curve of dependence of the absolute speed on the task size. Their design manages to delay the appearance of page faults, minimizing their number for medium task sizes. However, because any design can only delay paging but not avoid it, the number of page faults will start growing like a snowball, beginning from some threshold value of the task size. For such codes, the speed of the processor can be approximated accurately enough by a unit step function. One potential advantage of modeling the processor speed by unit step functions is that parallel algorithms with such models might be obtained by straightforward extensions of parallel algorithms with constant models.

At the same time, application MatrixMult (Fig. 4.1(b)), which implements a straightforward algorithm of multiplication of two dense square matrices and uses inefficient memory reference patterns, displays quite a smooth dependence of the speed on the task size. Page faults for this application start occurring much earlier than for its carefully designed counterpart, but the increase of their number will be much slower. A unit step function cannot accurately approximate the processor speed for such codes. Thus, if we want to have a single performance model covering the whole range of codes, the general functional model is a much better candidate than a model based on the unit step function.

4.2 DATA PARTITIONING WITH THE FUNCTIONAL PERFORMANCE MODEL OF HETEROGENEOUS PROCESSORS

In this section, we revisit some data partitioning problems that have been studied in Chapter 3 with constant performance models of heterogeneous processors. We will formulate and study them with the functional performance model.

We begin with the basic problem of partitioning a set of n (equal) elements between p heterogeneous processors. As we have seen in Chapter 3, the problem is a generalization of the problem of distributing independent computation units over a unidimensional arrangement of heterogeneous processors. The problem can be formulated as follows:

- Given a set of p processors $P_1, P_2, \ldots, P_p$, the speed of each of which is characterized by a real function, $s_i(x)$
- Partition a set of n elements into p subsets so that
  - There is one-to-one mapping between the partitions and the processors
  - The partitioning minimizes $\max_i \dfrac{n_i}{s_i(n_i)}$, where n_i is the number of elements allocated to processor P_i $(1 \leq i \leq p)$

The motivation behind this formulation is obvious. If elements of the set represent computation units of equal size, then the speed of the processor can be understood as the number of computation units performed by the processor per one time unit. The speed depends on the number of units assigned to the processor and is represented by a continuous function s: $\mathbf{R}_+ \to \mathbf{R}_+$. As we assume that the processors perform their computation units in parallel, the overall execution time obtained with allocation $(n_1, n_2, \dots, n_p)$ will be given by $\max_i \dfrac{n_i}{s_i(n_i)}$. The optimal solution has to minimize the overall execution time.

Algorithm 4.1 (Lastovetsky and Reddy, 2007b). Optimal distribution for n equal elements over p processors of speeds $s_1(x), s_2(x), \dots, s_p(x)$:

- **Step 1: Initialization.** We approximate the n_i so that $\dfrac{n_i}{s_i(n_i)} \approx const$ and $n - 2 \times p \le n_1 + n_2 + \dots + n_p \le n$. Namely, we find n_i such that either $n_i = \lfloor x_i \rfloor$ or $n_i = \lfloor x_i \rfloor - 1$ for $1 \le i \le p$, where $\dfrac{x_1}{s_1(x_1)} = \dfrac{x_2}{s_2(x_2)} = \dots = \dfrac{x_p}{s_p(x_p)}$.

- **Step 2: Refining.** We iteratively increment some n_i until $n_1 + n_2 + \dots + n_p = n$.

Approximation of the n_i (Step 1) is not that easy as in the case of constant speeds s_i of the processors when n_i can be approximated as $\left\lfloor \dfrac{s_i}{\Sigma_1^p s_i} \times n \right\rfloor$ (see Section 3.1). The algorithm is based on the following observations:

- Let $\dfrac{x_1}{s_1(x_1)} = \dfrac{x_2}{s_2(x_2)} = \dots = \dfrac{x_p}{s_p(x_p)}$.

- Then all the points $(x_1, s_1(x_1)), (x_2, s_2(x_2)), \dots, (x_p, s_p(x_p))$ will lie on a straight line passing through the origin of the coordinate system, being intersecting points of this line with the graphs of the speed functions of the processors. This is shown in Figure 4.2.

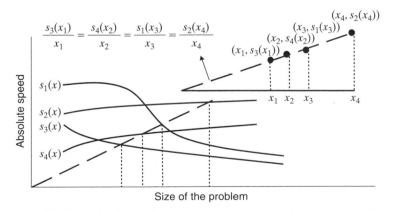

Figure 4.2. "Ideal" optimal solution showing the geometric proportionality of the number of elements to the speed of the processor.

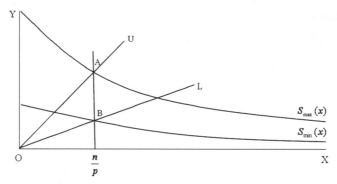

Figure 4.3. Selection of the initial two lines L and U. Here, n is the number of elements and p is the number of processors.

This algorithm is seeking for two straight lines passing through the origin of the coordinate system such that:

- The "ideal" optimal line (i.e., the line that intersects the speed graphs in points $(x_1, s_1(x_1))$, $(x_2, s_2(x_2))$, ... , $(x_p, s_p(x_p))$ such that $\dfrac{x_1}{s_1(x_1)} = \dfrac{x_2}{s_2(x_2)} = \ldots = \dfrac{x_p}{s_p(x_p)}$ and $x_1 + x_2 + \ldots + x_p = n$) lies between the two lines.

- There is no more than one point with integer x coordinate on either of these graphs between the two lines.

Algorithm 4.2 (Lastovetsky and Reddy, 2007b). Approximation of the n_i so that either $n_i = \lfloor x_i \rfloor$ or $n_i = \lfloor x_i \rfloor - 1$ for $1 \leq i \leq p$, where $\dfrac{x_1}{s_1(x_1)} = \dfrac{x_2}{s_2(x_2)} = \ldots = \dfrac{x_p}{s_p(x_p)}$ and $x_1 + x_2 + \ldots + x_p = n$:

- **Step 1.** The upper line U is drawn through the points $(0, 0)$ and $\left(\dfrac{n}{p}, \ \max_i \left\{ s_i \left(\dfrac{n}{p}\right)\right\}\right)$, and the lower line L is drawn through the points $(0, 0)$ and $\left(\dfrac{n}{p}, \ \min_i \left\{ s_i \left(\dfrac{n}{p}\right)\right\}\right)$, as shown in Figure 4.3.

- **Step 2.** Let $x_i^{(U)}$ and $x_i^{(L)}$ be the coordinates of the intersection points of lines U and L with the function $s_i(x)$ $(1 \leq i \leq p)$. If there exists $i \in \{1, \ldots, p\}$ such that $x_i^{(L)} - x_i^{(U)} \geq 1$ **then** go to Step 3 **else** go to Step 5.

- **Step 3.** Bisect the angle between lines U and L by the line M. Calculate coordinates $x_i^{(M)}$ of the intersection points of the line M with the function $s_i(x)$ for $1 \le i \le p$.
- **Step 4. If** $\Sigma_{i=1}^p x_i^{(M)} \le n$ **then** $U = M$ **else** $L = M$. Go to Step 2.
- **Step 5.** Approximate the n_i so that $n_i = \lfloor x_i^{(U)} \rfloor$ for $1 \le i \le p$.

Proposition 4.1 (Lastovetsky and Reddy, 2007b). Let functions $s_i(x)$ $(1 \le i \le p)$ be canonical speed functions. Then Algorithm 4.2 finds the n_i such that either $n_i = \lfloor x_i \rfloor$ or $n_i = \lfloor x_i \rfloor - 1$ for $1 \le i \le p$, where $\dfrac{x_1}{s_1(x_1)} = \dfrac{x_2}{s_2(x_2)} = \dots = \dfrac{x_p}{s_p(x_p)}$ and $x_1 + x_2 + \dots + x_p = n$.

See Appendix B for proof.

Algorithm 4.3 (Lastovetsky and Reddy, 2007b). Iterative incrementing of some n_i until $n_1 + n_2 + \dots + n_p = n$:

- **Step 1. If** $n_1 + n_2 + \dots + n_p < n$ **then** go to Step 2 **else** stop the algorithm.
- **Step 2.** Find $k \in \{1, \dots, p\}$ such that $\dfrac{n_k + 1}{s_k(n_k + 1)} = \min_{i=1}^p \left\{ \dfrac{n_i + 1}{s_i(n_i + 1)} \right\}$.
- **Step 3.** $n_k = n_k + 1$. Go to Step 1.

Note. It is worth to stress that Algorithm 4.3 cannot be used to search for the optimal solution beginning from an arbitrary approximation n_i satisfying inequality $n_1 + n_2 + \dots + n_p < n$, but only from the approximation found by Algorithm 4.2.

Proposition 4.2 (Lastovetsky and Reddy, 2007b). Let the functions $s_i(x)$ $(1 \le i \le p)$ be canonical speed functions. Let $(n_1, n_2, \dots, n_p)$ be the approximation found by Algorithm 4.2. Then Algorithm 4.3 returns the optimal allocation.

See Appendix B for proof.

Definition. The heterogeneity of the set of p physical processors $P_1, P_2, \dots, P_p$ of respective speeds $s_1(x), s_2(x), \dots, s_p(x)$ is *bounded* if and only if there exists a constant c such that $\max_{x \in R_+} \dfrac{s_{max}(x)}{s_{min}(x)} \le c$, where $s_{max}(x) = \max_i s_i(x)$ and $s_{min}(x) = \min_i s_i(x)$.

Proposition 4.3 (Lastovetsky and Reddy, 2007b). Let speed functions $s_i(x)$ $(1 \le i \le p)$ be canonical and the heterogeneity of processors $P_1, P_2, \dots, P_p$ be bounded. Then, the complexity of Algorithm 4.2 can be bounded by $O(p \times \log_2 n)$.

See Appendix B for proof.

Proposition 4.4. Let speed functions $s_i(x)$ $(1 \leq i \leq p)$ be canonical and the heterogeneity of processors P_1, P_2, ... , P_p be bounded. Then, the complexity of Algorithm 4.1 can be bounded $O(p \times \log_2 n)$.

Proof. If $(n_1, n_2, ... , n_p)$ is the approximation found by Algorithm 4.2, then $n - 2 \times p \leq n_1 + n_2 + ... + n_p \leq n$ and Algorithm 4.3 gives the optimal allocation in at most $2 \times p$ steps of increment, so that the complexity of Algorithm 4.3 can be bounded by $O(p^2)$. This complexity is given by a naïve implementation of Algorithm 4.3. The complexity of this algorithm can be reduced down to $O(p \times \log_2 p)$ by using *ad hoc* data structures. Thus, overall, the complexity of Algorithm 4.1 will be $O(p \times \log_2 p + p \times \log_2 n) = O(p \times \log_2(p \times n))$. Since $p < n$, then $\log_2(p \times n) < \log_2(n \times n) = \log_2(n^2) = 2 \times \log_2 n$. Thus, the complexity of Algorithm 4.1 can be bounded by $O(2 \times p \times \log_2 n) = O(p \times \log_2 n)$. Proposition 4.4 is proved.

The low complexity of Algorithm 4.2 and, hence, of Algorithm 4.1 is mainly due to the bounded heterogeneity of the processors. This very property guarantees that each bisection will reduce the space of possible solutions by a fraction that is lower bounded by some finite positive number independent of n. The assumption of bounded heterogeneity will be inaccurate if the speed of some processors becomes too slow for large n, effectively approaching zero. In this case, Algorithm 4.2 may become inefficient. For example, if $\frac{s_i(x)}{x} \sim e^{-x}$ for large x, then the number of bisections of the angle will be proportional to n for large n, resulting in the complexity of $O(p \times n)$.

The first approach to this problem is to use algorithms that are not that sensitive to the shape of speed functions for large task sizes. One such algorithm is obtained by a modification of Algorithm 4.2 (Lastovetsky and Reddy, 2004a).

To introduce the modified algorithm, let us reformulate the problem of finding the optimal straight line as follows. We define the space of solutions as the set of all straight lines drawn through the origin of the coordinate system and intersecting the speed functions of the processors so that the x coordinate of at least one intersection point will be an integer. We search for a line from this set, closest to the "ideal" optimal line.

Step 3 of Algorithm 4.2 halves the angle between two lines, not the space of solutions. The modified algorithm tries to halve the space of solutions rather than the angle where the desired solution lies as illustrated in Figures 4.4 and 4.5. At each iteration of this algorithm, we first find a processor P_i, whose speed function $s_i(x)$ is intersected by the maximal number of lines from the space of solutions between upper and lower lines U and L. In practice, the processor that maximizes $\left(x_i^{(L)} - x_i^{(U)}\right)$ can be chosen. Then we bisect the angle between U and L so that each subangle contains approximately the same number of lines from the space of solutions intersecting $s_i(x)$. To do it, we can draw a line passing through $(0, 0)$ and the point $\left(\left(\frac{x_i^{(L)} - x_i^{(U)}}{2}\right), s_i\left(\frac{x_i^{(L)} - x_i^{(U)}}{2}\right)\right)$. This

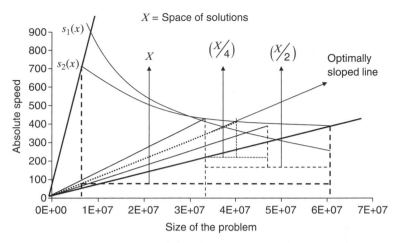

Figure 4.4. Halving the space of solutions.

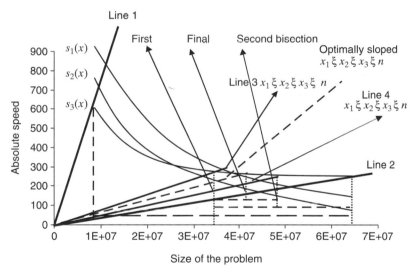

Figure 4.5. The modified bisection algorithm based on halving the space of solutions rather than the angle containing the solution. n is the number of elements.

algorithm guarantees that after p such bisections, the number of solutions in the region will be reduced by at least 50%. This means that we need no more than $p \times \log_2 n$ steps to arrive at the sought line. Correspondingly, the complexity of this algorithm will be $O(p^2 \times \log_2 n)$.

The second approach to the problem of unbounded heterogeneity is to use a model (Lastovetsky and Reddy, 2005) that represents the speed of the processor by a continuous function only until some threshold task size, beginning

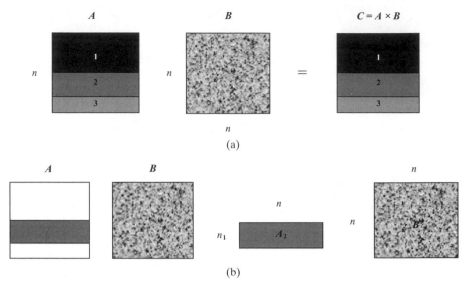

Figure 4.6. (a) Matrix operation $C = A \times B$ with matrices A, B, and C. Matrices A and C are horizontally sliced such that the number of elements in the slice is approximately proportional to the speed of the processor. (b) Serial matrix multiplication $A_2 \times B$ of matrix A_2 of size $n_1 \times n$ and matrix B of size $n \times n$ to estimate the absolute speed of processor 2.

from which the speed of the processor becomes so low that it makes no sense to use it for computations. Correspondingly, the model approximates the speed of the processor by zero for all task sizes greater than this threshold value. Data partitioning with this model is discussed in Section 4.3.

To demonstrate how the presented set partitioning algorithms can be applied to the design of heterogeneous parallel and distributed algorithms, we will use the same basic parallel algorithm of multiplication of two dense square $n \times n$ matrices, $C = A \times B$, on p heterogeneous processors, which we used in Chapter 3 (see also Fig. 4.6). First, we partition matrices A and C identically into p horizontal slices such that there will be one-to-one mapping between these slices and the processors. Each processor will store its slices of matrices A and C and the whole matrix B. Then all processors will compute their C slices in parallel.

The key step of this algorithm is the partitioning of matrices A and C. An optimal partitioning will minimize the execution time of computations. For this application, we first obtain the absolute speed of the processor for the task of multiplying two dense matrices of size $n_1 \times n$ and $n \times n$, respectively, as shown in Figure 4.6(b). The size of this task is represented by two parameters,

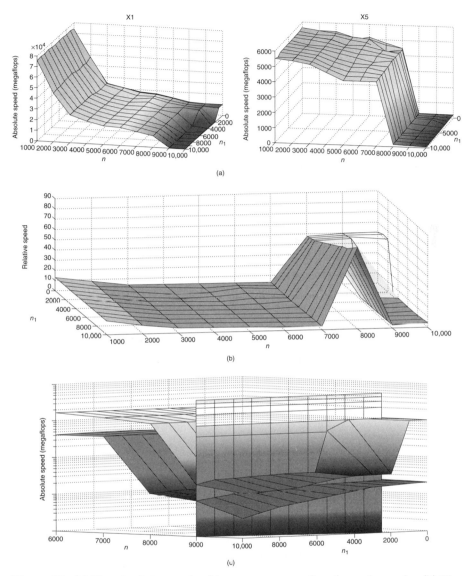

Figure 4.7. (a) The absolute speeds of two processors as functions of n_1 and n. (b) The relative speed of the two processors. (c) Surfaces representing the absolute speeds of the processors are sectioned by a plane $n = 9000$. Curves on this plane represent the absolute speeds of the processors against n_1, given n is fixed and equal to 9000.

n_1 and n. Let one unit of computation be a combined computation unit, which is made up of one addition and one multiplication. Assuming that n is large enough, the total number of computation units needed to solve this task will be approximately equal to $n_1 \times n \times n$. Therefore, for task size (n_1, n) we can calculate the absolute speed of the processor as $n_1 \times n \times n$ divided by the execution time of the application. This gives us a function, f: $\mathbf{N}^2 \rightarrow \mathbf{R}_+$, mapping task sizes to processor speeds. The functional performance model of the processor is obtained by the continuous approximation of function f: $\mathbf{N}^2 \rightarrow \mathbf{R}_+$ by function g: $\mathbf{R}_+^2 \rightarrow \mathbf{R}_+$ such that the latter satisfies all the necessary assumptions about the shape of speed function. The speed function is geometrically represented by a surface as shown in Figure 4.7(a) for two real processors. Figure 4.7(b) shows the geometrical representation of the relative speed of these two processors calculated as the ratio of their absolute speeds. One can see that the relative speed varies significantly depending on the value of variables n_1 and n.

Now, to partition a square matrix of any given size $N \times N$, we use the fact that the width of all partitions is the same, namely, equal to N. Therefore, we first section the surfaces representing the absolute speeds of the processors by a plane $n = N$, which is parallel to the axes representing parameter n_1 and the absolute speed of the processor and having an intercept of N on the axis representing the parameter n. This is illustrated in Figure 4.7(c) for two surfaces and $N = 9000$. This way we obtain a set of p curves on this plane that represent the absolute speeds of the processors against variable n_1 given parameter n is fixed. Then we apply a set partitioning algorithm to this set of p curves to obtain the optimal partitioning of n rows of matrices A and C between the p processors.

The next partitioning problem with the functional performance model that has been studied is the problem of partitioning a matrix for parallel dense factorization on p heterogeneous processors (Lastovetsky and Reddy, 2007c). The problem can be formulated as follows:

- Given
  - A dense $n \times n$ matrix A and
  - p ($n > p$) heterogeneous processors $P_1, P_2, \ldots , P_p$ of respective speeds $S = \{s_1(x,y), s_2(x,y), \ldots , s_p(x,y)\}$, where $s_i(x,y)$ is the speed of the update of a $x \times y$ matrix by the processor P_i, measured in operations per time unit and represented by a continuous function $R_+ \times R_+ \rightarrow R_+$
- Assign the columns of the matrix A to the p processors so that the

  assignment minimizes $\displaystyle\sum_{k=1}^{n} \max_{i=1}^{p} \frac{V(n-k, n_i^{(k)})}{s_i(n-k, n_i^{(k)})}$, where $V(x,y)$ is the number

  of operations needed to update an $x \times y$ matrix and $n_i^{(k)}$ is the number of columns updated by the processor P_i at step k of the parallel LU factorization

This formulation is motivated by the n-step parallel LU factorization algorithm presented in Section 3.3. One element of matrix A may represent a single number with computations measured in arithmetical operations. Alternatively, it can represent a square matrix block of a given fixed size $b \times b$. In this case, computations are measured in $b \times b$ matrix operations. The formulation assumes that the computation cost is determined by the update of the trailing matrix and fully ignores the communication cost. Therefore, the execution time of the k-th step of the LU factorization is estimated by $\max_{i=1}^{p} \dfrac{V(n-k, n_i^{(k)})}{s_i(n-k, n_i^{(k)})}$, and the optimal solution has to minimize the overall execution time, $\sum\limits_{k=1}^{n} \max_{i=1}^{p} \dfrac{V(n-k, n_i^{(k)})}{s_i(n-k, n_i^{(k)})}$.

Unlike the constant optimization problem considered in Section 3.3, the functional optimization problem cannot be reduced to the problem of minimizing the execution time of all n individual steps of the LU factorization. Correspondingly, this functional matrix-partitioning problem cannot be reduced to a problem of partitioning a well-ordered set. The reason is that in the functional case, there may be no globally optimal allocation of columns minimizing the execution time of all individual steps of the LU factorization. This complication is introduced by the use of the functional performance model of heterogeneous processors instead of the constant one. A simple example supporting this statement can be found in Appendix B.4.

Although there has been no formal proof of this fact, the above functional matrix-partitioning problem seems NP-complete. At least, no efficient algorithm that always returns its optimal solution has been proposed yet. At the same time, one approach to the design of efficient algorithms returning approximate solutions was proposed and studied in Lastovetsky and Reddy (2007c). The approach is to extend algorithms, which use constant performance models of processors, to the functional performance model. In particular, extensions of the Dynamic Programming (DP) and Reverse algorithms presented in Section 3.3 were designed and experimentally tested. The main idea of the extensions is that all allocations of columns are made using the functional performance model, giving accurate estimation of the speed of the processors at each step of the LU factorization depending on the number of columns of the trailing matrix updated by each processor at this step.

The Functional Reverse (FR) Algorithm (Lastovetsky and Reddy, 2007c). This algorithm extends the Reverse algorithm. The inputs to the algorithm are

- p, the number of processors,
- n, the size of the matrix,
- $S = \{s_1(x,y), s_2(x,y), \ldots, s_p(x,y)\}$, the speed functions of the processors, and
- $Proc(k, p, \Delta, w, d)$, a procedure searching for the optimal allocation of a group of $w + 1$ columns, $(k, k + 1, \ldots, k + w)$, given columns $1, \ldots, k - 1$ have been allocated and the total number of columns to be assigned to processor P_i is specified by the i-th element of integer array Δ.

The output d is an integer array of size n, the i-th element of which contains the index of the processor to which the column i is assigned.

The algorithm can be summarized as follows:

```
(d₁,…, dₙ) = (0,…, 0);
w=0;
(n₁,…, nₚ) = HSPF(p,  n,  S);
for  (k=1;  k<n;  k=k+1)  {
    ( n′₁ ,…, n′ₚ )=  HSPF(p,  n-k,  S);
    if  (w==0)
    then if  ((∃!j∈[1,p])(nⱼ  ==  n′ⱼ+1)  ∧  (∀i ≠ j)(nᵢ  ==  n′ⱼ))
            then  {dₖ=j;  (n₁,…, nₚ)  =  ( n′₁ ,…, n′ₚ );}
            else  w=1;
    else if  ((∃i∈[1,p])(nᵢ  <  n′ᵢ))
            then  w=w+1;
            else  {
                for  (i=1;  i≤p;  i=i+1)  {Δᵢ  =  nᵢ  -  n′ᵢ;}
                Proc(k,  p,  Δ,  w,  d);
                (n₁,…, nₚ)  =  ( n′₁ ,…, n′ₚ );
                w=0;
            }
}
if  ((∃i∈[1,p])(nᵢ  =  1))
then  dₙ=i;
```

Here, HSPF(p,m,S) (HSPF stands for heterogeneous set partitioning using the functional model of processors) returns the optimal distribution of a set of m equal elements over p heterogeneous processors $P_1, P_2, \ldots , P_p$ of respective speeds $S = \{s_1(m,y), s_2(m,y), \ldots , s_p(m,y)\}$ using Algorithm 4.1. The distributed elements represent columns of the $m \times m$ trailing matrix at step $(n - m)$ of the LU factorization. Function $f_i(y) = s_i(m,y)$ represents the speed of processor P_i depending on the number of columns of the trailing matrix, y, updated by the processor at the step $(n - m)$ of the LU factorization. Figure 4.8 gives a geometrical interpretation of this step of the matrix-parttioning algorithm:

1. Surfaces $z_i = s_i(x,y)$ representing the absolute speeds of the processors are sectioned by the plane $x = n - k$ (as shown on Fig. 4.8(a) for three surfaces). A set of p curves on this plane (as shown in Fig. 4.8(b)) will represent the absolute speeds of the processors against variable y, given parameter x is fixed.
2. Algorithm 4.1 is applied to this set of curves to obtain an optimal distribution of columns of the trailing matrix.

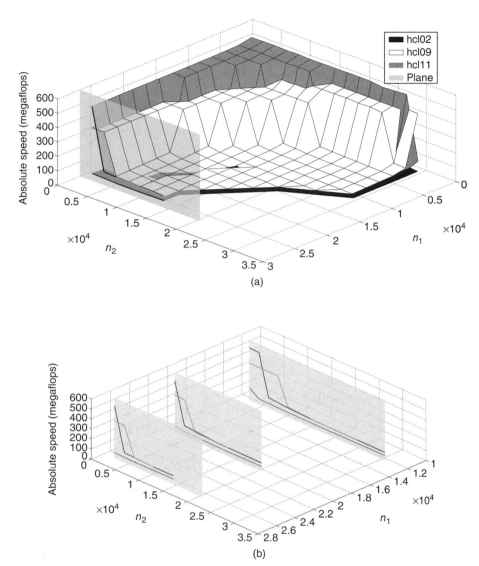

Figure 4.8. (a) Three surfaces representing the absolute speeds of three processors (hcl02, hcl09, hcl11) are sectioned by a plane $x = m$. (b) Curves on the plane represent the absolute speeds of the processors against variable y, given parameter x is fixed. (See color insert.)

Proposition 4.5. If assignment of a column panel is performed at each step of the algorithm, the FR algorithm returns the optimal allocation.

Proof. If a column panel is assigned at each iteration of the FR algorithm, then the resulting allocation will be optimal by design. Indeed, in this case, the distribution of column panels over the processors will be produced by the HSPF, and hence, be optimal for each step of the LU factorization.

Proposition 4.6. If the speed of the processor is represented by a constant function of problem size, the FR algorithm returns the optimal allocation.

Proof. If the speed of the processor is represented by a constant function of problem size, the FR algorithm is functionally equivalent to the reverse algorithm presented earlier. We have already proved that the reverse algorithm returns the optimal allocation when the constant performance model of heterogeneous processors is used.

Proposition 4.7. Let the functions $s_i(x,y)$ $(1 \leq i \leq p)$ be canonical speed functions for any fixed x (i.e., along variable y) and the heterogeneity of processors $P_1, P_2, \ldots, P_p$ be bounded. Then, if assignment of a column panel is performed at each step of the algorithm, the complexity of the FR algorithm can be bounded by $O(p \times n \times \log_2 n)$.

Proof. At each iteration of this algorithm, we apply the HSPF. Intersection of p surfaces by a plane to produce p curves will be of complexity $O(p)$. Application of Algorithm 4.1 to these curves will be of complexity bounded by $O(p \times \log_2 n)$ (Proposition 4.4). Testing the condition $(\exists! j \in [1, p])(n_j == n'_j + 1) \wedge (\forall i \neq j)(n_i == n'_i)$ is of complexity $O(p)$. Since there are n such iterations, the overall complexity of the algorithm will be bounded by $n \times O(p \times \log_2 n) + n \times O(p) + n \times O(p) = O(p \times n \times \log_2 n)$. *End of proof of Proposition 4.7.*

If the FR algorithm does not assign a column at each iteration of its main loop, then the optimality of the returned allocation is not guaranteed. The reason is that when we are forced to allocate a group of columns, $(k, k + 1, \ldots, k + w)$, then even if procedure *Proc* finds a locally optimal allocation, minimizing the sum of the execution times of the steps $k, k + 1, \ldots, k + w$ of the LU factorization (given columns $1, \ldots, k - 1$ have been allocated), this allocation may not minimize the global execution time. Hence, suboptimal allocations of the group of columns may be as good, or even better, as the exact optimal allocation. Therefore, in practice, it does not make much sense to use an exact but expansive algorithm in the implementation of procedure *Proc*. It has been shown (Lastovetsky and Reddy, 2007c) that many simple approximate algorithms of low complexity, which do not change the upper bound $O(p \times n \times \log_2 n)$ of the overall complexity fo the FR algorithm, return group allocations that are, in average, as good as exact optimal allocations.

The Functional DP (FDP) Algorithm. This algorithm extends the DP algorithm. The inputs to the algorithm are

- p, the number of processors,
- n, the size of the matrix, and

- $S = \{s_1(x,y), s_2(x,y), \dots, s_p(x,y)\}$, the speed functions of the processors.

The outputs are

- c, an integer array of size p, the i-th element of which contains the number of column panels assigned to processor P_i, and
- d, an integer array of size n, the i-th element of which contains the index of the processor to which the column panel i is assigned.

The algorithm can be summarized as follows:

```
(c₁,…,cₚ)=(0,…,0);
(d₁,…,dₙ)=(0,…,0);
for(k=1; k≤n; k=k+1)  {
    Cost_min=∞;
    (n₁,…,nₚ)=HSPF(p, k, S);
    for(i=1; i≤p; i++)  {
        Cost=(cᵢ+1)/nᵢ;
        if (Cost < Cost_min) { Cost_min= Cost; j=i;}
    }
    d_{n-k+1}=j;
    cⱼ=cⱼ+1;
}
```

Proposition 4.8. If the functions $s_i(x,y)$ $(1 \le i \le p)$ are canonical speed functions for any fixed x (i.e., along variable y) and the heterogeneity of processors $P_1, P_2, \dots, P_p$ is bounded, the complexity of the FDP algorithm can be bounded by $O(p \times n \times \log_2 n)$.

Proof. The complexity of HSPF is $O(p \times \log_2 n)$. The complexity of the inner **for** loop is $O(p)$. Therefore, the complexity of one iteration of the main loop of this algorithm will be $O(p \times \log_2 n) + O(p)$. Since there are n iterations, the complexity of the algorithm can be upper bounded by $n \times (O(p \times \log_2 n) + O(p)) = O(p \times n \times \log_2 n)$. *End of proof of Proposition 4.8.*

Thus, we see that the FR and FDP algorithms have the same complexity. At the same time, the FR algorithm has much more room for optimization as it does not have to assign a column at each iteration. Therefore, column allocations returned by the FR algorithm will be closer to the optimal allocation, resulting in faster LU factorization. Experimental results validating this statement are presented in Lastovetsky and Reddy (2007c).

4.3 OTHER NONCONSTANT PERFORMANCE MODELS OF HETEROGENEOUS PROCESSORS

4.3.1 Stepwise Functional Model

We have noted in Section 4.1 that for some scientific codes, which efficiently use memory hierarchy and demonstrate a sharp and distinctive curve of dependence of the absolute speed on the task size, the speed of the processor can be approximated by a unit step function. Such a model was also studied in Drozdowski and Wolniewicz (2003). More precisely, under this model, the performance of the processor is characterized by the execution time of the task, represented by a piecewise linear function of its size. The problem of *asymptotically optimal* partitioning a set was formulated with this model as a linear programming problem. As such, it relies on the state of the art in linear programming. Currently, little is known (especially, theoretically) about practical and efficient algorithms for the linear programming problem. Moreover, if the unknown variables in the linear programming problem are all required to be integers, then the problem becomes an integer linear programming problem, which is known to be NP-hard in many practical situations. This means that the linear programming model can hardly be used in the design of efficient algorithms returning the optimal *exact* solution of the set-partitioning problem.

4.3.2 Functional Model with Limits on Task Size

We have seen in Section 4.2 that the functional performance model can become inefficient if the speed of some processors is too slow for large task sizes, effectively approaching zero. In addition, it will be prohibitively expansive to build the model for large task sizes. To deal with the problems, a modified functional model (Lastovetsky and Reddy, 2005) can be used in this case. This model represents the speed of the processor by a continuous function only until some threshold task size, beginning from which the speed of the processor becomes so low that it makes no sense to use it for computations. Correspondingly, the model approximates the speed of the processor by zero for all task sizes greater than this threshold value. The basic problem of partitioning a set of n (equal) elements between p heterogeneous processors has been formulated and solved with this model (Lastovetsky and Reddy, 2005). The problem is formulated as follows:

- Given
  - A set of p processors $P = \{P_1, P_2, \ldots, P_p\}$, the speed of which is characterized by real functions $S = \{s_1(x), s_2(x), \ldots, s_p(x)\}$
  - Upper bounds $B = \{b_1, \ldots, b_p\}$ limiting the number of elements allocated to processors P
- Partition a set of n elements into p subsets so that
  - There is one-to-one mapping between the partitions and the processors
  - $n_i \leq b_i$, where n_i is the number of elements allocated to processor P_i ($1 \leq i \leq p$)
  - The partitioning minimizes $\max_i \dfrac{n_i}{s_i(n_i)}$

Algorithm 4.4. Optimal distribution for n equal elements over p processors P of speeds S and limits B:

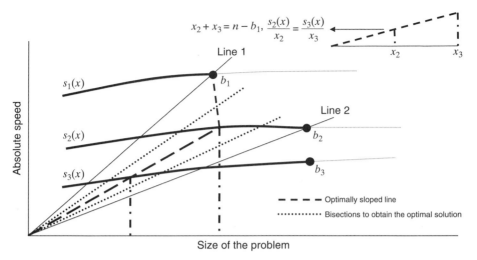

Figure 4.9. Distribution of n elements over three processors with limits on the number of allocated elements. The bold curves represent the experimentally obtained speed functions. The dotted curves represent reasonable extensions of the speed functions in a continuous manner. First, we assign to the processor, represented by speed function $s_1(x)$, the number of elements equal to its limit b_1. Then we partition the set of remaining $n - b_1$ elements over the processors represented by speed functions $s_2(x)$ and $s_3(x)$.

- **Step 1.** Apply Algorithm 4.1 to the distribution of n equal elements over p processors P of speeds S, $n_1 + n_2 + \ldots + n_p = n$.
- **Step 2.** If $(\forall i \in \{1 \ldots, p\})(n_i \le b_i)$ **then** stop the algorithm.
- **Step 3. forall** $(i \in \{1, \ldots, p\})$ if $(n_i > b_i)$ **then** $\{n_i = b_i; n = n - b_i;$ remove processor P_i from P; remove $s_i(x)$ from S; remove b_i from B; $p = p - 1\}$.
- **Step 4.** Recursively apply Algorithm 4.4 to the distribution of the updated set of n elements over p processors P of speeds S and limits B.

The algorithm is illustrated in Figure 4.9. In order to apply this algorithm, we experimentally build the speed functions only for $x \le b_i$ and just continuously extend them for $x > b_i$.

Proposition 4.9 (Lastovetsky and Reddy, 2005). Let the speed functions $s_i(x)$ $(1 \le i \le p)$ be canonical and $\sum_{i=1}^{p} b_i \ge n$. Then, Algorithm 4.4 returns the optimal distribution.

Proposition 4.10. If the functions $s_i(x)$ $(1 \le i \le p)$ are canonical speed functions, then the complexity of Algorithm 4.4 can be bounded by $O(p^2 \times \log_2 n)$.

Proof. The complexity of HSPF is $O(p \times \log_2 n)$. The complexity of the inner **for** loop is $O(p)$. Therefore, the complexity of one iteration of the main loop of this algorithm will be $O(p \times \log_2 n) + O(p)$. Since there are n iterations, the complexity of the algorithm can be upper bounded by $n \times (O(p \times \log_2 n) + O(p)) = O(p \times n \times \log_2 n)$. *End of proof of Proposition 4.8.*

Application of the modified functional model and Algorithm 4.4 is quite straightforward. Namely, they can seamlessly replace the functional model and Algorithm 4.1 in all presented algorithms where the solution of the set-partitioning problem is used as a basic building block.

4.3.3 Band Model

We have discussed in Chapters 1 and 2 that in general-purpose local and global networks integrated into the Internet, most computers periodically run some routine processes interacting with the Internet, and some computers act as servers for other computers. This results in constant unpredictable fluctuations in the workload of processors in such a network. This changing transient load will cause fluctuations in the speed of processors, in that the speed of the processor will vary when measured at different times while executing the same task. The natural way to represent the inherent fluctuations in the speed is to use a speed band rather than a speed function. The width of the band characterizes the level of fluctuation in the performance due to changes in load over time. Although some research on the band performance model and its use in the design of heterogeneous algorithms have been done (Higgins and Lastovetsky, 2005; Lastovetsky and Twamley, 2005), very little is known about the effectiveness and efficiency of data partitioning algorithms at this point.

CHAPTER 5

Communication Performance Models for High-Performance Heterogeneous Platforms

5.1 MODELING THE COMMUNICATION PERFORMANCE FOR SCIENTIFIC COMPUTING: THE SCOPE OF INTEREST

Modeling the performance of communication networks is a vast and diverse area of research and development that can hardly be covered by a single book, let alone a section. We also have no ambition to give a comprehensive overview of the area. Instead, in this section, we focus on a quite small subarea, the most directly related to the topic of the book, which is the design and implementation of scientific applications on heterogeneous platforms.

The whole area of communication performance modeling consists of two main fields. Each of the fields has its own research and development community, and the communities practically do not intersect and hardly interact with one another. They have different goals and use different approaches.

The first field is the design of communication networks. The goal of modeling in this field is to design a communication network satisfying some given (performance) criteria. The approach is to simulate the behavior of the communication network in order to predict its functioning for different design configurations and modes of use. Such a model is typically very detailed and includes a large number of design parameters, which are the primary parameters of the model. Performance parameters are secondary, being functions of the design parameters. The model allows the designer to see how the change of the design parameters will change the performance characteristics of the network. Optimization of the design parameters is the ultimate goal of the modeling. The techniques used include message queues, statistical methods, and so on. The field of network design is completely out of the scope of this book.

The second field is the optimal use of a given communication network. More specifically, we are interested in the optimal use of the network for high-performance scientific computing. The design and performance charac-teristics of the communication network are given and cannot be changed. The goal of modeling the communication performance in this case is to use the model in the design and implementation of scientific applications in order to improve their performance. Communication models for scientific computing are usually simple and efficient. They describe the network by a small number of (measurable) performance parameters. The models allow the application designer to predict the communication cost of the application and find the optimal communication scheme that minimizes the cost.

Invocation of a communication operation in a scientific application acti-vates a whole stack of communication software, higher levels of which are built upon lower ones. Modeling the performance of lower-level communication layers is mainly needed for the efficient implementation of the higher com-munication level. Many interesting results have been obtained in this area. One example of an active topic is the efficient implementation of MPI for different interconnects such as Ethernet, Myrinet, and Infiniband.

Some of the specialized, high-performance networks (e.g., Myrinet's MX, Open Fabrics (Infiniband), Quadrics) include hardware-level support for MPI. Network interface cards (NICs) for these networks have processing power to off-load protocol processing from the host CPU. They can bypass the operating system and interact directly with MPI processes. This reduces the overall latency of communication and can increase the bandwidth as the amount of local buffering can be reduced by allowing the NIC to write directly to user memory. Often, point-to-point communication requests can be matched on the NIC itself as well.

Our book, however, does not cover the area of efficient implementation of the stack of communication software used in high-performance scientific com-puting. Instead, we are looking at communications through the eyes of the application programmer. We consider the communication platform as a given combination of hardware and software and are interested in the prediction of the execution time of communication operations at the level of the communica-tion middleware used in the scientific application. For example, if the application uses MPI for communications, we will be interested in modeling the perfor-mance of MPI communication operations. In this case, the MPI communication platform, encapsulating all the hardware and software involved in passing mes-sages between MPI processes, will be the object of performance modeling.

Numerous setting parameters and installation parameters can be used for tuning and tweaking of the hardware equipment and the software components. For example, the design of computational clusters mainly deals with the opti-mization of such parameters (Sterling, Lusk, and Gropp, 2003). Obviously, these low-level parameters have a significant impact on the performance of application-level communication operations. The task of optimizing low-level parameters of the communication platform is similar to the task of network design and, like the latter, is out of scope of the book. Application program-mers have no way of changing most of the parameters. Therefore, at the application level, the low-level parameters are considered given and fixed and, as such, effectively do not exist for optimizing the performance of communications.

Thus, in this chapter, we will give an overview of the communication performance models proposed and used for application-level communication platforms. The chapter mainly focuses on models for heterogeneous clusters (Section 5.2). Communication performance models for other heterogeneous platforms such as general-purpose local networks and geographically distributed interconnected systems are still a subject of research. Currently used predictive models are rather simplistic and inaccurate. Section 5.3 gives a quick look at the area.

5.2 COMMUNICATION MODELS FOR PARALLEL COMPUTING ON HETEROGENEOUS CLUSTERS

Most analytical predictive communication models used for heterogeneous clusters are inherently homogeneous; that is, they were originally designed for homogeneous clusters. According to these models, the execution time of any communication operation depends only on its topology and the number of participating processors, not on which particular processors are involved in the operation.

There are two main issues associated with any predictive communication model. The first issue is the design of the parameterized analytical model itself. The second issue is the efficient and accurate estimation of the parameters of the model for each particular platform from the targeted class.

The basis of a homogeneous predictive model is a point-to-point communication model characterized by a set of integral parameters having the same value for each pair of processors. Collective operations are expressed as a combination of the point-to-point parameters, and the collective communication execution time is analytically predicted for different message sizes and the number of processors involved. The core of this approach is the choice of such a point-to-point model that is the most appropriate to the targeted platform, allowing for the easy and natural expression of different algorithms of collective operations.

For homogeneous clusters, the point-to-point parameters are found statistically from the measurements of the execution time of communications between any two processors. When such a homogeneous communication model is applied to a cluster of heterogeneous processors, its point-to-point parameters are found by averaging the values obtained for every pair of processors, and the averaged values are then used in modeling collective communication operations. Thus, in this case, the heterogeneous cluster will be treated as homogeneous in terms of the performance of communication operations.

According to the Hockney model (Hockney, 1994), the execution time of point-to-point communication is evaluated as $\alpha + \beta \times m$, where

- α is the latency (the message startup time, which includes the time to prepare the message [copy to system buffer, etc.], and the time for the first byte of the message to arrive at the receiver),
- β is the transfer time per byte, referred to as the bandwidth, and
- m is the message size.

The time to receive message is $\alpha + \beta \times m$, but the time when the sending process can start sending another message can be defined in a number of ways. In a worst-case scenario, no communication overlap is allowed, thus the sender must wait for the receiver to receive the message fully before it is allowed to initiate another send. In a best-case scenario, a process is allowed to initiate a second send after the latency has expired.

The parameters of the Hockney model can be estimated directly from point-to-point tests for different message sizes with the help of linear regression. Each test measures the time of a roundtrip. The roundtrip can consist of sending and receiving a message of size m. Alternatively, it can be a combination of sending a message of size m and receiving a zero-sized message.

The LogP model (Culler *et al.*, 1993) predicts the time of network communication for small fixed-sized messages in terms of the following parameters:

- L: an upper bound on the *latency*, or delay, incurred in sending a message from its source processor to its target processor.
- o: the *overhead*, defined as the length of time that a processor is engaged in the transmission or reception of each message; during this time, the processor cannot perform other operations.
- g: the *gap* between messages, defined as the minimum time interval between consecutive message transmissions or consecutive message receptions at a processor. The reciprocal of g corresponds to the available per-processor communication bandwidth for short messages.
- P: the number of processors.

According to LogP, the time of point-to-point communication can be estimated by $L + 2 \times o$. The gap parameter is added for every message sent sequentially, so that the network bandwidth can be expressed as L/g. This implies that the network allows transmission of $\lfloor L/g \rfloor$ messages simultaneously at most.

The LogP model is extended in Alexandrov *et al.* (1995) for messages of an arbitrary size, m, by introducing the gap per byte, G (to capture the cost of sending large messages across the network), with the point-to-point communication time estimated by $L + 2 \times o + (m - 1) \times G$ (the LogGP model).

In the parameterized LogP (PLogP) model (Kielmann, Bal, and Verstoep, 2000), some parameters are piecewise linear functions of the message size, the send and receive overheads are distinguished, and the meaning of the parameters slightly differs from that in LogP. The end-to-end latency, L, is a constant, combining all fixed contribution factors such as copying to/from network interfaces and the transfer over network. The send, $o_s(m)$, and receive, $o_r(m)$, overheads are the times the source and destination processors are busy during communication. They can be overlapped for sufficiently large messages. The gap, $g(m)$, is the minimum time between consecutive transmissions or receptions; it is the reciprocal value of the end-to-end bandwidth between two processors for messages of a given size m. The gap is assumed to cover the overheads: $g(m) \geq o_s(m)$ and $g(m) \geq o_r(m)$.

The *logp_mpi* library (Kielmann, Bal, and Verstoep, 2000) is widely used for the estimation of the point-to-point parameters of PLogP and other LogP-based models for MPI communication platforms.

The overhead $o_s(m)$ is found directly by measuring the execution time of sending a message of m bytes. For each message size, the value of $o_s(m)$ is obtained by averaging the results of a sufficient number of tests.

The overhead $o_r(m)$ is found directly from the time of receiving a message of m bytes in the roundtrip $i \underset{m}{\overset{0}{\rightleftharpoons}} j$, consisting of sending an empty message from processor i to processor j and receiving a nonempty reply of the size of m bytes. In this experiment, after completion of the send operation, processor i waits for some time, sufficient for the reply to reach the processor, and only then will it post a receive operation. The execution time of the receive operation is assumed to approximate $o_r(m)$. For each message size, the value of $o_s(m)$ is obtained by averaging the results of a sufficient number of tests. These tests are initially run a small number of times, which is successively increased until the variance of the results becomes acceptably small. Typically, the total number of roundtrips stays sufficiently small (of the order of tens).

This *logp_mpi* package implements two techniques of estimating the gap parameter $g(m)$: direct and optimized. In the direct method, the gap values $g(m)$ are found from the execution time $s_n(m)$ of sending without reply a large number n of messages of size m. As the execution time of sending n messages in a row is $s(m_1, \dots , m_n) = g(m_1) + \dots + g(m_n)$ on the sender side, the gap value will be equal to $g(m) = s_n(m)/n$. The number of messages n is obtained within the saturation process. The execution time $RTT_n(m)$ of a roundtrip consisting of n sending of the message of m bytes and a single zero reply is measured for n that is doubled until $\dfrac{RTT_{2n}(m)/2n - RTT_n(m)/n}{RTT_n(m)/n} \times 100\%$ changes less than 1%. The saturation ensures that the roundtrip time is dominated by bandwidth rather than latency. As a result, n will be quite large (of the order of thousands and more), and the saturation will take a major portion of the overall execution time. Thus, the direct technique of estimating the parameter $g(m)$ is very expensive. As a result, an indirect optimized method for estimating the parameter has been proposed.

The optimization technique for finding the gap $g(m)$ described in Kielmann, Bal, and Verstoep (2000) is based on a single point-to-point roundtrip message timing and the assumption that the roundtrip time can be expressed as

$RTT(m) = RTT_1(m) = L + g(m) + L + g(0)$. We do not understand how the roundtrip time can be expressed by this formula for a single point-to-point roundtrip message, given that there are no additional messages sent. Nevertheless, based on this assumption, the authors of *logp_mpi* replace the direct finding of the gap for each message size by measuring the execution time of a single roundtrip: $g(m) = RTT(m) - RTT(0) + g(0)$, with only the gap value of $g(0)$ found directly within the saturation process. The latency is found from a single roundtrip with empty messages: $L = RTT(0)/2 - g(0)$.

In general, the assumption used in the optimized method for the estimation of $g(m)$ is wrong. Therefore, the values of the gap obtained by this method may be quite inaccurate. For example, in experiments on switch-based Ethernet clusters, it was observed that the estimation of the gap obtained by the indirect method could be several times less than the (accurate) value obtained by the direct method. Moreover, the gap values found with the optimized technique are often less than the send/receive overheads for small and medium messages, which contradicts the assumption that $g(m) \geq o_s(m)$ and $g(m) \geq o_r(m)$. Thus, in *logp_mpi*, the direct method is the only reliable way of accurately estimating gap values. The *logp_mpi* library without the optimized method can still be used for the efficient estimation of the LogP/LogGP parameters because, in this case, only the measurements for three different message sizes (0, 1, and m bytes, where m is sufficiently large) are required (Table 5.1).

The presented point-to-point communication models are used to analyze and optimize the communication cost of parallel applications on computational clusters. One typical application of the models is the optimization of collective communications in the applications. Collective communications can be implemented by using different combinations of point-to-point communications. Therefore, it is possible to design analytical predictive models of collective communications by combining the parameters of the point-to-point communication models. For example, the Hockney model was used by Thakur, Rabenseifner, and Gropp (2005) to estimate the communication performance of different algorithms of collective operations. For a particular collective operation, switching between algorithms is suggested in order to choose the fastest one for each given message size and number of processors.

Previous studies of application usage show that the performance of collective communications is critical to high-performance computing. Profiling

TABLE 5.1 LogP/LogGP Parameters Expressed in Terms of PLogP

LogP/LogGP	PLogP
L	$L + g(1) - o_s(1) - o_r(1)$
o	$(o_s(1)+o_r(1))/2$
g	$g(1)$
G	$g(m)/m$, for a sufficiently large m
P	P

studies have shown that some applications spend more than 80% of the transfer time in collective operations. Thus, it is essential for MPI implementations to provide high-performance collective operations. Collective operations encompass a wide range of possible algorithms, topologies, and methods. The optimal implementation of a collective for a given system depends on many factors, including, for example, the physical topology of the system, the number of processes involved, the message sizes, and the location of the root node (where applicable). Furthermore, many algorithms allow explicit segmentation of the message that is being transmitted, in which case the performance of the algorithm also depends on the segment size in use. Some collective operations involve local computation (e.g., reduction operations), in which case the local characteristics of each node need to be considered as they could affect our decision on how to overlap communication with computation.

A simple, yet time-consuming, way to find even a semioptimal implementation of a collective operation is to run an extensive set of tests over a parameter space for the collective on a dedicated system. However, running such detailed tests, even on relatively small clusters (32–64 nodes), can take a substantial amount of time. If one were to analyze all the MPI collectives in a similar manner, the tuning process could take days. Still, many of the current MPI implementations use "extensive'" testing to determine switching points between the algorithms. The decision of which algorithm to use is semistatic and based on predetermined parameters that do not model all possible target systems.

Alternatives to the static decisions include running a limited number of performance and system evaluation tests. This information can be combined with predictions from parallel communication models to make runtime decisions to select the near-optimal algorithms and segment sizes for a given operation, communicator, message size, and rank of the root process.

There are many parallel communication models that predict the performance of any given collective operation based on standardized system parameters. Hockney, LogP, LogGP, and PLogP models are frequently used to analyze parallel algorithm performance. Assessing the parameters for these models within a local area network is relatively straightforward, and the methods to approximate them have already been established and are well understood.

In Pjesivac-Grbovic et al. (2007), the direct comparison of Hockney-, LogP/LogGP-, and PLogP-based parallel communication models applied to the optimization of intracluster MPI collective operations is provided. They quantitatively compare the predictions of the models with experimentally gathered data and use models to obtain the optimal implementation of broadcast collective. They have assessed the performance penalty of using model-generated decision functions versus the ones generated by exhaustive testing of the system. The results indicate that all of the models can provide useful insights into the various aspects of the collective algorithms and their relative performance. The results of Pjesivac-Grbovic et al. (2007) also demonstrate the importance of an accurate modeling of the gap between sending consecutive messages to a single destination and to a set of different destination processes. Experiments show that the value of the gap between consecutive send operations depends on the number of unique destination nodes. Unfortunately, neither of the models is able to capture this behavior correctly. This shortcoming is reflected in underestimating the benefit of using segmentation for the binomial reduce algorithm and the inaccurate prediction of switching points between available broadcast methods for large messages. Additionally, neither of the point-to-point models used considers network congestion directly. Nonetheless, for the communicator and the message size range considered, PLogP and LogP/LogGP models are able to model pairwise-exchange all-to-all algorithm successfully.

We believe that parallel communication models can still be used to perform focused tuning of collective operations. Based on the measured parameter values coupled with a small number of test runs, which would be used to verify predictions and adjust model parameters, one could use the models to decrease the number of physical tests needed to construct semioptimal decision functions for a particular collective.

Predictive models of collective communications analytically deduced from the presented point-to-point communication models will be obviously deterministic just because the point-to-point models themselves are deterministic. Moreover, as a rule, collective communication models designed upon linear point-to-point models, such as the Hockney, LogP, and LogGP models, are also linear. At the same time, recent research shows that the real behavior of collective communication operations on many popular message-passing platforms can be nondeterministic and nonlinear (Lastovetsky and O'Flynn, 2007).

In particular, in Lastovetsky and O'Flynn (2007), the gather and scatter operations are studied for the different combinations of MPI implementations and single-switched cluster platforms. The distinctive nondeterministic behavior of the gather operation is observed for all the studied MPI-based platforms, given the communication stack includes the TCP/IP layer and the gather operation is implemented straightforwardly, that is, using the flat tree topology, as specified in the MPI standard (Message Passing Interface Forum, 1995):

```
if (rank==root) {
  memcpy(recvbuf, sendbuf, recvcount);
  for (i=1; i<n; i++) {
    MPI_Irecv(recvbuf+recvcount*i, recvcount, recvtype, i, 0, comm);
  }
  MPI_Waitall(n-1);
}
else {
  MPI_Send(sendbuf, sendcount, sendtype, root, 0, comm);
}
```

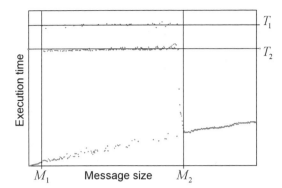

Figure 5.1. The execution time of the gather collective communication against the message size.

Figure 5.1 shows the typical behavior of the gather communication in these cases. We can see that the execution time is deterministic and linearly proportional to the message size for small messages, $m < M_1$. At the same time, for medium-sized messages, $M_1 \leq m \leq M_2$, in addition to the expected linear response to the increase of message size, sharp escalations of the execution time to a small number of discrete levels are also observed. Occurrence of the escalations is nondeterministic, and sometimes for the same operation in the same setup, there may be no escalation. In the absence of escalation, the execution time can be accurately predicted by the same linear model as for small messages. The escalations may be quite significant (of the order of tens and even hundreds of times). The frequency of the escalations increases with the increase of message size. For large messages, $m > M_2$, the execution time resumes a deterministic linear predictability for increasing message sizes.

In order to describe the observed nondeterministic deviations from the linear behavior for medium-sized messages, the traditional linear deterministic communication model is extended in Lastovetsky and O'Flynn (2007) by the following parameters, which are specific for every given combination of the cluster platform of size N and the MPI implementation:

- The minimum size of message, M_1, beginning from which escalations can be observed
- The maximum size of message, M_2, beginning from which the escalations stop occurring
- The number of levels of escalation, k
- The execution time of the gather operation at each level of escalation, T_i, $i = \{1, \dots, k\}$
- The probability of escalation to each of the levels as a function of the message size m $(M_1 \leq m \leq M_2)$ and the number of processors n $(3 \leq n \leq N)$ involved in the operation, $f_i(n,M)$, $i = \{1, \dots, k\}$

Parameter M_2 is observed to be a constant that does not depend on the number of processors n involved in the operation. Parameter M_1 depends on n. Parameter k is a constant that does not depend on n or on the size of message m. Parameters $\{T_i\}_{i=1}^k$ are also constants independent of n and m.

In general, the linear approximation of the gather execution time for large messages, $m > M_2$, may not be a continuation of that for small and medium messages, $m \leq M_2$. They may also have different slopes. The reason is that MPI implementations normally use an asynchronous communication mode for small and medium messages, allowing for parallel communications, and a synchronous mode for large messages, which results in serialized communications.

In addition to the nondeterministic behavior of the gather operation, a significant leap in the execution time of the scatter operation is also observed, given this operation is implemented straightforwardly, that is, using the flat tree topology, as specified in the MPI standard:

```
if (rank==root) {
  memcpy(recvbuf, sendbuf, recvcount);
  for (i=1; i<n; i++) {
    MPI_Isend(sendbuf+sendcount*i, sendcount, sendtype, i, 0, comm);
  }
  MPI_Waitall(n-1);
}
else {
  MPI_Recv(recvbuf, recvcount, recvtype, root, 0, comm);
}
```

Figure 5.2 shows the typical behavior of the scatter communication in these cases. We can see that there exists a message size, S, separating small and large messages for this operation. The linear approximations of the scatter execution time for small and large messages are given by different linear functions. As

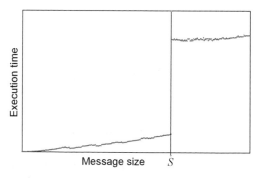

Figure 5.2. The execution time of the scatter collective communication against the message size.

reported in Lastovetsky and O'Flynn (2007), $S = M_2$ for all the studied platforms. The leap is explained by switching from an asynchronous to a synchronous communication mode when scattered messages become large.

One simple application of this more accurate model is given in Lastovetsky, O'Flynn, and Rychkov (2007). It is based on the observation that for many MPI implementations, native `MPI_Gather` and `MPI_Scatter` display the behavior shown in Figures 5.1 and 5.2, respectively. The idea is to replace the native collective operations by their optimized versions that avoid the `MPI_Gather` time escalations and the `MPI_Scatter` leap in the execution time. The optimization uses parameters S, M_1, and M_2, which are supposed to be computed upon the installation of the optimized version of the corresponding MPI implementation. One interesting feature of the optimization design is that the implementation of the optimized operation only uses its native counterpart and not point-to-point nor low-level communications.

The optimized `MPI_Gather` reinvokes the native `MPI_Gather` for small and large messages. The gathering of medium-sized messages, $M_1 \leq m \leq M_2$, is implemented by an equivalent sequence of N native `MPI_Gather` operations with messages of a size that fits into the range of small messages: $\dfrac{m}{N} < M_1$, $\dfrac{m}{N-1} \geq M_1$. Small-sized gatherings are synchronized by barriers, which remove communication congestions on the receiving node. The pseudocode is as follows:

```
if (M₁≤m≤M₂) {
    find N such that   m/N < M₁ and   m/(N-1) ≥ M₁;
    for (i=0; i<N; i++) {
        MPI_Barrier(comm);
        MPI_Gather(sendbuf + i* m/N , m/N );
    }
}
else MPI_Gather(sendbuf, m);
```

Note that if `MPI_Barrier` is removed from this code, the resulting implementation will behave exactly as the native `MPI_Gather`. It means that this synchronization is essential for preventing communication congestions on the receiving side.

The implementation of an optimized `MPI_Scatter` uses parameter S of the model. For small messages, $m < S$, the native `MPI_Scatter` is reinvoked. The scattering of large messages is implemented by an equivalent sequence of N native `MPI_Scatter` operations with messages of a size less than S: $\dfrac{m}{N} < S$, $\dfrac{m}{N-1} \geq S$. The pseudocode of the optimized scatter is as follows:

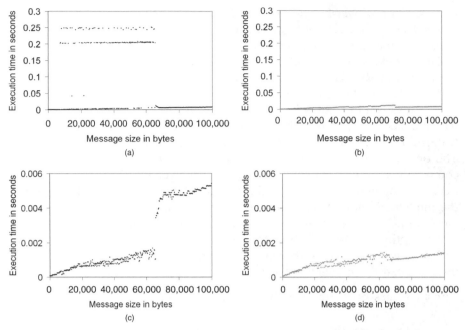

Figure 5.3. Performance of (a) native `MPI_Gather`, (b) optimized `MPI_Gather`, (c) native `MPI_Scatter`, and (d) optimized `MPI_Scatter` on a 16-node single-switched gigabit Ethernet-based cluster.

```
if (m≥S) {
        find N such that  m/N < S  and  m/(N-1) ≥ S;
        for (i=0; i<N; i++)
            MPI_Scatter(recvbuf + i*m/N, m/N);
}
else MPI_Scatter(recvbuf, m);
```

Figure 5.3 gives the comparison of the native and optimized `MPI_Gather` and `MPI_Scatter` operations on a real MPI platform using the LAM 7.1.1 MPI implementation and a 16-node single-switched gigabit Ethernet-based cluster.

None of the above point-to-point models reflects the heterogeneity of the processors. When applied to a cluster of heterogeneous processors, the point-to-point parameters of the models are found by averaging the values obtained for every pair of processors, and the averaged values are then used in modeling collective communication operations. When some processors in the heterogeneous cluster significantly differ in performance, the predictions based on the homogeneous communication models may become inaccurate. More accurate performance models would not average the point-to-point communication parameters but would have different point-to-point parameters reflecting nodal contributions in the communication execution time.

One such heterogeneous model (Lastovetsky, Mkwawa, and O'Flynn, 2006) is designed for computational clusters based on a single-switched network. This model does reflect the heterogeneity of processors in terms of node-specific fixed and variable processing delays. The drawback of this model is the significant increase of the number of parameters, which makes the problem of their accurate (and efficient!) estimation particularly difficult. As we will see, the traditional approach to the estimation of parameters cannot be applied to the heterogeneous model for two reasons. First, roundtrips between two processors, which are traditionally used in communication experiments, cannot give enough independent data to find the values of the point-to-point parameters of the heterogeneous model. Second, even if they did, we would have to perform the same set of measurements for each pair of heterogeneous processors, which would require numerous measurements and take an unacceptably long time.

Like most point-to-point communication models, except for PLogP, the heterogeneous point-to-point model (Lastovetsky, Mkwawa, and O'Flynn, 2006) is linear, representing the communication time by a linear function of the message size. Namely, the execution time of sending a message of m bytes from processor i to processor j in the heterogeneous model, $i \xrightarrow{m} j$, is estimated by $C_i + m \times t_i + C_j + m \times t_j + \dfrac{m}{\beta_{ij}}$, where C_i, C_j are the fixed processing delays, t_i, t_j are the delays of processing of a byte, and β_{ij} is the transmission rate. Different parameters for nodal delays reflect the heterogeneity of processors. For networks with a single switch, it is realistic to assume that $\beta_{ij} = \beta_{ji}$.

In terms of the Hockney model (applied to two connected processors i and j),

$C_i + C_j = \alpha$ and $m \times t_i + m \times t_j + \dfrac{m}{\beta_{ij}} = \beta \times m$. In comparison with the Hockney

model, the heterogeneous model reflects the heterogeneity of processors by introducing different fixed and variable delays. The values of the α parameters of the Hockney model for $i \xrightarrow{m} j$, $j \xrightarrow{m} k$, $k \xrightarrow{m} i$ point-to-point communications can be used to find the fixed processing delays of the heterogeneous model:

$$\begin{pmatrix} 1 & 1 & 0 \\ 0 & 1 & 1 \\ 1 & 0 & 1 \end{pmatrix} \times \begin{pmatrix} C_i \\ C_j \\ C_k \end{pmatrix} = \begin{pmatrix} \alpha_{ij} \\ \alpha_{jk} \\ \alpha_{ki} \end{pmatrix}.$$

Unfortunately, the data are not sufficient to determine the variable processing delays and transmission rates of the heterogeneous model, as we have $n + C_n^2$ unknowns but only C_n^2 equations.

In terms of the LogP/LogGP model, the sum of the fixed processing delays $C_i + C_j$ could be equal to $L + 2 \times o$ or $L + 2 \times o - G$, and

$m \times t_i + m \times t_j + \dfrac{m}{\beta_{ij}} = m \times G$. Similar to the Hockney model, the fixed processing delays could be found from every three point-to-point communications,

$$\begin{pmatrix} 1 & 1 & 0 \\ 0 & 1 & 1 \\ 1 & 0 & 1 \end{pmatrix} \times \begin{pmatrix} C_i \\ C_j \\ C_k \end{pmatrix} = \begin{pmatrix} (L+2\times o)_{ij} \\ (L+2\times o)_{jk} \\ (L+2\times o)_{ki} \end{pmatrix}$$

or

$$\begin{pmatrix} 1 & 1 & 0 \\ 0 & 1 & 1 \\ 1 & 0 & 1 \end{pmatrix} \times \begin{pmatrix} C_i \\ C_j \\ C_k \end{pmatrix} = \begin{pmatrix} (L+2\times o - G)_{ij} \\ (L+2\times o - G)_{jk} \\ (L+2\times o - G)_{ki} \end{pmatrix},$$

but it is not sufficient to find the other parameters.

As for the PLogP model, the meaning of its parameters and the assumption that the execution time of a roundtrip is $RTT(m) = L + g(m) + L + g(0)$ make impossible the use of the values of its parameters in finding the parameters of the heterogeneous point-to-point model.

Of course, the presented heterogeneous point-to-point communication model only makes sense if its parameters can be accurately and efficiently estimated. The design of the communication experiments that provide sufficient data for the accurate estimation of the parameters while keeping the total number of experiments (and their total execution time) reasonably small is proposed in Lastovetsky and Rychkov (2007).

For a cluster of n processors, there will be $2 \times n + C_n^2$ unknowns: n fixed processing delays, n variable processing delays, and C_n^2 transmission rates. The most accurate way to measure the execution time of MPI point-to-point communications is the measurement of roundtrip messaging. The execution time of sending m_1 bytes and receiving m_2 bytes between nodes $i \underset{m_2}{\overset{m_1}{\rightleftarrows}} j$ is equal to

$$T_{ij}(m_1,m_2) = \left(C_i + m_1 \times t_i + C_j + m_1 \times t_j + \dfrac{m_1}{\beta_{ij}}\right) + \left(C_i + m_2 \times t_i + C_j + m_2 \times t_j + \dfrac{m_2}{\beta_{ij}}\right).$$

First, we measure the execution time of the roundtrips with empty messages between each pair of processors $i < j$ (C_n^2 experiments). The fixed processing delays can be found from $T_{ij}(0) = 2 \times C_i + 2 \times C_j$ solved for every three roundtrips $i \underset{0}{\overset{0}{\rightleftarrows}} j$, $j \underset{0}{\overset{0}{\rightleftarrows}} k$, and $k \underset{0}{\overset{0}{\rightleftarrows}} i$ ($i < j < k$):

$$\begin{pmatrix} 2 & 2 & 0 \\ 0 & 2 & 2 \\ 2 & 0 & 2 \end{pmatrix} \times \begin{pmatrix} C_i \\ C_j \\ C_k \end{pmatrix} = \begin{pmatrix} T_{ij}(0) \\ T_{jk}(0) \\ T_{ki}(0) \end{pmatrix}$$

Since C_i can be found from the systems for different j and k, it makes sense to take C_i as an average of $\dfrac{(n-1)\times(n-2)}{2}$ values obtained from all the different systems of equations.

The C_n^2 experiments $i \underset{0}{\overset{m}{\rightleftarrows}} j\,(i<j)$ give us the same number of the following equations: $t_i + t_j + \dfrac{1}{\beta_{ij}} = \dfrac{T_{ij}(m) - 2\times C_i - 2\times C_j}{m}$. To find n variable processing delays t_i and C_n^2 transmission rates β_{ij}, we need at least n more independent equations. The equations are obtained from the communications $i \underset{0}{\overset{m}{\rightleftarrows}} j, k$, where the source processor sends the messages of the same size to two other processors and receives zero-sized messages from them.

The design of these additional experiments takes into account the possible nondeterministic and nonlinear behavior of MPI one-to-many and many-to-one communications that were observed on switched networks (Lastovetsky and O'Flynn, 2007). Namely, the execution time of many-to-one gather-like communications can nondeterministically escalate for a particular range of medium message sizes. Therefore, zero-sized messages are chosen to be gathered in order to avoid the nondeterministic escalations. Also, a leap in the execution time of one-to-many scatter-like operations for large messages is observed (Lastovetsky and O'Flynn, 2007). Therefore, m is taken as small enough. In this case, the source node does not wait until the current message has reached the destination node and can start sending the next message. In this communication, the contribution of the source node to the execution time will be $4 \times C_i + 2 \times m \times t_i$. The total time of transmission and processing on the destinations will be equal to the maximal value among the destination processors $\max\left\{2\times C_j + m\times t_j + \dfrac{m}{\beta_{ij}}, 2\times C_k + m\times t_k + \dfrac{m}{\beta_{ik}}\right\}$. Thus, the execution time $T_i(m)$ of one-to-two communications with root i can be expressed by

$$T_i(m) = 4\times C_i + 2\times m\times t_i + \max\left\{2\times C_j + m\times t_j + \dfrac{m}{\beta_{ij}}, 2\times C_k + m\times t_k + \dfrac{m}{\beta_{ik}}\right\}.$$

Let τ_j denote $2\times C_j + m\times t_j + \dfrac{m}{\beta_{ij}}$. Removing the maximum and rewriting the equation, we get

$$\begin{cases} 2\times t_i + t_j + \dfrac{1}{\beta_{ij}} = \dfrac{T_i(m) - 4\times C_i - 2\times C_j}{m}, & \tau_j > \tau_k \\ 2\times t_i + t_k + \dfrac{1}{\beta_{ik}} = \dfrac{T_i(m) - 4\times C_i - 2\times C_k}{m}, & \tau_k > \tau_j \end{cases}$$

Both alternatives less the equations for the point-to-point roundtrips with empty reply $i \underset{0}{\overset{m}{\rightleftarrows}} j$, $i \underset{0}{\overset{m}{\rightleftarrows}} k$ will give us the expression for the variable processing delay:

$$t_i = \begin{cases} \dfrac{T_i(m) - T_{ij}(m) - 2 \times C_i}{m}, & \tau_j > \tau_k \\ \dfrac{T_i(m) - T_{ik}(m) - 2 \times C_i}{m}, & \tau_k > \tau_j \end{cases},$$

where $T_{ij}(m)$ and $T_{ik}(m)$ are the execution times of the roundtrips. The inequalities can be simplified by adding $2 \times C_i + m \times t_i$ to both sides; the condition $\tau_j > \tau_k$ will turn into $T_{ij}(m) > T_{ik}(m)$. For the communications with other roots $j \underset{0}{\overset{m}{\rightleftharpoons}} i, k,\ k \underset{0}{\overset{m}{\rightleftharpoons}} i, j$, there will be similar expressions for t_j and t_k:

$$t_j = \begin{cases} \dfrac{T_j(m) - T_{ji}(m) - 2 \times C_j}{m}, & T_{ji}(m) > T_{jk}(m) \\ \dfrac{T_j(m) - T_{jk}(m) - 2 \times C_j}{m}, & T_{jk}(m) > T_{ji}(m) \end{cases},$$

$$t_k = \begin{cases} \dfrac{T_k(m) - T_{ki}(m) - 2 \times C_k}{M}, & T_{ki}(m) > T_{kj}(m) \\ \dfrac{T_k(m) - T_{kj}(m) - 2 \times C_k}{m}, & T_{kj}(m) > T_{ki}(m) \end{cases}.$$

We assume that $\beta_{ij} = \beta_{ji}$, therefore $T_{ij}(m) = T_{ji}(m)$. All we need is to compare the values of $T_{ij}(m)$, $T_{jk}(m)$, and $T_{ik}(m)$ and select the equations that satisfy the conditions. Then, the transmission rates can be expressed as $\dfrac{1}{\beta_{ij}} = \dfrac{T_{ij}(m) - 2 \times C_i - 2 \times C_j}{m} - t_i - t_j$. Thus, we have six equations with three conditions. For example, if $T_{ij}(m) > T_{ik}(m)$, $T_{ji}(m) > T_{jk}(m)$, and $T_{ki}(m) > T_{kj}(m)$, then the system of equations will look as follows:

$$\begin{cases} t_i = \dfrac{T_i(m) - T_{ij}(m) - 2 \times C_i}{m} \\ t_j = \dfrac{T_j(m) - T_{ji}(m) - 2 \times C_j}{m} \\ t_k = \dfrac{T_k(m) - T_{ki}(m) - 2 \times C_k}{m} \end{cases},$$

$$\frac{1}{\beta_{ij}} = \frac{T_{ij}(m) - 2 \times C_i - 2 \times C_j}{m} - t_i - t_j$$

$$\frac{1}{\beta_{jk}} = \frac{T_{jk}(m) - 2 \times C_j - 2 \times C_k}{m} - t_j - t_k .$$

$$\frac{1}{\beta_{ki}} = \frac{T_{ki}(m) - 2 \times C_k - 2 \times C_i}{m} - t_k - t_i$$

If $i < j < k$, there will be $3 \times C_n^3$ one-to-two experiments. The variable processing delays t_i can be obtained from $\dfrac{(n-1) \times (n-2)}{2}$ different triplets the processor i takes part in, and can then be averaged. The transmission rates β_{ij} can be averaged from $n - 2$ values.

This approach can also be extended to the communications $i \underset{0}{\overset{m}{\rightleftarrows}} j_1, \ldots, j_k \, (j_1 < \ldots < j_k)$. This will require $(1+k) \times C_n^{1+k}$ experiments to perform, $(k + 1) \times (k - 1)$ inequalities to check, and $1 + k + C_{k+1}^2$ equations to solve.

The above design is optimal in terms of the execution time taken for estimating point-to-point parameters. The total execution time depends on

- the number of measurements ($2 \times C_n^2$ one-to-one and $3 \times C_n^3$ one-to-two measurements),
- the execution time of every single measurement (fast roundtrips between two and three processors), and
- the complexity of calculations ($3 \times C_n^3$ comparisons, $12 \times C_n^3$ simple formulae for the calculation of the values of the parameters of the model, and averaging of $2 \times n + C_n^2$ values).

As the parameters of the point-to-point heterogeneous model are found in a small number of experiments, they can be sensitive to the inaccuracy of measurements. Therefore, it makes sense to perform a series of measurements for one-to-one and one-to-two experiments and to use the averaged execution times in the corresponding linear equations. One advantage of this design is that these series do not have to be long (typically, up to 10 in a series) because all the parameters have been already averaged within the procedure of their finding.

The models presented in the section are fundamental, addressing the basic communication properties of heterogeneous computational clusters. They constitute a basis for more complicated communications models, which use the basic models as building blocks. One simple example is given by various communication models of hierarchical heterogeneous clusters designed as multi-level hierarchies of basic communication models.

5.3 COMMUNICATION PERFORMANCE MODELS FOR LOCAL AND GLOBAL NETWORKS OF COMPUTERS

In this section, we briefly look at communication performance models for heterogeneous platforms other than dedicated heterogeneous clusters. The platforms include

- a general-purpose local network of computers,
- geographically distributed computers interconnected via dedicated communication channels, and
- geographically distributed computers interconnected via the Internet.

The models currently used for these platforms are just simplified versions of the models used for dedicated heterogeneous clusters. For example, the execution time of point-to-point communication between geographically distributed computers is typically estimated as $\beta \times m$, where m is the message size and β is the bandwidth of the communication link. This estimation can be accurate in the case of a dedicated communication link. If the two computers are connected via the Internet, then the bandwidth of the virtual communication link becomes unpredictable and the linear predictive model will be of little help. In other words, this simple model does not address a specific challenge imposed by the Internet-based platform, namely, that the bandwidth of Internet links is unpredictable. Local networks of computers impose a similar challenge as the traffic in the network is variable and unpredictable, making the performance characteristics of the network difficult to predict.

Research on communication performance models addressing specific challenges imposed by general-purpose local networks and distributed Internet-connected systems has not produced many results yet, and the results are anything but conclusive. Therefore, it would be fair to say that modeling the performance of these platforms is still a subject of research.

Some results that might be mentioned include the observation made in Casanova (2005) that Internet links can sustain multiple simultaneous data transfer between two nodes with the same end-to-end bandwidths. This observation is used in Gupta and Vadhiyar (2007) to design an algorithm for all-gather on Internet-based distributed systems utilizing available Internet bandwidths.

CHAPTER 6

Performance Analysis of Heterogeneous Algorithms

6.1 EFFICIENCY ANALYSIS OF HETEROGENEOUS ALGORITHMS

The methods for performance analysis of homogeneous parallel algorithms are well studied. They are based on models of parallel computers that assume a parallel computer to be a homogeneous multiprocessor. The theoretical analysis of a homogeneous parallel algorithm is normally accompanied by a relatively small number of experiments on a homogeneous parallel computer system. The purpose of these experiments is to show that the analysis is correct and that the analyzed algorithm is really faster than its counterparts are.

Performance analysis of heterogeneous parallel algorithms is a much more difficult task that is wide open for research. Very few techniques have been proposed; none of which is accepted as a fully satisfactory solution. In this chapter, we briefly outline the proposed techniques.

One approach to performance analysis of heterogeneous parallel algorithms is based on the fact that the design of such algorithms is typically reduced to the problem of optimal data partitioning of one or other mathematical object such as a set, a rectangle, and so on. As soon as the corresponding mathematical optimization problem is formulated, the quality of its solution is assessed rather than the quality of the solution of the original problem. As the optimization problem is typically NP-hard, some suboptimal solutions are proposed and analyzed. The analysis is mostly statistical: The suboptimal solutions for a large number of generated inputs are compared with each other and with the optimal one. This approach is used in many papers (Crandall and Quinn, 1995; Kaddoura, Ranka, and Wang, 1996; Beaumont et al., 2001b,c). It estimates the heterogeneous parallel algorithm indirectly, and additional experiments are still needed to assess its efficiency in real heterogeneous environments.

Another approach is to experimentally compare the execution time of the heterogeneous algorithm with that of its homogeneous prototype or

High-Performance Heterogeneous Computing, by Alexey L. Lastovetsky and Jack J. Dongarra
Copyright © 2009 John Wiley & Sons, Inc.

heterogeneous competitor. A particular heterogeneous network is used for such experiments. In particular, this approach is used in Kalinov and Lastovetsky (1999a), Kalinov and Lastovetsky (2001), Dovolnov, Kalinov, and Klimov (2003), and Ohtaki *et al.* (2004). This approach directly estimates the efficiency of heterogeneous parallel algorithms in some real heterogeneous environment but still leaves an open question about their efficiency in general heterogeneous environments. Another problem with this approach is that real-life heterogeneous platforms are often shared by multiple users, which makes their performance characteristics, and hence experimental performance results, difficult to reproduce.

One possible approach to the problems of diversity of heterogeneous platforms and reproducibility of their performance characteristics could be the use of simulators, similar to those used for simulation of grid environments (see Sulistio, Yeo, and Buyya (2004) for an overview of this topic). Although the accuracy of such simulation can be open to question, it seems to be the only realistic solution for the experimental analysis of algorithms for large-scale distributed environments.

In the case of heterogeneous computational clusters, a more natural and reliable solution would be the use of a reconfigurable and fully controlled environment for the reproducible experiments. This environment might include both reconfigurable hardware and software components, altogether providing reproducible performance characteristics of processors and communication links. One simple, practical, and easy-for-implementation design of such an environment is proposed in Canon and Jeannot (2006). The idea is to take a dedicated homogeneous cluster and degrade the performance of its computing nodes and communication links independently by means of a software in order to build a "heterogeneous" cluster. Then, any application can be run on this new cluster without modifications. The corresponding framework, called Wrekavoc, targets the degradation of the following characteristics:

- CPU power,
- network bandwidth,
- network latency, and
- memory (not implemented yet).

For degradation of CPU performance, Wrekavoc implements three software-based methods: managing CPU frequency through a kernel interface; burning a constant portion of the CPU by a CPU burner; and suspending the processes when they have used more than the required fraction of the CPU with a CPU limiter.

Limiting latency and bandwidth is done based on modern software tools allowing advanced IP routing. The tools allow the programmer to control both incoming and outgoing traffic, control the latency of the network interface, and alter the traffic using numerous and complicated rules based on IP addresses, ports, and so on.

The framework itself is implemented using the client–server model. A server, with administrator privileges, is deployed on each node of the instrumental homogeneous cluster and runs as a daemon. The client reads a configuration file, which specifies the required configuration of the target heterogeneous cluster, and sends orders to each node in the configuration. The client can also order the nodes to recover the original state.

Another related approach to the performance analysis of heterogeneous parallel algorithms is based on a performance model of heterogeneous environments. This model-based approach is aimed at the prediction of the execution time of the algorithms without their real execution in heterogeneous environments. This approach is proposed and implemented in the framework of the mpC programming system (Lastovetsky, 2002). The algorithm designer can describe the analyzed algorithm in a dedicated specification language. This description is typically parameterized and includes the following information:

- The number of parallel processes executing the algorithm
- The absolute volume of computations performed by each of the processes measured in some fixed computational units
- The absolute volume of data transferred between each pair of processes
- The scenario of interaction between the parallel processes during the algorithm execution

The heterogeneous environment is modeled by a multilevel hierarchy of interconnected sets of heterogeneous multiprocessors. The hierarchy reflects the heterogeneity of communication links and is represented in the form of an attributed tree. Each internal node of the tree represents a homogeneous communication space of the heterogeneous network. Attributes associated with the node allow one to predict the execution time of communication operations. Each terminal node in the tree represents an individual (homogeneous) multiprocessor computer that is characterized by the following:

- The time of execution of one computational unit by a processor of the computer; the computational unit is supposed to be the same as the one used in the description of the analyzed algorithm
- The number of physical processors
- The attributes of the communication layer provided by the computer

The description of the algorithm is compiled to produce a program that uses the performance model of the heterogeneous environment to predict the execution time of the algorithm for each particular mapping of its processes onto the computers of the environment.

The approach proposed in Lastovetsky and Reddy (2004b) is to carefully design a relatively small number of experiments in a natural or engineered heterogeneous environment in order to experimentally compare the efficiency of the heterogeneous parallel algorithm with some experimentally obtained ideal efficiency (namely, the efficiency of its homogeneous prototype in an equally powerful homogeneous environment). Thus, this approach compares the heterogeneous algorithm with its homogeneous prototype and assesses the heterogeneous modification rather than analyzes this algorithm as an isolated entity. It directly estimates the efficiency of heterogeneous parallel algorithms, providing relatively high confidence in the results of such an experimental estimation.

The basic postulate of this approach is that the heterogeneous algorithm cannot be more efficient than its homogeneous prototype. This means that the heterogeneous algorithm cannot be executed on the heterogeneous network faster than its homogeneous prototype on the *equivalent* homogeneous network. A homogeneous network of computers is equivalent to the heterogeneous network if

- its aggregate communication characteristics are the same as that of the heterogeneous network,
- it has the same number of processors, and
- the speed of each processor is equal to the average speed of the processors of the heterogeneous network.

The heterogeneous algorithm is considered *optimal* if its efficiency is the same as that of its homogeneous prototype.

This approach is relatively easy to apply if the target architecture of the heterogeneous algorithm is a set of heterogeneous processors interconnected via a homogeneous communication network. In this case, all that is needed is to find a (homogeneous) segment in the instrumental LAN and select two sets of processors in this segment so that

- both sets consist of the same number of processors,
- all processors comprising the first set are identical,
- the second set includes processors of different speeds, and
- the aggregate performance of the first set of processors is the same as that of the second one.

The first set of interconnected processors represents a homogeneous network of computers, which is equivalent to the heterogeneous network of computers represented by the second set of processors just by design. Indeed, these two networks of computers share the same homogeneous communication segment and, therefore, have the same aggregate communication characteristics. Results that are more reliable are obtained if the intersection of the two sets of processors is not empty. This allows us to better control the accuracy of experiments by checking that the same processor has the same speed in the heterogeneous network running the heterogeneous algorithm and in the homogeneous network running its homogeneous prototype. Higher confidence of the experimental assessment can be achieved by experimenting with several different pairs of processor sets from different segments. This approach is used in Lastovetsky and Reddy (2004b), Plaza, Plaza, and Valencia (2006, 2007), and Plaza (2007).

If the target architecture for the heterogeneous algorithm is a set of heterogeneous processors interconnected via a heterogeneous communication network, the design of the experiments becomes much more complicated. Although comprehensive solution of this problem is still a subject for research, one simple but quite typical case has been analyzed (Lastovetsky and Reddy, 2004b). Let the communication network of the target heterogeneous architecture consist of a number of relatively fast homogeneous communication segments interconnected by slower communication links. Let parallel communications between different pairs of processors be enabled within each of the segments (e.g., by using a switch, the number of ports of which is no less than the number of computers in the segment). Let communication links between different segments only support serial communication. Further design depends on the analyzed heterogeneous algorithm. Assume that the communication cost of the algorithm comes mainly from relatively rare point-to-point communications separated by a significant amount of computations, so that it is highly unlikely for two such communication operations to be performed in parallel. Also, assume that each such communication operation consists in passing a relatively long message. Those assumptions allows us to use a very simple linear communication model when time $t_{A \to B}(d)$ of transferring a data block of size d from processor A to processor B is calculated as $t_{A \to B}(d) = s_{A \to B} \times d$, where $s_{A \to B}$ is the constant speed of communication between processors A and B and $s_{A \to B} = s_{B \to A}$. Thus, under all these assumptions, the only aggregate characteristic of the communication network that has an impact on the execution time of the algorithm is the average speed of point-to-point communications.

To design experiments on the instrumental LAN in this case, we need to select two sets of processors so that

- both sets consist of the same number of processors,
- all processors comprising the first set are identical and belong to the same homogeneous communication segment,
- the second set includes processors of different speeds that span several communication segments,
- the aggregate performance of the first set of processors is the same as that of the second one, and
- the average speed of point-to-point communications between the processors of the second set is the same as the speed of point-to-point communications between the processors of the first set.

The first set of interconnected processors will represent a homogeneous network of computers, equivalent to the heterogeneous network of computers represented by the second set.

In a mathematical form, this problem can be formulated as follows. Let n be the number of processors in the first set, v be their speed, and s be the communication speed of the corresponding segment. Let the second set of processors, P, span m communication segments $S_1, S_2, \ldots, S_m$. Let s_i be the communication speed of segment S_i, n_i be the number of processors of set P belonging to S_i, and v_{ij} be the speed of the j-th processor belonging to segment S_i ($i = 1, \ldots, m; j = 1, \ldots, n_i$). Let s_{ij} be the speed of the communication link between segments S_i and S_j ($i, j = 1, \ldots, m$). Then,

$$\frac{\sum_{i=1}^{m} s_i \times \frac{n_i \times (n_i - 1)}{2} + \sum_{i=1}^{m} \sum_{j=i+1}^{m} n_i \times n_j \times s_{ij}}{\frac{n \times (n-1)}{2}} = s, \tag{6.1}$$

$$\sum_{i=1}^{m} n_i = n, \tag{6.2}$$

$$\sum_{i=1}^{m} \sum_{j=1}^{n_i} v_{ij} = n \times v. \tag{6.3}$$

Equation (6.1) states that the average speed of point-to-point communications between the processors of the second set should be equal to the speed of point-to-point communications between the processors of the first set. Equation (6.2) states that the total number of processors in the second set should be equal to the number of processors in the first set. Equation (6.3) states that the aggregate performance of the processors in the second set should be equal to the aggregate performance of the processors in the first set.

6.2   SCALABILITY ANALYSIS OF HETEROGENEOUS ALGORITHMS

The methods presented in the previous section are mainly aimed at the comparative analysis of the efficiency of different homogeneous and heterogeneous algorithms in given heterogeneous environments. Some researchers consider scalability at least as important a property of heterogeneous parallel algorithms as efficiency. *Scalability* refers to the ability of an algorithm to increase the performance of the executing parallel system with incremental addition of processors to the system. The analysis of scalability is particularly important if the algorithm is designed for large-scale parallel systems.

Scalability of a parallel application has two distinct flavors:

- *Strong* scalability—where the problem size is fixed and the number of processors increases, and our goal is to minimize the time to solution.

Here, scalability means that speedup is roughly proportional to the number of processors used. For example, if you double the number of processors, but you keep the problem size constant, then the problem takes half as long to complete (i.e., the speed doubles).

- *Weak* scalability—where the problem size and the number of processors expand, and our goal is to achieve constant time to solution for larger problems. In this case, scalability means the ability to maintain a fixed time to solution for solving larger problems on larger computers. For example, if you double the number of processors and double the problem size, then the problem takes the same amount of time to complete (i.e., the speed doubles).

Weak scaling is easier to achieve, at least relatively speaking. Weak scalability means, basically, that as you scale up the problem to a larger size, each processor does the same amount of computing. For example, if you double the size of a three-dimensional mesh in each dimension, you need eight times more processors.

Strong scaling, on the other hand, may not be as easy to achieve. Strong scalability means that for a given problem, as you scale up, say, from 100 to 800 processors, you apply this greater number of processors to the same mesh, so that each processor is now doing one-eighth as much work as before. You would like the job to run eight times faster, and to do that may require restructuring how the program divides the work among processors and increases the communication between them.

An example of an implementation demonstrating strong scalability comes from a molecular dynamics application called NAMD (Kumar *et al.*, 2006). NAMD is a C++-based parallel program that uses object-based decomposition and measurement-based dynamic load balancing to achieve its high performance, and a combination of spatial decomposition and force decomposition to generate a high degree of parallelism. As a result, NAMD is one of the fastest and most scalable programs for bimolecular simulations. It shows strong scalability up to 8192 processors. For NAMD, the overlapping of communication with computation is critical to achieving such scalability.

Weak scalability of homogeneous algorithms designed for execution on homogeneous parallel systems has been intensively studied (Gustafson, Montry, and Benner, 1988; Zorbas, Reble, and VanKooten, 1989; Karp and Platt, 1990; Grama, Gupta, and Kumar, 1993; Zhang, Yan, and He, 1994; Dongarra, van de Geijn, and Walker, 1994; Chetverushkin *et al.*, 1998). Nonetheless, the studies did not result in a unified method of scalability analysis that would be adopted by the research community. Among others, the *isoefficiency* approach (Grama, Gupta, and Kumar, 1993) is probably the most widely used. It is based on the notion of *parallel efficiency*, which is defined as the ratio of the speedup achieved by the algorithm on the parallel system to the number of processors involved in the execution of the algorithm:

$$E(n, p) = \frac{A(n, p)}{p}.$$

It is important that the parallel efficiency is defined as a function of the size of the task solved by the algorithm, n, and the number of processors, p. The parallel efficiency characterizes the level of utilization of the processors by the algorithm. While sometimes the parallel efficiency can be greater than 1 due to the superlinear speedup effects, it typically ranges from 0 to 1. Moreover, if the task size is fixed, the parallel efficiency of the algorithm will typically decrease with the increase of the number of processors involved in its execution. This is due to the increase of the overhead part in the execution time. On the other hand, the efficiency of the use of the same number of processors by the parallel algorithm usually increases with the increase of the task size.

Intuitively, the algorithm is *scalable* if it can use, with the same efficiency, the increasing number of processors for solution of tasks of increasing size. Mathematically, the level of scalability is characterized by a so-called *isoefficiency function*, $n = I(p)$, that determines how the task size should increase with the increase of the number of processors in order to ensure constant efficiency. The isoefficiency function is found from the *isoefficiency condition*, $E(n,p) = k$, where k denotes a positive constant. The isoefficiency function of a scalable algorithm should monotonically increase. The slower the function increases, the more scalable the algorithm is.

Extension of the isoefficiency approach to the scalability analysis of algorithms for heterogeneous parallel systems needs a new, more general, definition of parallel efficiency. Two definitions have been given so far (independently by several researchers). The first one defines the parallel efficiency as the ratio of the real and ideal speedups (Chetverushkin *et al.*, 1998; Mazzeo, Mazzocca, Villano, 1998; Bazterra *et al.*, 2005). The real speedup is the one achieved by the parallel algorithm on the heterogeneous parallel system. The ideal speedup is defined as the sum of speeds of the processors of the executing heterogeneous parallel system divided by the speed of a base processor (Chetverushkin *et al.*, 1998). All speedups are calculated relative to the serial execution of the algorithm on the base processor.

According to the second definition, the parallel efficiency is the ratio of the ideal and real execution times (Zhang and Yan, 1995; Chamberlain, Chace, and Patil, 1998; Pastor and Bosque, 2001; Kalinov, 2006). In particular, in Kalinov (2006), the parallel efficiency of the algorithm solving a task of size n on p heterogeneous processors of the speeds $S = \{s_1, s_2, \ldots, s_p\}$ is defined as

$$E(n, p, S) = \frac{T_{\text{ideal}}(n, s_{\text{seq}}, p, S)}{T_{\text{par}}(n, p, S)},$$

where s_{seq} is the speed of the base processor. The ideal parallel execution time is calculated under the assumptions that the communication and other overheads of the parallel execution are free and that the computational load of the processors is perfectly balanced:

$$T_{\text{ideal}}(n, s_{\text{seq}}, p, S) = \frac{s_{\text{seq}}}{\sum_{i \in [1,p]} s_i} \times T_{\text{seq}}(n, s_{\text{seq}}) = \frac{s_{\text{seq}}}{p s_{\text{aver}}} \times T_{\text{seq}}(n, s_{\text{seq}}),$$

where s_{aver} is the average speed of the p processors and $T_{\text{seq}}(n, s_{\text{seq}})$ is the execution time of the sequential solution of this task (of size n) on the base processor. Thus, the parallel efficiency will be given by

$$E(n, p, S) = \frac{s_{\text{seq}}}{s_{\text{aver}}} \times \frac{T_{\text{seq}}(n, s_{\text{seq}})}{p T_{\text{par}}(n, p, S)}.$$

For a homogeneous system, $s_{\text{seq}} = s_i = s_{\text{aver}} = const$, and the formula takes its usual form

$$E(n, p) = \frac{T_{\text{seq}}(n)}{p T_{\text{par}}(n, p)} = \frac{A(n, p)}{p}.$$

For a heterogeneous system, the isoefficiency condition $E(n, p, S) = k$ is used to find the isoefficiency function $n = I(p, S)$. In Kalinov (2006), this approach is used for the scalability analysis of heterogeneous modifications of the SUMMA parallel matrix multiplication algorithm (van de Geijn and Watts, 1997) under the additional assumption that the minimal (s_{min}), maximal (s_{max}), and average (s_{aver}) processor speeds do not change with the increase in the number of processors (p) in the heterogeneous system. In this case, the formulae for the isoefficiency functions only include the integral characteristics of the heterogeneous parallel system, namely, p, s_{min}, s_{max}, and s_{aver}, making the isoefficiency functions only functions of the number of processors, not functions of the speeds of the processors. Moreover, for some algorithms, s_{min} and s_{max} appear in the formulae only in the form of their ratio, which characterizes the level of heterogeneity of the considered parallel systems.

Another approach to scalability, the *isospeed* approach (Sun and Rover, 1994), is based on the notion of speed of a computer system defined as the work performed by the computer system divided by the execution time. This approach has been extended to heterogeneous systems (Sun, Chen, and Wu, 2005). The average speed of a processor is defined as the ratio of the speed achieved by the parallel system to the number of processors. The algorithm will be scalable if the average speed of a processor can be maintained at a constant level by increasing the size of the problem when the number of processors increases. A software tool for scalability testing and analysis based on the isospeed approach has been also developed (Chen and Sun, 2006).

PART III

PERFORMANCE: IMPLEMENTATION AND SOFTWARE

In this part, we analyze issues arising during the implementation of parallel and distributed algorithms for heterogeneous platforms and outline programming tools available for their implementation.

CHAPTER 7

Implementation Issues

7.1 PORTABLE IMPLEMENTATION OF HETEROGENEOUS ALGORITHMS AND SELF-ADAPTABLE APPLICATIONS

Parallel programming for heterogeneous platforms is a more difficult and challenging task than that for traditional homogeneous ones. The heterogeneity of processors means that they can execute the same code at different speeds. The heterogeneity of communication networks means that different communication links may have different bandwidths and latency. As a result, traditional parallel algorithms that distribute computations and communications evenly over available processors and communication links will not, in general, be optimal for heterogeneous platforms. Heterogeneous algorithms can be designed to achieve top performance on heterogeneous networks of computers. Such algorithms would distribute computations and communications unevenly, taking into account the heterogeneity of both the processors and the communication network.

The design of heterogeneous parallel algorithms introduced in Part II of this book has been an active research area over the last decade. A number of highly efficient heterogeneous algorithms have been proposed and analyzed. At the same time, there is practically no available scientific software based on these algorithms. The prime cause of this obvious disproportion in the number of heterogeneous parallel algorithms that have been designed and the scientific software based on these algorithms is that the implementation of a heterogeneous parallel algorithm is itself a difficult and nontrivial task. The point is that the program implementing the algorithm only makes sense if it is portable and able to automatically tune itself to any executing heterogeneous platform in order to achieve top performance. This poses additional challenges that should be addressed by scientific programmers. Let us take a closer look at these challenges.

As we have seen in Part II of this book, a heterogeneous parallel algorithm is normally designed in a generic, parameterized form. Parameters of the algorithm can be divided into three groups (Lastovetsky, 2006):

High-Performance Heterogeneous Computing, by Alexey L. Lastovetsky and Jack J. Dongarra
Copyright © 2009 John Wiley & Sons, Inc.

- problem parameters,
- algorithmic parameters, and
- platform parameters.

Problem parameters are the parameters of the problem to be solved (e.g., the size of the matrix to be factorized). These parameters can only be provided by the user.

Algorithmic parameters are the parameters representing different variations and configurations of the algorithm. Examples are the size of a matrix block in local computations for linear algebra algorithms, the total number of processes executing the algorithm, and the logical shape of their arrangement. The parameters do not change the result of computations but can have an impact on the performance. This impact may be very significant. On some platforms, a multifold speedup can be achieved due to the optimization of the algorithmic parameters rather than using their default values. The influence of algorithmic parameters on the performance can be due to different reasons. The total amount of computations or communications can depend on some parameters such as the logical shape of how the processes are arranged. Others do not change the volume of computations and communications but can change the fraction of computations performed on data located at higher levels of memory hierarchy, and hence, change the fraction of computations performed at a higher speed (the size of a matrix block in local computations for linear algebra algorithms is of this type). The program straightforwardly implementing the algorithm would require its users to provide (optimal) values of such parameters. This is the easiest way for the scientific programmer to implement the algorithm, but it makes the use of the program rather inconvenient. An alternative approach, which is more convenient for the end users, is to delegate the task of finding the optimal values of the algorithmic parameters to the software implementing the algorithm, making the software self-adaptable to different heterogeneous platforms.

Platform parameters are the parameters of the performance model of the executing heterogeneous platform such as the speed of the processes and the bandwidth and latency of communication links between the processes. The parameters have a major impact on the performance of the program implementing the algorithm. Indeed, consider an algorithm distributing computations in proportion to the speed of processors and based, say, on a simple constant performance model of heterogeneous processors. The algorithm should be provided with a set of positive constants representing the relative speed of the processors. The efficiency of the corresponding application will strongly depend on the accuracy of estimation of the relative speed. If this estimation is not accurate enough, the load of the processors will be unbalanced, resulting in poor execution performance.

The traditional approach to this problem is to run a test code to measure the relative speed of the processors in the network and then use this estimation when distributing computation across the processors. Unfortunately, the problem of accurate estimation of the relative speed of processors is not as easy as it may look. Of course, if two processors only differ in clock rate, it will not be a problem to accurately estimate their relative speed. A single test code can be used to measure their relative speed, and the relative speed will be the same for any application. This simple approach may also work if the processors used in computations have very similar architectural characteristics. But if the processors are of very different architectures, the situation will change drastically. Everything in the processors may be different: sets of instructions, number of instruction execution units, numbers of registers, structures of memory hierarchy, sizes of each memory level, and so on. Therefore, the processors may demonstrate different relative speeds for different applications. Moreover, processors of the same architecture but of different models or configurations may also demonstrate different relative speeds on different applications. Even different applications of the same narrow class may be executed by two different processors at significantly different relative speeds.

Another complication comes up if the network of computers allows for multi-tasking. In this case, the processors executing the parallel application may be also used for other computations and communications. Therefore, the real performance of the processors can dynamically change depending on the external computations and communications. Accurate estimation of the platform parameters for more advanced performance models (using, say, the functional model of processors) is obviously even more a difficult problem.

Therefore, if scientific software implementing the heterogeneous algorithm requires the user to provide the platform parameters, its performance will strongly depend on the accuracy of the provided parameters, making the software rather useless for the majority of potential users. Indeed, even relatively small inaccuracies in the estimation of these parameters can completely distort the performance. For example, let only one slow processor be wrongly estimated by the user as a fast one (say, because of the use of a nonrepresentative test code). Then, this processor will be assigned by the software a disproportional large amount of computation and slow down the application as the other processors will be waiting for it at points of data transfer and synchronization.

Thus, good scientific software implementing a heterogeneous parallel algorithm should provide

- accurate platform parameters of the algorithm and
- optimal values of algorithmic parameters.

If implemented this way, the application will be portable and self-adaptable, automatically tuning to the executing heterogeneous platform in order to provide top performance. In terms of implementation, this means that, in addition to the core code of the program implementing the algorithm for each valid combination of the values of its parameters, the scientific programmer has to write a significant amount of nontrivial code responsible for the solution of the above tasks.

Note. It should be noted that one fundamental assumption is implicitly made about all algorithms considered in this book. Namely, we assume that the volume of computations and communications performed during the execution of an algorithm is fully determined by its problem and algorithmic parameters and does not depend on the value of input data such as matrices. Algorithms that may perform different amounts of computations or communications depending on the value of the input data are out of the scope of this book.

How can a programming system help the scientific programmer write all the code? First of all, it does not look realistic to expect that the programming system can significantly automate the writing of the core code of the program. Actually, if this was the case, it would mean that the possibility of an automatic generation of good heterogeneous parallel algorithms from some simple specifications would be realized. As we have seen, the design of heterogeneous parallel algorithms is a very difficult and challenging task that is wide open for research. This research area is just taking its first steps, and thus requires a lot of skill and creativity from contributors. In other words, it is unrealistic to expect that parallel programming systems for heterogeneous computing can help common users having no idea about heterogeneous parallel algorithms but are willing, with minimal efforts, to obtain a good parallel program efficiently solving their problems in heterogeneous environments. On the other hand, given the algorithm is well described, the implementation of the core code is rather a straightforward engineering exercise.

What the programming system can do is to help qualified algorithm designers write the code responsible for providing accurate platform parameters and for the optimization of algorithmic parameters. The code provided by the programming system comes in two forms. The first one is the application-specific code generated by a compiler from the specification of the implemented algorithm provided by the application programmer. The second type of code is not application specific and comes in the form of run-time support systems and libraries. It is worthwhile to note that the size and complexity of such code is very significant and can account for more than 90% of the total code for some algorithms.

Programming systems for heterogeneous parallel computing can help not only in the implementation of original heterogeneous parallel algorithms but also in the efficient implementation of traditional homogeneous parallel algorithms for heterogeneous platforms. This approach can be summarized as follows:

- The whole computation is partitioned into a large number of equal chunks.
- Each chunk is performed by a separate process.
- The number of processes run by each processor is proportional to the relative speed of the processor.

Thus, while distributed evenly across parallel processes, data and computations are distributed unevenly over processors of the heterogeneous network so that each processor performs the volume of computations proportional to its speed. Again, the code responsible for the accurate estimation of platform parameters, optimization of algorithmic parameters, and optimal mapping of processes to the processors can be provided by the programming system. The main responsibility of the application programmer is to provide an accurate specification of the implemented algorithm. The practical value of this approach is that it can be used to port legacy parallel software to heterogeneous platforms.

7.2 PERFORMANCE MODELS OF HETEROGENEOUS PLATFORMS: ESTIMATION OF PARAMETERS

Accurate estimation of parameters of the performance model of the heterogeneous platform used in the design of a heterogeneous algorithm (platform parameters) is a key to the efficient implementation of the algorithm. If these parameters are estimated inaccurately, the heterogeneous algorithm will distribute computations and communications based on wrong assumptions about the performance characteristics of the executing platform, which will result in poor performance. It can be even much poorer than the performance of the homogeneous counterpart of the algorithm. Therefore, the problem of accurate estimation of parameters of heterogeneous performance models is very important.

7.2.1 Estimation of Constant Performance Models of Heterogeneous Processors

As can be seen from Part II, most of the heterogeneous algorithms that have been designed so far are based on the simplest performance model, whose parameters include

- p, the number of the processors, and
- $S = \{s_1, s_2, \dots, s_p\}$, the relative speeds of the processors in the form of positive constants s_i, $\Sigma_{i=1}^{p} s_i = 1$.

Although some of these algorithms are originally formulated in terms of absolute speeds of the processors, we have shown that it is not necessary and the algorithms will work correctly if reformulated in terms of relative speeds (see Note on Algorithm 3.1 in Chapter 3). The absolute speeds in such algorithms are used only to make them more intuitive.

The general approach to the estimation of relative speeds of a set of heterogeneous processors is to run some benchmark code and use its execution time on each of the processors for calculation of their relative speeds. As we have discussed in Section 2.1, the same heterogeneous processors can execute different applications at significantly different relative speeds. Therefore, it is impossible to design a single, universally applicable benchmark code. The benchmark code accurately estimating the relative speeds of the processors is application specific and should be carefully designed for each particular application.

The efficiency of the benchmark code will not be a big issue if the application is supposed to be executed multiple times on the same set of heterogeneous processors having the stable and reproducible performance characteristics. In this case, the benchmark code can be separated from the main application code and run just once in order that the obtained estimation of relative speeds could be used in all subsequent runs of the application. The execution time of the benchmark code is not that substantial in this scenario as it will be negligible compared to the total execution time of all the subsequent executions of the application.

If every execution of the application is seen unique, running in a heterogeneous environment with different performance characteristics, the benchmark code will have to be a part of the application, being executed at run time. In this case, the efficiency of the benchmark code becomes an issue. The overhead of the accurate estimation of the performance parameters should not exceed gains due to the use of the heterogeneous algorithm. Therefore, the amount of computations performed by the benchmark code should be relatively small compared with the main body of the application's computations. At the same time, in order to accurately estimate the speeds of the processors, the benchmark code should be representative of the main body of the code, reproducing the data layout and computations of the application during its execution.

The design of the benchmark code is relatively straightforward for data parallel applications using the one-process-per-processor configuration and performing iterative computations such that

- The data layout is static, not changing during the execution of the algorithm
- At each iteration, the processor solves the same task of the same size performing the same computations; the processed data may be different for different iterations but will still have the same pattern
- For all processors, the size of the task solved by one iteration of the main loop will be the same

In this case, the benchmark code made of any one iteration of the main loop of the implemented algorithm will be both efficient and well representative of the application. Let us illustrate this design with an application that we used in Section 3.1. This application implements a heterogeneous parallel algorithm of multiplication of two dense square $n \times n$ matrices, $C = A \times B$, on p processors based on one-dimensional partitioning of matrices A and C into p horizontal slices (see Fig. 3.1). There is one-to-one mapping between these slices and the processors. All the processors compute their C slices in parallel by executing a loop, each iteration of which computes one row of the resulting matrix C by multiplying the row of matrix A by matrix B.

In this application, the size of the task solved by one iteration of the main loop will be the same for all processors because the task is the multiplication of an n-element row by an $n \times n$ matrix. The load of the heterogeneous processors will be balanced by different numbers of iterations of the main loop performed by different processors. The execution time of computations performed by a processor will be equal to the execution time of multiplication of an n-element row by an $n \times n$ matrix multiplied by the number of iterations. Therefore, the relative speed demonstrated by the processors during the execution of this application will be equal to their relative speed of the multiplication of an n-element row by an $n \times n$ matrix.

Although the execution of the above benchmark code typically takes just a small fraction of the execution of the whole application, it can be made even more efficient. Indeed, the relative speed of the processors demonstrated during the multiplication of an n-element row by an $n \times n$ matrix should be equal to their relative speed of multiplication of an n-element row by an n-element column of the matrix. Therefore, the relative speed of the processors for this application can be measured by multiplying an n-element row by an n-element column, given the column used in this computation is one of the columns of a whole $n \times n$ matrix stored in the memory of the processor. The latter requirement is necessary in order to reproduce in the benchmark code the same pattern of access to the memory hierarchy as in the original application. In practice, this more efficient benchmark code can be too lightweight and less accurate due to possible minor fluctuations in the load of the processors. The optimal solution would be the multiplication of a row by a number of columns of the matrix. The number should be the smallest number that guarantees the required accuracy of the estimation.

Relaxation of the above restrictions on applications makes the design of the benchmark code less straightforward. Indeed, let us remove the third bulleted restriction allowing at one iteration different processors to solve tasks of different sizes. This relaxation will lead to the additional problem of finding the most representative task size of the benchmark. To illustrate this problem, consider the application that implements a heterogeneous parallel algorithm of multiplication of two dense square $n \times n$ matrices, $C = A \times B$, on p processors based on the Cartesian partitioning of the matrices, which was presented in Section 3.4 (see Fig. 3.13). The algorithm can be summarized as follows:

- Matrices A, B, and C are identically partitioned into a Cartesian partitioning such that
  - There is one-to-one mapping between the rectangles of the partitioning and the processors
  - The shape of the partitioning, $p = q \times t$, minimizes $(q + t)$
  - The sizes of the rectangles, h_i and w_j, are returned by Algorithm 3.5
- At each step k of the algorithm
  - The pivot column of $r \times r$ blocks of matrix $A, a_{\bullet k}$, is broadcast horizontally

◦ The pivot row of $r \times r$ blocks of matrix B, $b_{k\bullet}$, is broadcast vertically
◦ Each processor P_{ij} updates its rectangle c_{ij} of matrix C with the product of its parts of the pivot column and the pivot row, $c_{ij} = c_{ij} + a_{ik} \times b_{kj}$

In that application, at each iteration of the main loop, processor P_{ij} solves the same task of the same size, namely, it updates an $h_i \times w_j$ matrix by the product of $h_i \times r$ and $r \times w_j$ matrices. The arrays storing these matrices are the same at all iterations. The execution time of computations performed by the processor will be equal to the execution of the task of updating an $h_i \times w_j$ matrix by the product of $h_i \times r$ and $r \times w_j$ matrices multiplied by the total number of iterations. Therefore, the speed of the processor will be the same for the whole application and for an update of an $h_i \times w_j$ matrix.

Unlike the first application, in this case, all processors perform the same number of iterations, and the load of the processors is balanced by using different task sizes. Therefore, whatever task size we pick for the benchmark code updating a matrix, it will not be fully representative of the application as it does not reproduce in full the data layout and computations during the real execution. Nevertheless, for any heterogeneous platform, there will be a range of task sizes where the *relative* speeds of the processors do not depend significantly on the task size and can be quite accurately approximated by constants. Hence, if all matrix partitions fall into this range, then the benchmark code updating a matrix of any size from this range will accurately estimate their relative speeds for the application. In particular, a matrix of the size $\frac{n}{q} \times \frac{n}{t}$ can be used in the benchmark code.

Finding the optimal task size for the benchmark will be more difficult if at different iterations, the processor solves tasks of different sizes. Applications implementing heterogeneous parallel LU factorization algorithms from Section 3.3 are of that type. Indeed, at each iteration of the algorithm, the main body of computations performed by the processor falls into the update $\tilde{A}_{22} \leftarrow A_{22} - L_{21}U_{12} = L_{22}U_{22}$ of its columns of the trailing submatrix A_{22} of matrix A. The size of this submatrix and the number of columns processed by the processor will become smaller and smaller with each next step of the algorithm, asymptotically decreasing to zero. Therefore, during the execution of the application, the sizes of the task solved by each processor will vary in a very wide range—from large at initial iterations to very small at final ones. It is unrealistic to assume that the relative speed of the heterogeneous processors will remain constant within such a wide range of task sizes. More likely, their relative speed will gradually change as the execution proceeds. In this case, no task size will accurately estimate the relative speed of the processors for *all* iterations. At the same time, given that different iterations have different computation cost, we can only focus on the iterations making the major contribution to the total computation time, namely, on some number of first iterations. If the sizes of the tasks solved by the processors at these iterations fall into the range where the relative speeds of the processors can be approximated by constants, then the benchmark code updating a matrix of any size from this range will accurately estimate their relative speeds for the entire application.

Thus, the benchmark code solving the task of some fixed size, which represents one iteration of the main loop of the application, can be efficient and accurate for many data parallel applications performing iterative computations. This approach has been used in some parallel applications designed to automatically tune to the executing heterogeneous platform (Lastovetsky, 2002).

There are also programming systems providing basic support for this and other approaches to accurate estimation of relative speeds of the processors. These systems are mpC (Lastovetsky, 2002, 2003), the first language for heterogeneous parallel programming, and HeteroMPI (Lastovetsky and Reddy, 2006), an extension of MPI for high-performance heterogeneous computing. HeteroMPI and mpC allow the application programmer to explicitly specify benchmark codes representative of computations in different parts of the application. It is assumed that the relative speed demonstrated by the processors during the execution of the benchmark code will be approximately the same as the relative speed of the processors demonstrated during the execution of the corresponding part of the application. It is also assumed that the time of execution of this code is much less than the time of the execution of the corresponding part of the application. The mpC application programmer uses a **recon** statement to specify the benchmark code and when this code should be run. During the execution of this statement, all processors execute the provided benchmark code in parallel, and the execution time elapsed on each processor is used to obtain their relative speed. Thus, the accuracy of estimation of the relative speed of the processors is fully controlled by the application programmer. Indeed, creative design of the benchmark code together with well-thought-out selection of the points and frequency of the **recon** statements in the program are the means for the efficient and accurate estimation of the relative speed of the processors during each particular execution of the application. In HeteroMPI, the **HMPI_Recon** function plays the same role as the **recon** statement in mpC.

7.2.2 Estimation of Functional and Band Performance Models of Heterogeneous Processors

In Chapter 4, we discussed the limitations of constant performance models of heterogeneous processors. The main limitation is the assumption that the application fits into the main memory of the executing parallel processors. This assumption is quite restrictive in terms of the size of problems that can be solved by algorithms based on the constant models. Therefore, functional and band performance models were introduced. The models are more general and put no restrictions on problem size. Of course, the design of heterogeneous algorithms with these models is a more difficult task than that with constant models, but the task is solvable. In Chapter 4, we have presented a number of efficient heterogeneous algorithms based on the nonconstant, mainly functional models.

The accurate estimation of a functional performance model can be very expensive. Indeed, in order to build the speed function of the processor for a given application with a given accuracy, the application may need to be executed for quite a large number of different task sizes. One straightforward approach is as follows:

- For simplicity, we assume that the task size is represented by a single variable, x.
- The original interval $[a, b]$ of possible values of the task size variable is divided into a number of equal subintervals $[x_i, x_{i+1}]$. The application is executed for each task size x_i, and a piecewise linear approximation is used as the first approximation of the speed function $f(x)$.
- At each next step,
  - each current subinterval is bisected and the application is executed for all task sizes representing the midpoints,
  - the speeds for these points, together with all previously obtained speeds, are used to build the next piecewise linear approximation of $f(x)$, and
  - this new approximation and the previous one are compared against some error criterion. If the criterion is satisfied, the estimation is finished; otherwise, this step is repeated.

It is very likely to have to execute the application for quite a large number of different task sizes before the above algorithm converges. The number will increase by orders of magnitude if the task size is represented by several variables. As a result, in real-life situations, this straightforward algorithm can be very expensive.

Minimizing the cost of accurate estimation of the speed function is a challenging research problem of significant practical importance. The problem is wide open. The only approach proposed and studied so far (Lastovetsky, Reddy, and Higgins, 2006) is based on the property of heterogeneous processors integrated into the network to experience constant and stochastic fluctuations in the workload. As have been discussed in Chapters 1, 2, and 4, this changing transient load will cause a fluctuation in the speed of the processor in the sense that the execution time of the same task of the same size will vary for different runs at different times. The natural way to represent the inherent fluctuations in the speed is to use a speed band rather than a speed function. The width of the band characterizes the level of fluctuation in the performance due to changes in load over time.

The idea of the approach (Lastovetsky, Reddy, and Higgins, 2006) is to use this inherent inaccuracy of any approximation of the speed function in order to reduce the cost of its estimation. Indeed, any function fitting into the speed

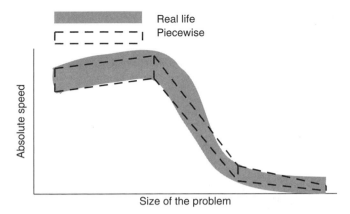

Figure 7.1. Real-life speed band of a processor and a piecewise linear function approximation of the speed band.

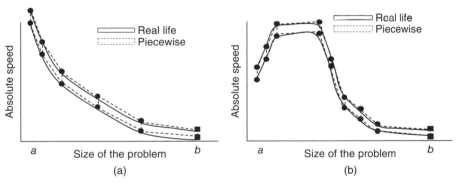

Figure 7.2. Piecewise linear approximation of speed bands for two processors. Circular points are experimentally obtained; square points are calculated using heuristics. (a) The speed band is built from five experimental points; the application uses the memory hierarchy inefficiently. (b) The speed band is built from eight experimental points; the application uses memory hierarchy efficiently.

band can be considered a satisfactory approximation of the speed function. Therefore, the approach is to find, experimentally, a piecewise linear approximation of the speed band as shown in Figure 7.1 such that it will represent the speed function with the accuracy determined by the inherent deviation of the performance of the processor. This approximation is built using a set of few experimentally obtained points as shown in Figure 7.2. The problem is to spend minimum experimental time to build the approximation.

The piecewise linear approximation of the speed band of the processor is built using a set of experimentally obtained points for different problem sizes. For simplicity, we assume that the problem size is represented by a single variable. To obtain an experimental point for a problem size x, the application is executed for this problem size and the ideal execution time t_{ideal} is measured. t_{ideal} is defined as the time it would require to solve the problem on a completely idle processor. For example, on Unix platforms, this information can be obtained by using the **time** utility or the **getrusage()** system call, summing the reported user and system CPU seconds a process has consumed.

The ideal speed of execution, s_{ideal}, is then equal to the volume of computations divided by t_{ideal}. Further calculations assume given two *load functions*, $l_{max}(t)$ and $l_{min}(t)$, which are the maximum and minimum load averages, respectively, observed over increasing time periods. The *load average* is defined as the number of active processes running on the processor at any time. Given the load functions, a prediction of the maximum and minimum average load, $l_{max,predicted}(x)$ and $l_{min,predicted}(x)$, respectively, that would occur during the execution of the application for the problem size x are made (note that unlike the load functions, which are functions of time, the minimum and maximum average load are functions of problem size). The creation of the functions $l_{max}(t)$ and $l_{min}(t)$ and prediction of the load averages will be explained in detail later. Using s_{ideal} and the load averages predicted, $s_{max}(x)$ and $s_{min}(x)$, for a problem size x are calculated as follows:

$$s_{max}(x) = s_{ideal}(x) - l_{min,predicted}(x) \times s_{ideal}(x)$$
$$s_{min}(x) = s_{ideal}(x) - l_{max,predicted}(x) \times s_{ideal}(x). \tag{7.1}$$

The experimental point is then given by a vertical line connecting the points $(x, s_{max}(x))$ and $(x, s_{min}(x))$. This vertical line is called a "cut" of the real band. This is illustrated in Figure 7.3(a).

The difference between the speeds $s_{max}(x)$ and $s_{min}(x)$ represents the level of fluctuation in the speed due to changes in load during the execution of the problem size x. The piecewise linear approximation is obtained by connecting these experimental points as shown in Figure 7.3(b). So the problem of building the piecewise linear function approximation is to find a set of such experimental points that can represent the speed band with sufficient accuracy and at the same time spend minimum experimental time to build the piecewise linear approximation.

Mathematically, the problem of building a piecewise linear approximation is formulated as follows:

- Given the functions $l_{min}(t)$ and $l_{max}(t)$ ($l_{min}(t)$ and $l_{max}(t)$ are functions of time characterizing the level of fluctuation in load over time)
- Obtain a set of n experimental points representing a piecewise linear approximation of the speed band of a processor, each point representing a cut given by $(x_i, s_{max}(x_i))$ and $(x_i, s_{min}(x_i))$, where x_i is the size of the problem and $s_{max}(x_i)$ and $s_{min}(x_i)$ are speeds calculated based on the functions $l_{min}(t)$ and $l_{max}(t)$ and ideal speed s_{ideal} at point i, such that
  - The nonempty intersectional area of the piecewise linear approximation with the real-life speed band is a simply connected topological space

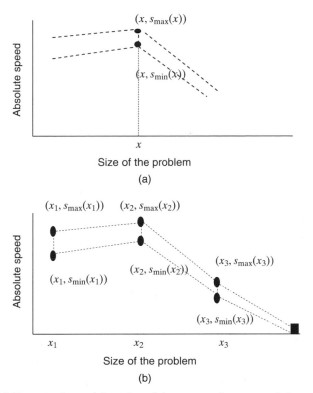

Figure 7.3. (a) The speeds $s_{max}(x)$ and $s_{min}(x)$ representing a cut of the real band used to build the piecewise linear approximation. (b) Piecewise linear approximation built by connecting the cuts.

(a topological space is said to be path connected if a path can be drawn from every point contained within its boundaries to every other point; a topological space is simply connected if it is path connected and has no "holes"; this is illustrated in Fig. 7.4)

○ The sum $\sum_{i=1}^{n} t_i$ of the times is minimal, where t_i is the experimental time used to obtain point i

The algorithm (Lastovetsky, Reddy, and Higgins, 2006) returning an approximate solution of this problem makes the following assumptions about the speed band:

• The upper and lower curves of the speed band are continuous functions of the problem size
• The permissible shapes of the speed band are

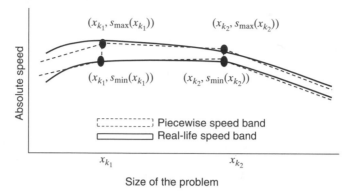

Figure 7.4. The nonempty intersectional area of a piecewise linear approximation with the real-life speed band is a simply connected topological space.

- ◦ The upper curve and the lower curve are both a nonincreasing function of the size of the problem for all problem sizes (Fig. 7.5(a); this shape is typical for applications inefficiently using memory hierarchy)
- ◦ The upper curve and the lower curve are both an increasing function of the size of the problem followed by a nonincreasing function (see Fig. 7.5(b); this shape is typical for applications efficiently using memory hierarchy)
- · A straight line connecting the endpoints of the upper (lower) curve of the speed band intersects the curve in no more than one point (as shown in Fig. 7.5(a),(b))
- · The width of the speed band decreases as the problem size increases

Experiments with diverse scientific kernels and different computers show that the above assumptions are realistic and the speed band of the processor can be approximated accurately enough by a band satisfying them within the accuracy of measurements (Lastovetsky and Twamley, 2005).

The algorithm (Lastovetsky, Reddy, and Higgins, 2006) that builds a piecewise linear approximation of the speed band of a processor is formulated in terms of cuts, cut projections, and operations on these objects:

- · *Cut C_x* (of the speed band) is a vertical line connecting the points $(x, s_{min}(x))$ and $(x, s_{max}(x))$.
- · *Projection I_x* of this cut is the interval $(s_{min}(x), s_{max}(x))$. By definition, $I_x \leq I_y$ if and only if $s_{max}(x) \leq s_{max}(y)$ and $s_{min}(x) \leq s_{min}(y)$. Obviously, $I_x = I_y$ if and only if $I_x \leq I_y$ and $I_y \leq I_x$.
- · $I_x \cap I_y$ is the intersection of the intervals $(s_{min}(x), s_{max}(x))$ and $(s_{min}(y), s_{max}(y))$. Obviously, that if $I_x \cap I_y = I_y$, then the interval $(s_{min}(x), s_{max}(x))$ contains the interval $(s_{min}(y), s_{max}(y))$, that is, $s_{max}(x) \geq s_{max}(y)$ and

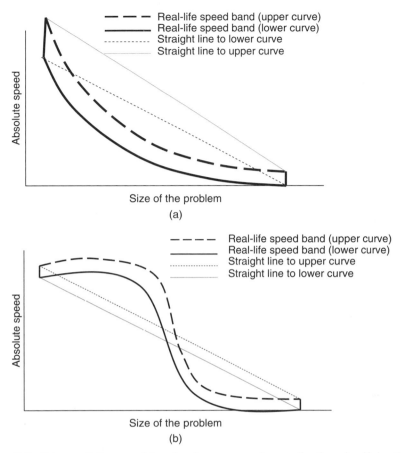

Figure 7.5. Shapes of the speed bands of processors for applications inefficiently (a) and efficiently (b) using memory hierarchy.

$s_{\min}(x) \le s_{\min}(y)$. If the intervals are disjoint, then $I_x \cap I_y = \emptyset$, where $\emptyset$ is an empty interval.

Algorithm 7.1 (Lastovetsky, Reddy, and Higgins, 2006). Building piecewise linear approximation of the speed band of a processor characterized by given load functions $l_{\max}(t)$ and $l_{\min}(t)$:

Step 1: Initialization. We select an interval $[a, b]$ of problem sizes, where a is some small size and b is the problem size large enough to make the speed of the processor practically zero. We obtain, experimentally, the speeds of the processor at point a given by $s_{\max}(a)$ and $s_{\min}(a)$ and we set the speed of the processor at point b to 0. Our initial approximation of the speed band is a band connecting cuts C_a and C_b. This is illustrated in Figure 7.6(a).

126

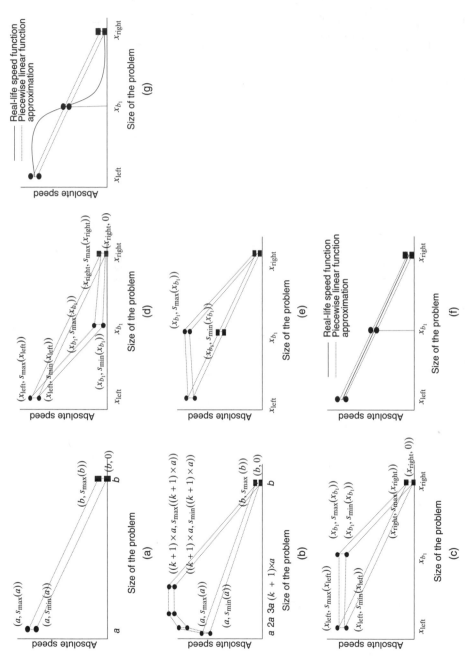

Figure 7.6. (a) Initial approximation of the speed band. (b) Approximation of the speed band. (c)–(e) Approximation of the nonincreasing section of the speed band. (f) and (g) Possible scenarios when the next experimental point falls in the area of the current trapezoidal approximation: (f) the current approximation is accurate; (g) the current approximation is inaccurate.

Step 2: Approximation of the Increasing Part of the Speed Band (If Any). First, we experimentally find cuts for problem sizes a and $2a$. If $I_{2a} \leq I_a$ or $I_{2a} \cap I_a = I_{2a}$ (i.e., the increasing section of the speed band, if any, ends at point a), the current trapezoidal approximation is replaced by two trapezoidal connected bands, the first one connecting cuts C_a and C_{2a} and the second one connecting cuts C_{2a} and C_b. Then, we set x_{left} to $2a$ and x_{right} to b and go to Step 3 dealing with the approximation of the nonincreasing section of the band.

If $I_a < I_{2a}$ (i.e., the band speed is increasing), Step 2 is recursively applied to pairs $(ka, (k + 1)a)$ until $I_{(k+1)a} \leq I_{ka}$ or $I_{(k+1)a} \cap I_{ka} = I_{(k+1)a}$. Then, the current trapezoidal approximation of the speed band in the interval $[ka, b]$ is replaced by two connected bands, the first one connecting cuts C_{ka} and $C_{(k+1) \times a}$ and the second one connecting cuts $C_{(k+1) \times a}$ and C_b. Then, we set x_{left} to $(k + 1)a$ and x_{right} to b and go to Step 3. This is illustrated in Figure 7.6(b).

It should be noted that the experimental time taken to obtain the cuts at problem sizes $\{a, 2a, 3a, \dots, (k + 1) \times a\}$ is relatively small (usually milliseconds to seconds) compared with that for larger problem sizes (usually minutes to hours).

Step 3: Approximation of the Nonincreasing Section of the Speed Band. We bisect the interval $[x_{\text{left}}, x_{\text{right}}]$ into subintervals $[x_{\text{left}}, x_{b_1}]$ and $[x_{b_1}, x_{\text{right}}]$ of equal length. We obtain, experimentally, the cut Cx_{b_1} at problem size x_{b_1}. We also calculate the cut of intersection of the line $x = x_{b_1}$ with the current approximation of the speed band connecting the cuts Cx_{left} and Cx_{right}. The cut of the intersection is given by $C'x_{b_1}$.

- If $Ix_{\text{left}} \cap Ix_{b_1} \neq \varnothing$, we replace the current trapezoidal approximation of the speed band with two connected bands, the first one connecting cuts Cx_{left} and Cx_{b_1} and the second one connecting cuts Cx_{b_1} and Cx_{right}. This is illustrated in Figure 7.6(c). We stop building the approximation of the speed band in the interval $[x_{\text{left}}, x_{b_1}]$ and recursively apply Step 3 to the interval $[x_{b_1}, x_{\text{right}}]$.

- If $Ix_{\text{left}} \cap Ix_{b_1} = \varnothing$ and $Ix_{\text{right}} \cap Ix_{b_1} \neq \varnothing$, we replace the current trapezoidal approximation of the speed band with two connected bands, the first one connecting cuts Cx_{left} and Cx_{b_1} and the second one connecting cuts Cx_{b_1} and Cx_{right}. This is illustrated in Figure 7.6(d). We stop building the approximation of the speed band in the interval $[x_{b_1}, x_{\text{right}}]$ and recursively apply Step 3 for the interval $[x_{\text{left}}, x_{b_1}]$.

- If $Ix_{\text{left}} \cap Ix_{b_1} = \varnothing$ and $Ix_{\text{right}} \cap Ix_{b_1} = \varnothing$ and $I'x_{b_1} < Ix_{b_1}$ (i.e., $I'x_{b_1} \leq Ix_{b_1}$ and $Ix_{b_1} \cap I'x_{b_1} = \varnothing$), we replace the current trapezoidal approximation of the speed band with two connected bands, the first one connecting cuts Cx_{left} and Cx_{b_1} and the second one connecting cuts Cx_{b_1} and Cx_{right}. This is illustrated in Figure 7.6(e). Then, we recursively apply Step 3 to the intervals $[x_{\text{left}}, x_{b_1}]$ and $[x_{b_1}, x_{\text{right}}]$.

- If $Ix_{\text{left}} \cap Ix_{b_1} = \emptyset$ and $Ix_{\text{right}} \cap Ix_{b_1} = \emptyset$ and $Ix_{b_1} \cap I'x_{b_1} \neq \emptyset$, then we may have two scenarios for each of the intervals $[x_{\text{left}}, x_{b_1}]$ and $[x_{b_1}, x_{\text{right}}]$ as illustrated in Figure 7.6(f),(g). Other scenarios are excluded by our assumptions about the shape of the speed band. In order to determine which situation takes place, we experimentally test each of these intervals as follows:

  ○ First, we bisect the interval $[x_{\text{left}}, x_{b_1}]$ at point x_{b_2}, obtaining, experimentally, cut Cx_{b_2} and calculating the cut of intersection $C'x_{b_2}$ of line $x = x_{b_2}$ with the current trapezoidal approximation of the speed band.

    ▪ If $Ix_{b_2} \cap I'x_{b_2} \neq \emptyset$, we have the first scenario shown in Figure 7.6(f). Therefore, we stop building the approximation in the interval $[x_{\text{left}}, x_{b_1}]$ and replace the current trapezoidal approximation in the interval $[x_{\text{left}}, x_{b_1}]$ by two connected bands, the first one connecting cuts Cx_{left} and Cx_{b_2} and the second one connecting points Cx_{b_1} and Cx_{b_2}. Since we have obtained the cut at problem size x_{b_2} experimentally, we use it in the approximation. This is chosen as the final piece of the piecewise linear approximation in the interval $[x_{\text{left}}, x_{b_1}]$.

    ▪ If $Ix_{b_2} \cap I'x_{b_2} = \emptyset$, we have the second scenario shown in Figure 7.6(g). Therefore, we recursively apply Step 3 to the intervals $[x_{\text{left}}, x_{b_2}]$ and $[x_{b_2}, x_{b_1}]$.

  ○ Then, we bisect the interval $[x_{b_1}, x_{\text{right}}]$ at point x_{b_3}, obtaining, experimentally, Cx_{b_3} and calculating $C'x_{b_3}$.

    ▪ If $Ix_{b_3} \cap I'x_{b_3} \neq \emptyset$, we have the first scenario shown in Figure 7.6(f) and can stop building the approximation for this interval.

    ▪ If $Ix_{b_3} \cap I'x_{b_3} = \emptyset$, we have the second scenario shown in Figure 7.6(g). Therefore, we recursively apply Step 3 to the intervals $[x_{b_3}, x_{\text{right}}]$ and $[x_{b_1}, x_{b_3}]$.

Algorithm 7.1 uses functions $l_{\max}(t)$ and $l_{\min}(t)$ in order to find cuts of the speed band from experimental runs of the application for different problem sizes. More precisely, for a problem size x, it uses these functions to find load averages $l_{\max,\text{predicted}}(x)$ and $l_{\min,\text{predicted}}(x)$, which give the maximum and minimum average numbers of extra active processes running in parallel with the application during the time of its execution for this problem size. These load averages are then used to calculate the cut according to (7.1).

Construction of the functions $l_{\max}(t)$ and $l_{\min}(t)$ and their translation into the load averages $l_{\max,\text{predicted}}(x)$ and $l_{\min,\text{predicted}}(x)$ are performed as follows (Lastovetsky, Reddy, and Higgins 2006).

The experimental method to obtain the functions $l_{\min}(t)$ and $l_{\max}(t)$ is to use the metric of *load average*. Load average measures the number of active processes at any time. High load averages usually means that the system is being used heavily and the response time is correspondingly slow. A Unix-like operating system maintains three figures for averages over 1-, 5-, and 15-minute periods. There are alternative measures available through many utilities on various platforms such as **vmstat** (Unix), **top** (Unix), and **perfmon** (Windows) or through performance probes, and they may be combined to more accurately represent utilization of a system under a variety of conditions (Spring, Spring, and Wolski, 2000). For simplicity, we will use the load average metric only.

The load average data is represented by two piecewise linear functions: $l_{max}(t)$ and $l_{min}(t)$. The functions describe load averaged over increasing periods of time up to a limit w as shown in Figure 7.7(b). This limit should be, at most, the running time of the largest foreseeable problem, which is the problem size where the speed of the processor can be assumed to be zero (i.e., given by problem size b discussed above). For execution of a problem with a running time greater than this limit, the values of the load functions at w may be

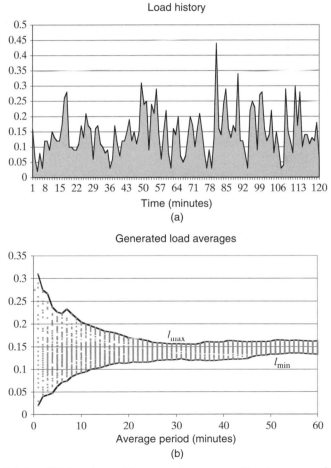

Figure 7.7. (a) Load history is used to generate a range of load averages. (b) $l_{max}(t)$ and $l_{min}(t)$, the maximum and minimum loads calculated from the matrix of load averages A.

extended to infinity. The functions are built from load averages observed every Δ time units. The convenient values for Δ are 1, 5, or 15 minutes as statistics for these time periods are provided by the operating system (using a system call **getloadavg()**). Alternate values of Δ would require additional monitoring of the load average and translation into Δ time unit load average.

The amount of load observations used in the calculation of $l_{max}(t)$ and $l_{min}(t)$ is given by h, the history. A sliding window with a length of w passes over the h most recent observations. At each position of the window, a set of load averages is created. The set consists of load averages generated from the observations inside the window. If Δ were 1 minute, a 1-minute average would be given by the first observation in the window, a 2-minute average would be the average of the first and second observations in the window, and so on. While the window is positioned completely within the history, a total of w load averages would be created in each set, the load averages having periods of $\Delta, 2\Delta, \dots, w\Delta$ time units. The window can move a total of w times, but after the $(h-w)$-th time, its end will slide outside of the history. The sets of averages created at these positions will not range as far as $w\Delta$, but they are still useful. From all of these sets of averages, maximum and minimum load averages for each time period $\Delta, 2\Delta, \dots, w\Delta$ are extracted and used to create the functions $l_{max}(t)$ and $l_{min}(t)$.

More formally, if we have a sequence of observed loads: $l_1, l_2, \dots, l_h$, then the matrix A of load averages created from observations is defined as follows:

$$A = \begin{pmatrix} a_{1,1} & \cdot & \cdot & a_{1,h} \\ \cdot & & & \times \\ \cdot & & \times & \times \\ a_{w,1} & \times & \times & \times \end{pmatrix} \quad \text{where } a_{ij} = \frac{\displaystyle\sum_{k=j}^{i+j-1} l_k}{i \cdot \Delta},$$

for all $i = 1 \dots h;\ j = 1 \dots w$ and $i + j < h$.

The elements marked as $\times$ in matrix A are not evaluated as the calculations would operate on observations taken beyond l_h. $l_{max}(t)$ and $l_{min}(t)$ are then defined by the maximum and minimum calculated j-th load averages, respectively, that is, the maximum or minimum value of a row j in the matrix (see Fig. 7.7(a),(b)). Points are connected in sequence by straight-line segments to give a continuous piecewise function. The points are given by

$$l_{max}(j) = \max_{i=1}^{h}(a_{ij}) \quad \text{and} \quad l_{min}(j) = \min_{i=1}^{h}(a_{ij}).$$

Initial generation of the array has been implemented with a complexity of $h \times w^2$. Maintaining the functions $l_{max}(t)$ and $l_{min}(t)$ after a new observation is made has a complexity of w^2. Δ, h, and w may be adjusted to ensure that the generation and maintenance of the functions is not an intensive task.

When building the speed functions $s_{min}(x)$ and $s_{max}(x)$, the application is executed for a problem size x. Then, the ideal time of the execution, t_{ideal}, is measured. t_{ideal} is defined as the time it would require to solve the problem on

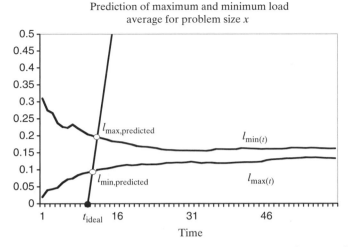

Figure 7.8. Intersection of load and running time functions (formula (7.2)).

a completely idle processor. On Unix platforms, it is possible to measure the number of CPU seconds a process has used during the total time of its execution. This information is provided by the **time** utility or by the **getrusage()** system call. The number of CPU seconds a process has used is assumed equivalent to the time it would take to complete execution on a completely idle processor: t_{ideal}. Then, the time of execution for the problem running under any load l can be estimated with the following function:

$$t(l) = \frac{1}{1-l} \times t_{ideal} \qquad (7.2)$$

This formula assumes that the system is based on a uniprocessor, that no jobs are scheduled if the load is one or greater, and that the task we are scheduling is to run as a **nice**'d process (*nice* is an operating system call that allows a process to change its priority), only using idle CPU cycles. These limitations fit the target of execution on nondedicated platforms. If a job is introduced onto a system with a load of, for example, 0.1, the system has a 90% idle CPU, then the formula predicts that the job will take 1/0.9 times longer than the optimal time of execution t_{ideal}.

In order to calculate the speed functions $s_{min}(x)$ and $s_{max}(x)$, we need to find the points where the function of performance degradation due to load (formula (7.2)) intersects with the history of maximal and minimal load $l_{max}(t)$ and $l_{min}(t)$ as shown in Figure 7.8. For a problem size x, the intersection points give the maximum and minimum predicted loads $l_{max,predicted}(x)$ and $l_{min,predicted}(x)$.

Using these loads, the speeds $s_{min}(x)$ and $s_{max}(x)$ for problem size x are calculated as follows:

$$s_{max}(x) = s_{ideal}(x) - l_{min,predicted}(x) \times s_{ideal}(x)$$
$$s_{min}(x) = s_{ideal}(x) - l_{max,predicted}(x) \times s_{ideal}(x),$$

where $s_{ideal}(x)$ is equal to the volume of computations involved in solving the problem of size x divided by the ideal time of execution t_{ideal}.

7.2.3   Benchmarking of Communication Operations

As has been discussed in Chapter 5, analytical predictive communication performance models play an important role in the optimization of parallel applications for homogeneous and heterogeneous computational clusters. The effectiveness of the model-based optimization techniques strongly depends on the accuracy of these models for each particular cluster. The parameters of the communication model are typically obtained from the experimentally estimated execution times of some communication operations. Therefore, the accuracy of the experimental estimation of the execution time of communication operations will have a significant impact on the accuracy of the communication model itself.

In this section, we discuss methods used for the experimental estimation of the execution time of MPI communication operations. We compare their accuracy and efficiency for homogeneous and heterogeneous clusters. The methods are presented in the context of MPI benchmarking suites (Grove and Coddington, 2001; Worsch, Reussner, and Augustin, 2002; Intel, 2004), software tools most commonly used for experimental estimation of the performance of MPI communications. The aim of these suites is to estimate the execution time of MPI communication operations as accurately as possible. In order to evaluate the accuracy of the estimation given by different suites, we need a unified definition of the execution time. As not all of the suites explicitly define their understanding of the execution time, we use the following as a natural definition (Lastovetsky, O'Flynn, and Rychkov, 2008). The execution time of a communication operation is defined as the real (wall clock) time elapsed from the start of the operation, given that all the participating processors have started the operation simultaneously, until the successful completion of the operation by the last participating processor. Mathematically, this time can be defined as the minimum execution time of the operation, given that the participating processors do not synchronize their start and are not participating in any other communication operation. It is important to note that the definition assumes that we estimate the execution time for a single isolated operation.

Estimation of the execution time of the communication operation includes

- selection of two events marking the start and the end of the operation, respectively, and
- measuring the time between these events.

First of all, the benchmarking suites differ in what they measure, which can be

- the time between two events on a single designated processor,
- for each participating processor, the time between two events on a processor, or
- the time between two events but on different processors.

The first two approaches are natural for clusters as there is no global time in these environments where each processor has its own clock showing its own local time. The local clocks are not synchronized and can have different clock rates, especially in heterogeneous clusters.

The only way to measure the time between two events on two different processors is to synchronize their local clocks before performing the measurement. Therefore, the third approach assumes the local clocks to be regularly synchronized. Unlike the first two, this approach introduces a measurement error as it is impossible to keep the independent clocks synchronized all the time with absolute accuracy.

Whatever time is measured, the suites repeat the same measurements in order to obtain statistically reliable values by averaging (or, sometimes, by minimizing [Grove and Coddington, 2001]) the results. Some suites (Grove and Coddington, 2001; Worsch, Reussner, and Augustin, 2002) make sure that the sequence of communication experiments consists of independent isolated experiments, not having an impact on the execution time of each other. This is achieved by using a barrier to synchronize the start of each individual experiment. The averaged measured time is then used as a direct estimate of the execution time.

In order to measure time, most of the benchmarking packages rely on the **MPI_Wtime** function. This function is used to measure the time between two events on the same processor (the local time). For example, the execution time of a roundtrip can be measured on one process and used as an indication of the point-to-point communication execution time (Intel, 2004; Worsch, Reussner, and Augustin, 2002). The execution time of a collective communication operation can also be measured at a designated process. For collective operations with a root, the root can be a natural selection for the measurement. As for many collective operations, the completion of the operation by the root does not mean its completion by all participating processes; short or empty messages can be sent by the processors to the root to confirm the completion. A barrier, reduce, or empty point-to-point communications can be used for this purpose. The final result must be corrected by the average time of the confirmation. The drawback of this approach is that the confirmation can be overlapped with the collective operation, and hence, it cannot simply be subtracted from the measured time. As a result, this technique may give negative values of the execution time for very small messages.

The accuracy of the approach based on measurements on a single dedicated process is strongly dependent on whether all processes have started the execution of the operation simultaneously. To ensure the, more or less, accurate synchronization of the start, a barrier, reduce, or empty point-to-point communications can be used. They can be overlapped with the collective operation to be measured and previous communications as well. To achieve even better synchronization, multiple barriers are used in the benchmarking suites (Grove and Coddington, 2001; Worsch, Reussner, and Augustin, 2002; Intel, 2004).

The second approach suggests that the local times can be measured on all processes involved in the communication, and the maximum can be taken as the communication execution time (Intel, 2004). This approach is also dependent on the synchronization of the processes before communication, for example, with a barrier.

To measure the time between two events on different processors, the local clocks of the processors have to be synchronized. Such synchronization can be provided by the MPI global timer if the MPI_WTIME_IS_GLOBAL attribute is defined and true. Alternatively, local clocks of two processors A and B can be synchronized by the following simple algorithm (Grove and Coddington, 2001):

- Processor A sends processor B a message, which contains the current time plus a half of the previously observed minimum roundtrip time.
- Processor B receives the message and returns it to A, which calculates the total time that the roundtrip took to complete. If the roundtrip time is the fastest observed so far, then the estimated time of arrival of the initial message is the most accurate yet. If so, processor B calculates the current approximation of the time offset as the message's value received in the next iteration.
- The processors repeat this procedure until a new minimum roundtrip time has not been observed for a prearranged number of repetitions.
- Given A being a base processor, this synchronization procedure is performed sequentially for all pairs (A, B_i).

A similar procedure is implemented in SKaMPI (Worsch, Reussner, and Augustin, 2002) to find offsets between local times of the root and the other processes:

```
delta_lb = -INFINITY;
delta_ub = INFINITY;
loop over repetitions
{
    if (rank == 0)
    {
        s_last = MPI_Wtime();
```

```
            MPI_Send(buffer, M, i, comm);
            MPI_Recv(&t_last, 1, i, comm);
            s_now = MPI_Wtime();
            delta_lb = max(t_last - s_now, delta_lb);
            delta_ub = min(t_last - s_last, delta_ub);
        }
        if (rank == i)
        {
            MPI_Recv(buffer, M, 0, comm);
            t_last = MPI_Wtime();
            MPI_Send(&t_last, 1, 0, comm);
        }
    }
}
if (rank == 0)
{
    delta = (delta_lb + delta_ub) / 2;
}
```

As local clocks can run at different speeds, especially in heterogeneous environments, the synchronization has to be regularly repeated. The synchronization procedures are quite costly and introduce a significant overhead in benchmarking when used. As soon as the global time has been set up, the time between two events on different processors can be measured (Grove and Coddington, 2001; Worsch, Reussner, and Augustin, 2002). The accuracy of this approach will depend on the accuracy of the clock synchronization and on whether processors start the communication simultaneously.

The global timing usually gives more accurate estimation because its design is closer to the natural definition of the communication execution time given in the beginning of this section. However, the methods based on local clocks are more time efficient and still can provide quite accurate results for many popular platforms and MPI implementations. Therefore, if the benchmarks are to be used in the software that requires the runtime results of the benchmarking, the methods based on local clocks will be the choice.

To obtain a statistically reliable estimate of the execution time, a series of the same experiments are typically performed in the benchmarking suites. If the communications are not separated from each other for this series, the successive executions may overlap, resulting in a so-called pipeline effect (Bernaschi and Iannello, 1998), when some processes finish the current repetition earlier and start the next repetition of the operation before the other processes have completed the previous operation. The pipeline affects the overall performance of the series of the operations, resulting in inaccurate averaged execution time. This is the case for the Intel MPI Benchmarks (IMB; former Pallas MPI Benchmark [PMB]) (Intel, 2004), where the repetitions in a series are not isolated, in the attempt to prevent the participation of the processes in third-party communications. The IMB measures the

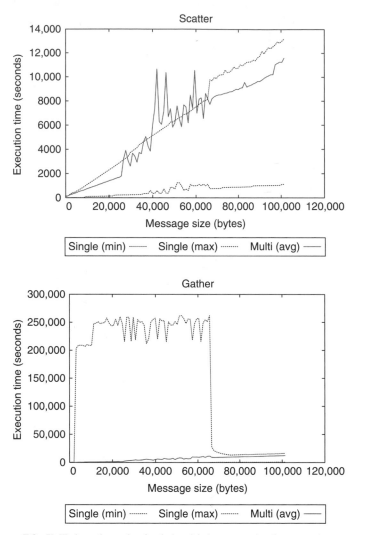

Figure 7.9. IMB benchmark: single/multiple scatter/gather measurements.

communication execution times locally on each process, and the minimum, maximum, and average times are then returned. Figure 7.9 shows the results returned by the IMB on a heterogeneous cluster for scatter and gather operations when single and multiple repetitions are used in the experiments (Lastovetsky, O'Flynn, and Rychkov, 2008). One can see that for the scatter experiments with a single repetition, the minimum time represents the execution time of a nonblocking send on the root, and is therefore relatively small. In the gather experiments with a single repetition, the maximum time is observed on the root, reflecting the communication congestion. The difference between the minimum and maximum times decreases with an increase in the number of repetitions. In both cases, we observe a clear impact of the pipeline effect on the measured execution time of the operation:

- Scatter: For small and large messages, the execution time of a repetition in the series is smaller than that measured in a single experiment. For medium-sized messages, escalations of the execution time are observed that do not happen in single experiments.
- Gather: Escalations of the execution time for medium-sized messages, observed for single experiments, disappear with the increase of the number of repetitions due to the pipelining.

Thus, the pipeline effect can significantly distort the actual behavior of the communication operation, given that we are interested in the accurate estimation of the time of its single and isolated execution.

In order to find an execution time of a communication operation that is not distorted, it should be measured in isolation from other communications. A barrier, reduce, or point-to-point communications with short or empty messages can be used between successive operations in the series. The approach with isolation gives more accurate results.

There are some particular collective operations and implementations of operations being measured that have the additional potential suitability to allow the use of more accurate and efficient methods that cannot be applied to other collective operations. One example is the method of measurement of linear and binomial implementations of the MPI broadcast on heterogeneous platforms proposed in de Supinski and Karonis (1999). It is based on measuring individual tasks rather than the entire broadcast; therefore, it does not need the global time. An individual task is a part of broadcast communication between the root and the i-th process (Fig. 7.10). In each individual task, the pipelining effect is eliminated by sending an acknowledgement message from the i-th process to the root. The execution time of the task is then corrected by the value of the point-to-point execution time as shown in the following code:

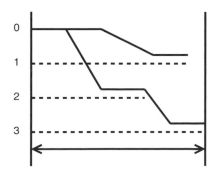

Figure 7.10. The time line of the binomial broadcast.

```
loop over comm size, i <> root
{
    if (rank == root)
    {
        start = MPI_Wtime();
        loop over repetitions
        {
            MPI_Send(buffer, M, i, comm);
            MPI_Recv(buffer, M, i, comm);
        }
        finish = MPI_Wtime();
        round = (finish - start) / repetitions;
        MPI_Bcast(comm);
        MPI_Recv(&ack, 1, i, comm);
        start = MPI_Wtime();
        loop over repetitions
        {
            MPI_Bcast(comm);
            MPI_Recv(ack, 1, i, comm);
        }
        finish = MPI_Wtime();
        time[i] = (finish - start) / repetitions -
round / 2;
    }
    else if (rank == i)
    {
        loop over repetitions
        {
            MPI_Recv(buffer, M, root, comm);
            MPI_Send(buffer, M, root, comm);
        }
        loop over repetitions + 1
        {
            MPI_Bcast(comm);
            MPI_Send(&ack, 1, root, comm);
        }
    }
    else
    {
        loop over repetitions + 1
            MPI_Bcast(comm);
    }
}
if (rank == root)
    time = max(time[i]);
```

The acquisition of detailed knowledge on the implementation of collective operations can prove useful toward improving the efficiency of measurement methodologies. This becomes particularly important for benchmarking performed at run time with on-the-fly optimization of communication operations.

Despite the different approaches to what and how to measure, the MPI benchmarking suites (Grove and Coddington, 2001; Worsch, Reussner, and Augustin, 2002; Intel 2004) have several common features:

- A single timing method is used
- Computing an average execution time of a series of the same communication experiments to get accurate results
- Measuring the communication time for different message sizes; the number of measurements can be fixed or adaptively increased for messages when time is fluctuating rapidly
- Performing simple statistical analysis by finding averages, variations, and errors

The MPI benchmarking suites are also very similar in terms of software design. Usually, they provide a single executable that takes a description of communication experiments to be measured and produces an output for plotting utilities to obtain graphs.

One more recent benchmarking package, MPIBlib (Lastovetsky, O'Flynn, and Rychkov, 2008), is implemented in the form of a library rather than a stand-alone application, and therefore can be used in parallel MPI applications. Unlike other benchmarking packages, it provides a range of efficient methods of measuring MPI communication operations, both universal and operation specific. This variety of methods allows users to optimize the cost of benchmarking by choosing the most efficient method for a given operation and required accuracy of estimation. MPIBlib provides three main operation-independent timing methods. Along with these universal timing methods, it provides methods of measuring some particular MPI communication operations or their implementations, which are usually unavailable in traditional MPI benchmarking suites.

7.3 PERFORMANCE MODELS OF HETEROGENEOUS ALGORITHMS AND THEIR USE IN APPLICATIONS AND PROGRAMMING SYSTEMS

As have been discussed in Section 7.1, algorithmic parameters can have a significant impact on the performance of the application implementing the heterogeneous algorithm. We have specified two types of algorithmic parameters. A parameter of the first type does not change the volume of computations and communications performed by the processors during the execution of the algorithm. Given the values of all other parameters are fixed, each processor will perform the same amount of the same arithmetic operations and communicate the same amount of data independent of the value of this parameter. Its impact on the performance is due to the different speeds of the execution of these operations because of variations in the use of the memory hierarchy for the different values of this parameter. The size of a matrix block in local computations for linear algebra algorithms is an example of a parameter of this type.

The predominant approach to the optimization of such a parameter is to locally run on each processor a representative benchmark code for a number of different values of the parameter in order to find the value maximizing the absolute speed of the processor. This experimental optimization can be done once, say, upon installation of the corresponding application. Alternatively, it can be performed at run time if its cost is much less than the cost of executing the whole application. It is still a problem which value should be selected if different processors have different optimal values of this parameter.

The Automatically Tuned Linear Algebra Software (ATLAS) package (Whaley, Petitet, and Dongarra, 2001) is an example of mathematical software parameterized by this type of algorithmic parameters and designed to automatically optimize the algorithmic parameters upon its installation on each particular processor. It implements a standard set of basic linear algebra subprograms known as BLAS (Dongarra *et al.*, 1990). The ATLAS design is based on a highly parameterized code generator that can produce an almost infinite number of implementations depending on the values of the algorithmic parameters. The ATLAS approach to the optimization of the algorithmic parameters is to optimize them for some particular performance critical operation. Namely, the ATLAS optimizes these parameters for the **matmul** operation that implements multiplication of two dense rectangular matrices, $C = A \times B$. In particular, its parameterized implementation provides the following options:

- Support for A and/or B being either standard form, or stored in transposed form.
- Register blocking of "outer product" form (the most optimal form for **matmul** register blocking). Varying the register blocking parameters provides many different implementations of **matmul**. The register blocking parameters are
  ◦ a_r: registers used for elements of A, and
  ◦ b_r : registers used for elements of B.

  Outer product register blocking then implies that $a_r \times b_r$ registers are then used to block the elements of C. Thus, if N_r is the maximal number of registers discovered during the floating-point unit probe, the search needs to try all a_r and b_r that satisfy $a_r \times b_r + a_r + b_r \leq N_r$.

- Loop unrollings: There are three loops involved in **matmul**, one over each of the provided dimensions (M, N, and K), each of which can have its associated unrolling factor (m_u, n_u, k_u). The M and N unrolling factors are restricted to varying with the associated register blocking (a_r and b_r, respectively), but the K-loop may be unrolled to any depth (i.e., once a_r is selected, m_u is set as well, but k_u is an independent variable).

- Choice of floating-point instruction:
  - Combined multiply/add with required pipelining
  - Separate multiply and add instructions, with associated pipelining and loop skewing
- User choice of utilizing generation-time constant or runtime variables for all loop dimensions (M, N, and K; for noncleanup copy L1 **matmul**, $M = N = K = N_B$). For each dimension that is known at generation, the following optimizations are made:
  - If unrolling meets or exceeds dimension, no actual loop is generated (no need for loop if fully unrolled).
  - If unrolling is non-one, correct cleanup can be generated with no if.

Even if a given dimension is a runtime variable, the generator can be told to assume particular, no, or general-case cleanup for arbitrary unrolling.

- For each operand array, the leading dimension can be generation-time constant (e.g., it is known to be N_B for copied L1 **matmul**), with associated savings in indexing computations, or a runtime variable.
- For each operand array, the leading dimension can have a stride (a stride of 1 is most common, but a stride of 2 can be used to support complex arithmetic).
- Generator can eliminate unnecessary arithmetic by generating code with special alpha (1, –1, and variable) and beta (0, 1, –1, and variable) cases. In addition, there is a special case for when alpha and beta are both variables, but it is safe to divide beta by alpha (this can save multiple applications of alpha).
- Various fetch patterns for loading A and B registers.

Algorithmic parameters of the second type have a direct effect on the performance of the application as the volume of computations and communications performed by each processor will depend on the values of these parameters. The logical shape of the processors' arrangement in heterogeneous linear algebra algorithms gives an example of a parameter of that type. Of course, there may be algorithms that will find the (sub)optimal shape themselves (see Chapter 3 for examples). However, if the shape is an input parameter of the algorithm and the performance depends on its value, then a good *self-adaptable* implementation should include a component finding its optimal or, at least, suboptimal value.

Moreover, in many cases, the number and the ordering of processors will be algorithmic parameters whose optimal values are to be found by the implementation. The reason is that straightforward implementation involving *all* available processors of any heterogeneous platform in the execution of the algorithm will not be universally optimal. It is quite likely that the extra communication cost caused by involving a larger number of processors will exceed gains due to the extra parallelization of computations. In this case, some subset of the processors will execute the algorithm faster than the entire set or any other subset. In addition, the ordering of processors in the subset may have an impact on the performance of the algorithm. Therefore, if the application implementing the algorithm is supposed to be self-adaptable it has to first find such an optimal (or suboptimal) subset and properly order it and only then execute the algorithm with this ordered subset provided as an input parameter.

Optimization of algorithmic parameters of the second type could be performed experimentally by running a representative benchmark code for a number of different values of the parameters, like that typically done for algorithmic parameters of the first type. At the same time, there is much more an efficient method to do it, that efficient that the optimization can be made a part of the application and performed at run time. This method is based on the concept of a *performance model of the algorithm*. It was originally proposed and implemented in the mpC language (Lastovetsky, 2002, 2003), and later used in HeteroMPI (Lastovetsky and Reddy, 2006).

The idea of the method is to allow the application programmer to describe the main features of the implemented heterogeneous parallel algorithm having an impact on the performance such as

- the number of processors executing the algorithm,
- the total volume of computations performed by each of these processors during the execution of the algorithm, and
- the total volume of data communicated between each pair of the processors during the execution of the algorithm.

Such a description is parameterized by the problem and algorithmic parameters of the algorithm and defines a performance model of the algorithm. The model does not specify *what* computations and communications are performed by the algorithm but rather *how* they are performed. The description is translated into a code used by the programming system at run time to estimate the execution time of the algorithm (without its real execution) for each combination of the values of its problem and algorithmic parameters. In particular, the mpC language provides an operator, **timeof**, whose only operand is a fully specified algorithm (i.e., an algorithm together with the values of its parameters), and the result is the estimated execution time of the algorithm. In HeteroMPI, similar functionality is provided by routine **HMPI_Timeof()**. Thus, the programmer implementing the algorithm in mpC or HeteroMPI can include in the application a piece of code finding (sub)optimal values of its algorithmic parameters (by comparing the estimated execution time for a number of candidate values) and then use the found values in the rest of the code. It is very important that when performing these estimations, the

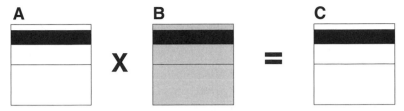

Figure 7.11. Matrix multiplication, $C = A \times B$, on a set of heterogeneous processors. The matrices A, B, and C are horizontally (and identically) sliced such that the number of elements in the slice is proportional to the speed of the processor.

programming system uses the performance characteristics of the platform at the time of the execution of the application. This makes the application self-adaptable not only to different executing heterogeneous platforms but also to different states of the same platform for different runs of the application.

In order to illustrate the method, let us consider the implementation of the following simple parallel algorithm of multiplication of two dense square $n \times n$ matrices, $C = A \times B$, on p heterogeneous processors:

- Matrices A, B, and C are identically partitioned into p uneven horizontal slices such that there will be one-to-one mapping between these slices and the processors. Each processor will store its slices of these matrices as shown in Figure 7.11.
- Each processor broadcasts its slice of matrix B to all other processors, resulting in all processors storing locally a copy of the whole matrix B.
- All processors compute their C slices in parallel such that each element c_{ij} in C is computed as $c_{ij} = \sum_{k=0}^{n-1} a_{ik} \times b_{kj}$.

The implementation will partition matrices A, B, and C over p heterogeneous processors by applying Algorithm 3.1 as described in Section 3.1. Namely, given speeds $s_1, \ldots, s_p$ of the processors, where s_i is the number of rows of matrix C computed by processor P_i per one time unit, Algorithm 3.1 finds the optimal distribution of n rows over these processors, which will minimize the computation time of matrix multiplication. After the implementation has found the optimal partitioning, it performs the communications and computations specified above.

In order to perform the partitioning, the implementation needs to obtain $s_1, \ldots, s_p$. The goal of the application is to minimize the *execution* time, not the *computation* time. Therefore, accurate estimation of the speeds of all processors running the application and optimal distribution of data over these processors are not enough as it will minimize the computation time, not the execution time of the application, which also includes the communication time. The application has to also find the optimal subset of the processors, minimizing the execution time. Let us assume, for simplicity, that our target heterogeneous platforms have a homogeneous communication layer. Then, the optimal subset will always consist of the fastest processors. Thus, given the problem size n and the total number q of available processors, the application can find the optimal number p of the involved processors and their speeds $s_1, \ldots, s_p$ as follows:

- Use the benchmark code multiplying one n-element row and a dense $n \times n$ matrix to estimate the speeds $s_1, \ldots, s_q$ of the processors.
- Rearrange the processors such that $s_1 \geq s_2 \geq \cdots \geq s_q$.
- Given $t_0 = \infty$, for $i = 1$ until $i \leq q$, do the following:
  ∘ Estimate the execution time t_i of the application given the matrices are optimally partitioned over processors $P_1, \ldots, P_i$.
  ∘ **If** $t_i < t_{i-1}$ **then** $i = i + 1$ and continue **else** $p = i$ and stop.

The code performing this procedure can be easily implemented in mpC or HeteroMPI (we will use mpC in this section). First of all, the performance model of the heterogeneous algorithm of matrix multiplication is described as follows:

```
algorithm AxB(int p, int n, int d[p])
{
  coord I=p;
  node { I>=0: bench*(d[I]); };
  link (J=p) { I!=J: length(double)*(d[I]*n) [J]->[I]; };
};
```

The first line of this description introduces the name $A \times B$ of the algorithvm and its three parameters: two scalar parameters p and n, and a p-element vector parameter d. We assume the following semantics of the parameters:

- p is the number of abstract processors performing the algorithm,
- n is the matrix size, and
- $d[i]$ is the number of rows in the horizontal matrix slice allocated to the i-th abstract processor.

The **coord** declaration specifies the arrangement (one-dimensional in this case) of the abstract processors performing the algorithm.

The **node** declaration specifies that the i-th processor will perform $d[i]$ computation units during the execution of the algorithm. A computation unit should be the same as the one used to estimate the speed of the processors, namely, multiplication of one n-element row and a dense $n \times n$ matrix. Obviously, given the amount of computations to be performed by the processor and an accurate estimation of its speed, both expressed in the same computation units, the programming system can easily estimate its computation time.

The **link** declaration specifies the total amount of data that will be sent from each processor j to each other processor i $(i \neq j)$ during the execution of the algorithm. Obviously, given this information and performance characteristics of the network (such as latency and bandwidth), the programming system can estimate the total time of communication between every ordered pair of processors.

Given the above description of the algorithm, the rest of relevant code will look as follows:

```
// Run a benchmark code in parallel by all
// physical processors to refresh the estimation of their speeds
{
  repl double *row, *matrix, *result;
  //memory allocation for row, matrix, and result
  //initialization of row, matrix, and result
  ...
  recon RowxMatrix(row, matrix, result, n);
}
// Get the total number of physical processors
q = MPC_Get_number_of_processors();
speeds = calloc(q, sizeof(double));
d = calloc(q, sizeof(int));
// Get the speed of the physical processors
MPC_Get_processors_info(NULL, speeds);
// Sort the speeds in descending order
qsort(speeds+1, q-1, sizeof(double), compar);
// Calculate the optimal number of physical processors
[host]:
  {
    int p;
    struct {int p; double t;} min;
    double t;
    min.p = 0;
    min.t = DBL_MAX;
    for(p=1; p<=q; p++)
    {
      // Calculate the size of C slice to be computed by
      // each of p involved physical processors
```

```
    Partition(p, speeds, d, n);
    // Estimate the execution time of matrix-matrix
    // multiplication on m physical processors
    t = timeof(algorithm AxB(p, n, d));
    if(t<min.t) { min.p = p; min.t = t; }
  }
  p = min.p;
}
```

The **recon** statement updates the estimate of the speed of physical processors by using a serial multiplication of an n-element row and an $n \times n$ matrix with function *SerialAxB*. The estimated speeds are then returned in the array *speeds* by function *MPC_Get_processors_info* and reordered in the decreasing order. This newly ordered array of speeds is then used in the following code, which finds the optimal number of processors. Namely, it is used by the function *Partition* performing the optimal matrix partitioning. The operator **timeof** uses the actual performance characteristics of the executing platform, such as the processors' speeds obtained by the most recent execution of the **recon** statement and the latency and bandwidth of the communication links, to estimate the execution time of the parallel algorithm $A \times B$ for specified values of its parameters. Thus, after execution of this code, the value of variable p will be equal to the very optimal number of processors.

Our description of the algorithm $A \times B$ says nothing about exactly how parallel processors are interacting during execution of the algorithm. Therefore, the operator **timeof** must make some assumptions about the interaction in order to calculate the execution time of the algorithm. Namely, to calculate the execution time it assumes that

- the processors execute all the communications in parallel,
- each processor executes all its computations in parallel with other processors, and
- a synchronization barrier exists between the execution of the computations and the communications.

This assumption is satisfactory for our algorithm of matrix multiplication. At the same time, in many parallel algorithms, there are data dependencies between computations performed by different processors. One processor may need data computed by other processors in order to start its computations. This serializes some computations performed by different parallel processors. As a result, the real execution time of the algorithm will be longer than the execution time calculated proceeding from the assumption about strictly parallel execution of computations.

On the other hand, some parallel algorithms are trying to overlap computations and communications to achieve better performance. The real execution time of those algorithms will be shorter than the execution time calculated proceeding from the assumption that computations and communications do not overlap.

Thus, when the calculation of the execution time of different parallel algorithms is based on the same scenario of interaction of parallel processors during the execution of the algorithm, the calculated execution time may be not accurate.

The mpC language addresses the problem. It allows the programmer to include the scenario of interaction of parallel processes during the execution of the parallel algorithm into the description of its performance model. This and other features of the mpC language are presented in detail in Chapter 8.

7.4 IMPLEMENTATION OF HOMOGENEOUS ALGORITHMS FOR HETEROGENEOUS PLATFORMS

As discussed in Section 7.1, the design and implementation of original heterogeneous algorithms is not the only approach to high-performance computing on heterogeneous platforms. Another approach consists in the efficient implementation of traditional homogeneous parallel algorithms. This approach, originally proposed in Kalinov and Lastovetsky (1999b) for the acceleration of ScaLAPACK applications on heterogeneous platforms, is based on a multiple-processes-per-processor configuration of the application implementing the homogeneous algorithm. While all processes are supposed to perform the same amount of computations, the load of the heterogeneous processors is balanced by the heterogeneous distribution of the parallel processes over the processors. This approach is known as *HeHo*, *He*terogeneous distribution of processes of the processors and *Ho*mogeneous distribution of data between the processes, in contrast to the *HoHe* approach, *Ho*mogeneous distribution of processes (one process per processor) and *He*terogeneous distribution of data between the processes (Kalinov and Lastovetsky, 2001).

The main problem of the HeHo approach is to find the optimal configuration of the application, namely,

- the optimal subset of the heterogeneous processors to be involved in the execution of the algorithm and
- the optimal distribution of processes over the processors as well as the optimal values of other algorithmic parameters.

This problem has been addressed in a number of research papers (Kalinov and Lastovetsky 1999b; Kalinov and Lastovetsky 2001; Kishimoto and Ichikawa 2004; Kalinov and Klimov 2005; Cuenca, Giménez, and Martinez, 2005; Reddy and Lastovetsky, 2006). In Kishimoto and Ichikawa (2004), a simple performance model of the target heterogeneous cluster is first built for the given parallel application from a large number of experimental runs of different configurations of the application. Then this performance model is used to find the optimal subset of the processors of the cluster and the optimal distribution of processes over the processors for that application on this cluster.

In Kalinov and Klimov (2005), the performance of a processor involved in the execution of the given application is represented by a function of the number of processes running on the processor and the amount of data distributed to the processor. A simple algorithm that finds the optimal number of processes and their optimal distribution over the processors based on this model is proposed.

The implementation of parallel dynamic programming algorithms for heterogeneous platforms is studied in Cuenca, Giménez, and Martinez (2005). It proposes heuristic algorithms for the estimation of the optimal configuration of applications implementing such algorithms.

In Reddy and Lastovetsky (2006), the mpC/HeteroMPI approach based on the specification of the performance model of the parallel algorithm is applied to a self-adaptable implementation of Parallel Basic Linear Algebra Subprograms (PBLAS) (Choi *et al.*, 1996b). The accurate estimation of platform parameters, optimization of algorithmic parameters (including the number of parallel processes and their arrangement), and optimal mapping of processes to the heterogeneous processors are performed automatically by the programming system based on the specification of the implemented homogeneous algorithm provided by the application programmer.

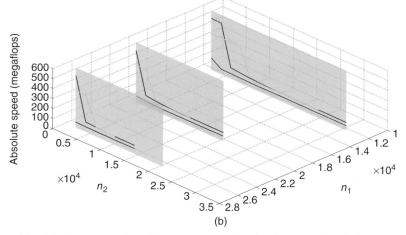

(b)

Figure 4.8. (b) Curves on the plane represent the absolute speeds of the processors against variable *y*, given parameter *x* is fixed. (See text for full caption.)

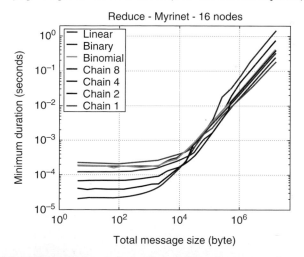

Figure 8.1. Multiple implementations of the MPI reduce operation on 16 nodes.

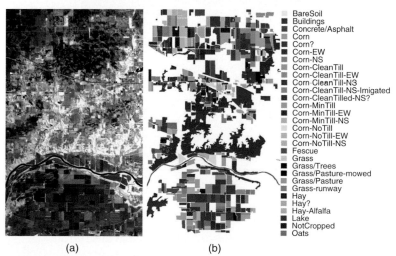

(a)   (b)

Figure 10.6. (a) Spectral band at 587 nm wavelength of an AVIRIS scene comprising agricultural and forest features at Indian Pines, Indiana. (b) Ground truth map with 30 mutually exclusive classes.

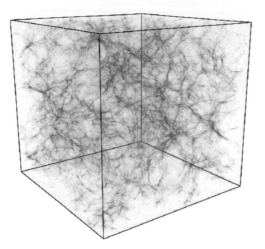

Figure 11.1. Example of a Hydropad output.

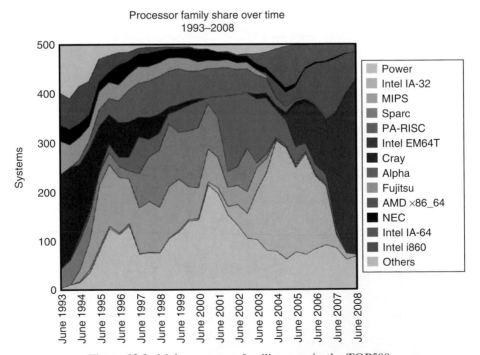

Figure 12.2. Main processor families seen in the TOP500.

CHAPTER 8

Programming Systems for High-Performance Heterogeneous Computing

In this chapter, we overview parallel and distributed programming systems used for high-performance computing on heterogeneous platforms. Parallel programming systems are outlined in Sections 8.1, 8.2, and 8.3, while Section 8.4 overviews programming systems for high-performance scientific distributed computing.

8.1 PARALLEL PROGRAMMING SYSTEMS FOR HETEROGENEOUS PLATFORMS

The area of parallel programming is littered with programming systems that have been designed and tested. Many of these are purely experimental and are not intended to be of practical use. Some have interesting implementations of parallel programming concepts but are not practical for general-purpose parallel applications. The two systems that have persisted are Message Passing Interface (MPI) and Open Multi-Processing (OpenMP).

Doing a comprehensive overview of this parallel programming world is a very challenging task that we will not take on in this book. Instead, we give an overview only on some parallel programming systems that are used for implementing real scientific applications on *heterogeneous* networks of computers. The systems can be broken into two groups. The systems of both groups allow the parallel applications to seamlessly run over a set of interconnected heterogeneous processors. The programming systems of the first group, which we call *traditional* systems, are more widely used but do not address performance issues caused by the heterogeneity of processors. The abstract parallel machine seen through their programming models is a set of interconnected homogeneous processors. This group includes such systems as MPI, parallel virtual machine (PVM), Linda, and High Performance Fortran (HPF). The systems of the second group are called *heterogeneous* parallel programming systems. While not yet as widely used as the traditional ones, they do provide a means of facilitating the implementation of portable applications that automatically adapt themselves to each particular executing heterogeneous platform in order to achieve top performance. The systems are mpC and Heterogeneous MPI (HeteroMPI).

8.2   TRADITIONAL PARALLEL PROGRAMMING SYSTEMS

Traditional parallel programming systems can be categorized according to whether they support an explicitly or implicitly parallel programming model. An explicitly parallel system requires that the programmer specify directly the activities of the multiple concurrent "threads of control" that form a parallel computation. In contrast, an implicitly parallel system allows the programmer to provide a higher-level specification of program behavior, in which parallelism is not represented directly. It is then the responsibility of the compiler or library to implement this parallelism efficiently and correctly.

Implicitly parallel systems can simplify programming by eliminating the need for the programmer to coordinate the execution of multiple processes. For example, in the implicitly parallel, primarily data-parallel language HPF, the programmer writes what is essentially a sequential Fortran 90 code, augmented with some directives. Race conditions cannot occur, and the HPF program need not be rewritten to take advantage of different parallel architectures.

Explicitly parallel systems provide the programmer with more control over program behavior, and hence can often be used to achieve higher performance. For example, an MPI implementation of an adaptive mesh-refinement algorithm may incorporate sophisticated techniques for computing mesh distributions, structuring communications among subdomains, and redistributing data when load imbalances occur. These strategies are beyond the capabilities of today's HPF compilers.

A parallel programming style that is becoming increasingly popular is to encapsulate the complexities of the parallel algorithm design within libraries (e.g., an adaptive mesh-refinement library, as just discussed). An application program can then consist of a sequence of calls to such library functions. In this way, many of the advantages of an implicitly parallel approach can be obtained within an explicitly parallel framework.

Explicitly parallel programming systems can be categorized according to whether they support a shared or distributed memory programming model. In a shared memory model, the programmer's task is to specify the activities of a set of processes that communicate by reading and writing shared, common memory. In a distributed memory model, processes have only local memory and must use some other mechanisms (e.g., message passing or remote procedure call) to exchange information. Shared memory models have the significant advantage that the programmer need not be concerned with data distribution issues. On the other hand, high-performance implementations may be difficult on computers that lack hardware support for shared memory, and race conditions tend to arise more easily.

Distributed memory models have the advantage that programmers have explicit control over data distribution and communication; this control facilitates high-performance programming on large distributed memory parallel computers.

8.2.1 Message-Passing Programming Systems

MPI. MPI is a specification for a set of functions for managing the movement of data among sets of communicating processes in a standard programming language.

Official MPI bindings are defined for C, Fortran, and C++; bindings for various other languages have been produced as well. MPI defines functions for point-to-point communication between two processes, collective operations among processes, parallel I/O, and process management. In addition, MPI's support for communicators facilitates the creation of modular programs and reusable libraries. Communication in MPI specifies the types and layout of data being communicated, allowing MPI implementations to both optimize for non-contiguous data in memory and support clusters of heterogeneous systems.

MPI programs are commonly implemented in terms of a single program multiple data (SPMD) model, in which all processes execute essentially the same program but may be at different points of execution within the program. MPI is, today, the technology of choice for constructing scalable parallel programs, and its ubiquity means that no other technology can beat it in portability. In addition, a significant body of MPI-based libraries that provide high-performance implementations of commonly used algorithms has emerged.

While MPI's Application Programming Interface (API) does not address the performance issues caused by the possible heterogeneity of processors, its portable implementations, such as MPICH (Gropp *et al.*, 2007) and Open MPI (Gabriel *et al.*, 2004), do address the communication performance issues caused by the diversity and heterogeneity of communication networks in a way transparent to the application programmers. In particular, Open MPI supports MPI communication over a wide variety of communication protocols, including shared memory, InfiniBand, Myrinet, Transmission Control Protocol (TCP) and the Internet Protocol (IP) (TCP/IP), and Portals. Open MPI uses two forms of optimization for higher performance of point-to-point communications in heterogeneous networks—it can stripe a single message to a single destination over multiple networks (of either the same or different communication protocols), and it can communicate to different peers using different communication protocols (Graham *et al.*, 2006).

In addition, in Open MPI, the idea of self-adapting and self-tuning has been applied to collective communication routines. Studies of application usage show that the performance of collective communications is critical to high-performance computing. A profiling study (Rabenseifner, 1999) showed that some applications spend more than 80% of transfer time in collective operations. Given this fact, it is essential for MPI implementations to provide high-performance collective operations. A general algorithm for a given collective communication operation may not give good performance on all systems due to the differences in architectures and network parameters and the buffering of the underlying MPI implementation. Hence, collective communications have to be tuned for the system on which they will be executed. In order to determine the optimum parameters of collective communications on a given system, the collective communications need to be modeled effectively at some level as exhaustive testing might not produce meaningful results in a reasonable time as system sizes increase.

Collective operations can be classified as either one-to-many/many-to-one (single producer or consumer) or many-to-many (every participant is both a producer and a consumer) operations. These operations can be generalized in terms of communication via virtual topologies. Experiments currently support a number of these virtual topologies such as flat-tree/linear, pipeline (single chain), binomial tree, binary tree, and K-chain tree (K fan out followed by K chains). Tests show that given the collective operation, message size, and number of processes, each of the topologies can be beneficial for some combination of input parameters. An additional parameter that we utilize is segment size. This is the size of a block of contiguous data into which the individual communications can be broken down. By breaking large, single communications into smaller communications and scheduling many communications in parallel, it is possible to increase the efficiency of any underlying communication infrastructure. Thus, for many operations, we need to specify both parameters—the virtual topology and the segment size.

Figure 8.1 shows how many crossover points between different implementations can exist for a single collective operation on a small number of nodes when finding the optimal (faster implementation). The number of crossovers demonstrates quite clearly why limiting the number of methods available per MPI operation at run time can lead to poor performance in many instances across the possible usage (parameter) range. The MPI operations currently supported within the Open MPI framework include barrier, broadcast, reduce, all-reduce, gather, all-to-all and scatter operations.

A simple, yet time-consuming, method to find an optimal implementation of an individual collective operation is to run an extensive set of tests over a parameter space for the collective operation on a dedicated system. However, running such detailed tests, even on relatively small clusters, can take a substantial amount of time (Vadhiyar, Fagg, and Dongarra, 2000). Tuning exhaustively for eight MPI collectives on a small (40 node) IBM SP-2 up to message sizes of 1 MB involved approximately 13,000 individual experiments and took 50 hours to complete. Even though this only needed to occur once, tuning all of the MPI collectives in a similar manner would take days for a moderately sized system, or weeks for a larger system.

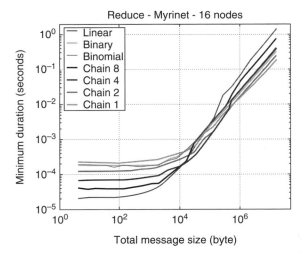

Figure 8.1. Multiple implementations of the MPI reduce operation on 16 nodes. (See color insert.)

Finding the optimal implementation of any given collective can be broken down into a number of stages. The first stage is dependent on message size, number of processors, and MPI collective operation. The second stage is an optimization at these parameters for the correct method (topology–algorithm pair) and segmentation size. Reducing the time needed for running the actual experiments can be achieved at many different levels, such as not testing at every point and interpolating results, that is, testing 8, 32, 128 processes rather than 8, 16, 32, 64, 128, and so on. Additionally, to reduce time one can use actual runs of applications that have been instrumented to build a table of those collective operations that are used in the application.

PVM. PVM represents another popular instantiation of the message-passing model that was one of the principal forerunners of MPI and the first *de facto* standard for the implementation of portable message-passing programs. Although PVM has been superseded by MPI for tightly coupled multiprocessors, it is still widely used on networks of commodity processors. The PVM's principal design goal was portability, even to nonhomogeneous collections of nodes, which was gained by sacrificing optimal performance. MPI, on the other hand, provides high-performance communication. MPI-1 provided only a nonflexible static process model, while MPI-2 adds a scalable dynamic process model.

Central to the design of PVM is the notion of a "virtual machine"—a set of heterogeneous hosts connected by a network that appears logically to the user as a single large parallel computer. PVM API functions provide the ability to (a) join or leave the virtual machine, (b) start new processes by using a number of different selection criteria, including external schedulers and resource managers, (c) kill a process, (d) send a signal to a process, (e) test to check that a process is responding, and (f) notify an arbitrary process if another disconnects from the PVM system.

Comparison between PVM and MPI. PVM is one of a number of parallel distributed computing environments (DCEs) (Rosenberry, Kenney, and Fisher, 1992) that were introduced to assist users wishing to create portable parallel applications (Turcotte, 1993). The system has been in use since 1992 (Geist *et al.*, 1994) and has grown in popularity over the years, leading to a large body of knowledge and a substantial quantity of legacy code accounting for many man-years of development.

Standardization efforts have attempted to address many of the deficiencies of the different DCEs and introduce a single stable system for message passing. These efforts culminated in the first MPI standard, introduced in June 1994 (MPI, 1994). Within a year, several different implementations of MPI were available, including both commercial and public systems.

One of MPI's prime goals was to produce a system that would allow manufacturers of high-performance massively parallel processors (MPPs) computers to provide highly optimized and efficient implementations. In contrast, PVM was designed primarily for networks of workstations, with the goal of portability, gained at the sacrifice of optimal performance. PVM has been ported successfully to many MPPs by its developers and by vendors, and several enhancements have been implemented with much success. Nevertheless, PVM's inherent message structure has limited overall performance when compared with that of native communications systems. Thus, PVM has many features required for operation on a distributed system consisting of many (possibly nonhomogeneous) nodes with reliable, but not necessarily optimal, performance.

MPI, on the other hand, provides high-performance communication and a nonflexible static process model.

Central to the design of PVM was the notion of a "virtual machine"—a set of heterogeneous hosts connected by a network that appears logically to the user as a single large parallel computer. One aspect of the virtual machine was how parallel tasks exchanged data. In PVM, this was accomplished using simple message-passing constructs. There was a strong desire to keep the PVM interface simple to use and understand. Portability was considered much more important than performance for two reasons: Communication across the internet was slow, and the research was focused on problems with scaling, fault tolerance, and heterogeneity of the virtual machine.

The PVM virtual machine is defined by the number and location of the running daemons. Although the number of hosts can be indicated by a fixed list at start-up time, there exists only a single point of failure, the first master daemon to start. All other hosts can join, leave, or fail without affecting the rest of the virtual machine.

PVM API functions allow the user to

- add or delete hosts,
- check that a host is responding,
- be notified by a user-level message that a host has been deleted (intentionally or not) or has been added, and
- shut down the entire virtual machine, killing attached processes and daemons.

PVM API functions provide the ability to

- join or leave the virtual machine,
- start new processes by using a number of different selection criteria, including external schedulers and resource managers,
- kill a process,
- send a signal to a process,
- test to check that it is responding, and
- notify an arbitrary process if another disconnects from the PVM system.

If an application is going to be developed and executed on a single MPP, then MPI has the advantage of expected higher communication performance. The application would be portable to other vendor's MPP so it would not need to be tied to a particular vendor. MPI has a much richer set of communication functions, therefore MPI is favored when an application is structured to exploit special communication modes not available in PVM. The most often cited example is the nonblocking send.

Some sacrifices have been made in the MPI specification in order to be able to produce high communication performance. Two of the most notable are the lack of interoperability between any of the MPI implementations, that is, one vendor's MPI cannot send a message to another vendor's MPI. The second is the lack of ability to write fault tolerant applications in MPI. The MPI specification states that the only thing that is guaranteed after an MPI error is the ability to exit the program.

Because PVM is built around the concept of a virtual machine, PVM has the advantage when the application is going to run over a networked collection of hosts, particularly if the hosts are heterogeneous. PVM contains resource management and process control functions that are important for creating portable applications that run on clusters of workstations and MPP.

If an application is going to be developed and executed on a single MPP, then MPI has the advantage of expected higher communication performance. In addition, MPI has a much richer set of communication functions, therefore it is favored when an application is structured to exploit special communication modes, such as nonblocking send, not available in PVM. PVM has the advantage when the application is going to run over a networked collection of hosts, particularly if the hosts are heterogeneous. PVM includes resource management and process control functions that are important for creating portable applications that run on clusters of workstations and MPPs. PVM is also to be favored when fault tolerance is required. MPI implementations are improving in all of these areas, but PVM still provides better functionality in some settings.

The larger the cluster of hosts, the more important PVM's fault tolerant features becomes. The ability to write long-running PVM applications that can continue even when hosts or tasks fail, or loads change dynamically due to outside influence, is quite important to heterogeneous distributed computing.

Programmers should evaluate the functional requirements and running environment of their application and choose the API that has the features they need.

8.2.2 Linda

Linda (Carriero *et al.*, 1994) is based on an associative shared virtual memory system, or tuple space. Rather than sending messages from one process to another, processes created, consumed, duplicated or evaluated data objects known as tuples.

Creating a tuple is performed by calling **out()**, which is then passed into a common shared space, which all other processes have access to. Reading a tuple is performed by either **rd()** or **in()**, where **rd()** just reads (duplicated) the tuple and **in()** consumes the tuple and removes it from the shared space. The matching of tuples is performed by specifying a template of possible fields in the tuple when calling either **rd()** or **in()**. **eval()** creates tuples asynchronously, with each field making the tuple evaluated in parallel (or at least in a nondeterministic order much like in the Occam ALT construct).

Linda allows for very simple but powerful parallel computer programs by simplifying addressing (no explicit addressing of processes, only the data they handled) and by removing the coupling between processes. In Linda, one cannot specify the consumer of a tuple, and the consumer may not even have existed when the tuple is created.

For example, in a conventional message-passing system, the following steps are required to pass a message from one process to another:

proc A	proc B
find address of 'B' (addrB)	**find address of 'A' (addrA)**
Send (outdata, addrB, messagetag)	**Recv (indata, addrA, messagetag)**

whereas in Linda, one could have:

proc A out (messagetag, outdata) exit

Some time later:

proc B in (messagetag, ?indata) {process data} exit

In this case, the tuple that contained **"messagetag"** as the first field would be consumed by process B (the "?" specifies a wildcard) upon which its data would be placed in the **indata** memory buffer. Neither process ever overlaps temporarily or knows of each others **"address"**.

Although initial implementations were slower than native libraries, later versions that utilized compile-time analysis of data fields used by application programs allowed the runtime system to select tuned low-level services that implemented the tuple space management and matching operations. On a number of tests (Deshpande and Schultz, 1992), some versions of Linda performed comparably with both networked message-passing systems such as PVM as well as native vendor message-passing libraries on a number of MPPs for medium to large message payloads.

8.2.3   HPF

HPF is a *de facto* standard language for writing data parallel programs for shared and distributed memory parallel architectures (High Performance Fortran Forum, 1997). HPF programs can be easier to write than conventional message-passing programs.

HPF is an extension to Fortran 90. It makes use of the fact that the array handling features of Fortran 90 are ideal for expressing parallel array operations. It also provides ways of describing parallel loops. The extensions to Fortran 90 include

- compiler directives: to guide the compiler to distribute the data in a given array across the available processors, or to label parallel DO loops,
- a FORALL statement and construct to complement the Fortran 90 WHERE
  ∘ both are parallel constructs in HPF,
- new intrinsic and library procedures: to extend the already rich set in Fortran 90,
- subset HPF is a version of HPF that omits from full HPF some Fortran 90 features plus those compiler directives related to the dynamic redistribution of data at runtime. It remains much more powerful than Fortran 77.

An HPF program should run effectively on a wide range of parallel machines, including distributed memory machines. On these, programmers have become used to writing "message-passing" programs, and resigned to the difficulties of doing this. HPF programs contain no message passing (although the compiler will inevitably insert some into the final code). An HPF program is as easy to write as a Fortran 90 program, and also as easy to read. Therefore, HPF provides a much friendlier programming paradigm for users who want their results fast, without needing to worry about the details of the parallelism.

The HPF approach is based on two fundamental observations. First, the overall performance of a program can be increased if operations are performed concurrently by multiple processors. Second, the efficiency of a single processor is highest if the processor performs computations on data elements stored locally. Based on these observations, the HPF extensions to Fortran 90 provide a means for the explicit expression of parallelism and data mapping. An HPF programmer can express parallelism explicitly, and using this information, the compiler may be able to tune data distribution accordingly to control load balancing and minimize communication.

An HPF program has essentially the same structure as a Fortran 90 program, but is enhanced with data distribution and alignment directives. When writing a program in HPF, the programmer specifies computations in a global data space. Array objects are aligned to abstract arrays with no data, called "templates." Templates are distributed according to distribution directives in "block" and "cyclic" fashions. All arrays aligned to such templates are implicitly distributed.

Parallelism can be explicitly expressed in HPF using the following language features:

- Fortran 90 array assignments
- masked array assignments
- WHERE statements and constructs
- HPF FORALL statements and constructs
- HPF INDEPENDENT directives
- intrinsic functions
- the HPF library
- EXTRINSIC functions

The compiler uses these parallel constructs and distribution information to produce a code suitable for parallel execution on each node of a parallel computer. The efficiency of an HPF application strongly depends on the quality of the compiler as the programmer has no language means to advise the compiler of the many features of the implemented parallel algorithm having significant impact on its performance, such as the optimal communication pattern.

8.3 HETEROGENEOUS PARALLEL PROGRAMMING SYSTEMS

Unlike traditional systems, heterogeneous parallel programming systems are designed specifically for the implementation of heterogeneous and homogeneous algorithms for sets of interconnected heterogeneous processors in the form of portable self-adaptable programs. There have been two such systems developed so far, mpC and HeteroMPI. These systems share the same design principles, and even some software components. In this book, we use HeteroMPI to introduce these principles. The reason is twofold. First, the mpC language has been well published since its first release in 1997 (Lastovetsky, 2002, 2003). HeteroMPI is a relatively recent development; its first release appeared in 2006. Second, HeteroMPI is defined as a small number of extensions to standard MPI, which makes it relatively easy to learn and understand. mpC is a new high-level language that introduces many novel programming concepts aimed at easier parallel programming. The drawback of this novelty is that mpC is not that easy to learn.

While MPI is the most popular programming tool for high-performance computing not only on homogeneous but also on heterogeneous distributed memory computer systems, it does not provide means that would address some additional challenges posed by heterogeneous platforms:

- *Heterogeneity of Processors.* A good parallel application for heterogeneous platforms must distribute computations unevenly, taking into account the speeds of the processors. The efficiency of the parallel application also depends on the accuracy of estimation of the speeds of the heterogeneous processors. This estimation is difficult because the processors may demonstrate different speeds for different applications due to differences in the instruction sets, the number of instruction execution units, the number of registers, the structure of memory hierarchy, and so on.
- *Ad Hoc Communication Network.* The communication network in a heterogeneous platform may be relatively slow and/or heterogeneous. This makes the problem of optimal distribution of computations and communications even more difficult.

HeteroMPI (Lastovetsky and Reddy, 2006) is a small set of extensions to MPI that help the programmer develop a parallel program distributing computations and communications unevenly, in accordance with the speeds of the processors and the latencies and bandwidths of communication links of the executing heterogeneous platform.

The standard MPI specification provides communicator and group constructors, which allow application programmers to create a group of processes that execute together a logical unit of the implemented parallel algorithm. The processes in the group are explicitly chosen from a preordered set of processes. This approach to group creation is acceptable if the MPI application runs on a homogeneous distributed memory computer system, one process per processor. In this case, the explicitly created group will execute the parallel algorithm with the same execution time as any other group with the same number of processes because the processors have the same computing power, and the latency and the bandwidth of communication links between different pairs of processors are the same.

On a heterogeneous cluster, there may be a group of processes executing the parallel algorithm faster than any other group. Finding such a group is a difficult task. It requires the programmers to write a lot of complex code, detecting the actual speeds of the processors and the latencies of the communication links between them and then using this information for selecting the optimal set of processes running on different computers of the heterogeneous network.

The main idea of HeteroMPI is to automate the process of finding the group of processes that would execute the implemented parallel algorithm faster than any other group.

The first step in this process of automation is the specification of the performance model of the implemented parallel algorithm. The performance model allows the application programmer to describe the main features of the underlying parallel algorithm having an impact on the performance. These features are

- the total number of processes executing the algorithm,
- the total volume of computations to be performed by each of the processes in the group during the execution of the algorithm,
- the total volume of data communicated between each pair of processes in the group during the execution of the algorithm, and
- the order of execution of the computations and communications by the parallel processes in the group, that is, how exactly the processes interact during the execution of the algorithm.

HeteroMPI provides a small and dedicated definition language for specifying this performance model, which it shares with mpC. This language has been briefly introduced in Section 7.3. A compiler translates the description of the performance model into a set of functions, which make up an algorithm-specific part of the HeteroMPI runtime system.

Having provided the description of the performance model of the algorithm, the application programmer can use a new operation, **HMPI_Group_ create**, to create a group of processes that would execute the algorithm faster than any other group of processes:

```
HMPI_Group_create(HMPI_Group* gid, const HMPI_Model* perf_model,
            const void* model_parameters)
```

The parameter **perf_model** is a handle of the performance model, and **model_parameters** are the parameters of the performance model (see example shown below). This function returns a HeteroMPI handle to the group of MPI processes in **gid**.

In HeteroMPI, groups are not absolutely independent of each other. Every newly created group has exactly one process shared with already existing groups. That process is called a *parent* of this newly created group, and is the connecting link through which the results of computations are passed if the group ceases to exist. **HMPI_Group_create** is a collective operation and must be called by the parent and all the processes that are not members of any HeteroMPI group.

During the creation of this group of processes, the HeteroMPI runtime system solves the problem of selecting the optimal set of processes to execute the algorithm. The solution to the problem is based on

- The performance model of the parallel algorithm
- The performance model of the executing heterogeneous platform, which reflects its state upon the execution of the parallel algorithm; this model considers the executing platform as a multilevel hierarchy of interconnected sets of heterogeneous multiprocessors, and takes into account the material nature of communication links and their heterogeneity

The algorithms used by the HeteroMPI runtime system to find an approximate solution of this problem are described in Lastovetsky (2002). The accuracy of the solution strongly depends on the accuracy of the estimation of the speeds of the processors in the performance model of the executing platform. HeteroMPI provides a new operation, **HMPI_Recon**, to dynamically update the estimation of processor speeds at run time:

```
typedef void (*HMPI_Benchmark_function)(const void*, int, void*);
int HMPI_Recon(HMPI_Benchmark_function func, const void* input_p,
        int num_of_parameters, void* output_p)
```

This is a collective operation and must be called by all the processes in the group associated with the predefined communication universe **HMPI_COMM_WORLD** of the HeteroMPI. The execution of the operation results in all the processors of the heterogeneous platform to run the benchmark function **func** in parallel, and the time elapsed on each of the processors to be used to refresh the estimation of its speed. Thus, the accuracy of the estimation of the speeds of the processors is fully controlled by the application programmer. Indeed, it is the programmer's responsibility to provide a representative benchmark code and to decide when it should be run.

Figure 8.2 illustrates the usage of **HMPI_Recon** to write parallel programs sensitive to both the differences in the speed of processors for different logical phases of computations and the dynamic variation of the workload of the executing computer system. As can be seen from the figure, the combination of calls **HMPI_Recon** and **HMPI_Group_create** can be used for each distinct phase of the parallel application to create a group of processes that executes the computations and communications in that phase with the best execution performance. The groups are created at each iteration of the main loop in

```
void Phase1_benchmark_code(const void*, int, void*);
void Phase2_benchmark_code(const void*, int, void*);
int main() {

   ...

   for (i = 0; i < number_of_iterations; i++) {
      double *phase1_speeds, *phase2_speeds;
      //Phase1
      if ((HMPI_Is_member(HMPI_COMM_WORLD_GROUP)) {
         HMPI_Recon(&Phase1_benchmark_code,...);
         HMPI_Get_processors_info(phase1_speeds);
      }
      //Distribute computations using the speeds
      HMPI_Group_create(...);
      //Execution of the computations and communications
      //Free the group
      //Phase2
      if ((HMPI_Is_member(HMPI_COMM_WORLD_GROUP)) {
         HMPI_Recon(&Phase2_benchmark_code,...);
         HMPI_Get_processors_info(phase2_speeds);
      }
      //Distribute computations using the speeds
      HMPI_Group_create(...);
      //Execution of the computations and communications
      //Free the group

      ...

   }

}
```

Figure 8.2. An example illustrating the usage of the operation **HMPI_Recon** to write parallel programs sensitive to dynamic changing loads.

order to guarantee that the distribution of computations and communications for this iteration is based on the most recent estimation of the speeds of the processors.

Another principal operation provided by HeteroMPI, **HMPI_Timeof**, allows the application programmer to predict the execution time of the algorithm without its real execution:

```
double HMPI_Timeof(const HMPI_Model* perf_model,
                   const void* model_parameters)
```

This is a local operation that can be called by any process of the HeteroMPI program. This function invokes the HeteroMPI runtime system to find the optimal set of processes for the execution of the parallel algorithm specified by its performance model, **perf_model**, and the parameters of this model, **model_parameters**. The estimated execution time of the algorithm by this optimal set of processes is then returned. The parameters of the model include problem and algorithmic parameters. The use of this operation for finding (at run time) the optimal values of algorithmic parameters of the implemented algorithm has been discussed in Section 7.3.

A typical HeteroMPI application starts with the initialization of the HeteroMPI runtime system using the operation

```
HMPI_Init (int argc, char** argv)
```

where **argc** and **argv** are the same as the arguments passed to **main**. After the initialization, application programmers can call any other HeteroMPI routines. In addition, MPI users can use normal MPI routines, with the exception of MPI initialization and finalization, including the standard group management and communicator management routines to create and free groups of MPI processes. However, they must use the predefined communication universe **HMPI_COMM_WORLD** of the HeteroMPI instead of **MPI_COMM_WORLD** of the MPI.

The only group constructor operation provided by HeteroMPI is the creation of the group using **HMPI_Group_create**, and the only group destructor operation provided by HeteroMPI is

```
HMPI_Group_free(HMPI_Group* gid)
```

where **gid** is the HeteroMPI handle to the group of MPI processes. This is a collective operation and must be called by all the members of this group.

The other additional group management operations provided by HeteroMPI apart from the group constructor and destructor are the following group accessors:

- **HMPI Group_rank** to get the rank of the process in the HeteroMPI group and
- **HMPI_Group_size** to get the number of processes in this group.

The initialization of the HeteroMPI runtime system is typically followed by

- Updating of the estimation of the speeds of processors with **HMPI_Recon**
- Finding the optimal values of the algorithmic parameters of the parallel algorithm with **HMPI_Timeof**

- Creation of a group of processes that will perform the parallel algorithm by using **HMPI_Group_create**
- Execution of the parallel algorithm by the members of the group. At this point, control is handed over to MPI. MPI and HeteroMPI are interconnected by the operation

```
const MPI_Comm* HMPI_Get_comm (const HMPI_Group* gid)
```

which returns an MPI communicator with the communication group of MPI processes defined by **gid**. This is a local operation not requiring interprocess communication. Application programmers can use this communicator to call the standard MPI communication routines during the execution of the parallel algorithm. This communicator can safely be used in other MPI routines
- Freeing the HeteroMPI groups with **HMPI_Group_free**
- Finalizing the HeteroMPI runtime system by using the operation

```
HMPI_Finalize (int exitcode)
```

A HeteroMPI application is like any other MPI application and can be deployed to run in any environment where MPI applications are used. HeteroMPI applications can be run in environments where batch queuing and resource management systems are used. However, HeteroMPI uses its own measurements and performance models of the underlying system for running parallel applications efficiently.

One simple application of HeteroMPI is the conversion of conventional parallel programs that are designed to run on MPPs such as ScaLAPACK programs to HeteroMPI programs with minor rewriting of these applications, which mainly includes the insertion of HeteroMPI group creation and destruction calls. These HeteroMPI programs do not aim to extract the maximum performance from a heterogeneous platform but instead provide an easy and simple way to execute the conventional parallel programs on heterogeneous processors with good performance improvements. To write such a HeteroMPI program, first, application programmers describe the performance model of their homogeneous algorithm. Second, the transformed HeteroMPI program uses a multiprocessing algorithm that allows more than one process involved in its execution to be run on each processor. The upper bound on the number of processes executed on each processor is roughly equal to the ratio of the speed of the fastest processor to the speed of the slowest processor on the executing network of computers. During the creation of a HeteroMPI group of processes, the mapping of the parallel processes to the executing network of computers is performed such that the number of processes running on each processor is proportional to its speed. In other words, while distributed evenly across parallel processes, data and computations are distributed unevenly over processors of the heterogeneous network, and this way, each processor performs the volume of computations proportional to its speed.

8.4 DISTRIBUTED PROGRAMMING SYSTEMS

8.4.1 NetSolve

NetSolve (Casanova and Dongarra, 1996) is a project that aims to bring together disparate computational resources connected by computer networks. It is a Remote Procedure Call (RPC)-based client/agent/server system that allows one to remotely access both hardware and software components.

The purpose of NetSolve is to create the middleware necessary to provide a seamless bridge between the simple, standard programming interfaces and desktop scientific computing environments (SCEs) that dominate the work of computational scientists and the rich supply of services supported by the emerging grid architecture, so that the users of the former can easily access and reap the benefits (shared processing, storage, software, data resources, etc.) of using the latter.

This vision of the broad community of scientists, engineers, research professionals, and students working with the powerful and flexible tool set provided by their familiar desktop SCEs and yet able to easily draw on the vast, shared resources of the grid for unique or exceptional resource needs or able to collaborate intensively with colleagues in other organizations and locations is the vision that NetSolve will be designed to realize.

NetSolve uses a client–server system that enables users to solve complex scientific problems remotely. The system allows users to access both hardware and software computational resources distributed across a network. NetSolve searches for computational resources on a network, chooses the best one available and, using retry for fault tolerance, solves a problem and returns the answers to the user. A load balancing policy is used by the NetSolve system to ensure good performance by enabling the system to use the computational resources available as efficiently as possible. The NetSolve framework is based on the premise that distributed computations involve resources, processes, data, and users, and that secure yet flexible mechanisms for cooperation and communication between these entities is the key to metacomputing infrastructures.

Some goals of the NetSolve project are ease-of-use for the user, efficient use of the resources, and the ability to integrate any arbitrary software component as a resource into the NetSolve system.

Interfaces in Fortran, C, Matlab, Mathematica, and Octave have been designed and implemented, which enable users to access and use NetSolve more easily. An agent-based design has been implemented to ensure the efficient use of system resources.

One of the key characteristics of any software system is versatility. In order to ensure the success of NetSolve, the system has been designed to incorporate any piece of software with relative ease. There are no restrictions on the type of software that can be integrated into the system.

8.4.2 Nimrod

Parametric computational experiments are becoming increasingly important in science and engineering as a means of exploring the behavior of complex systems. For example, an engineer may explore the behavior of a wing by running a computational model of the airfoil multiple times while varying key parameters such as angle of attack, air speed, and so on. The results of these multiple experiments yield a picture of how the wing behaves in different parts of parametric space.

Nimrod is a tool that manages the execution of parametric studies across distributed computers. It takes responsibility for the overall management of an experiment, as well as the low-level issues of distributing files to remote systems, performing the remote computation, and gathering the results. EnFuzion is a commercial version of the research system Nimrod. When a user describes an experiment to Nimrod, they develop a declarative plan file that describes the parameters, their default values, and the commands necessary for performing the work. The system then uses this information to transport the necessary files and schedule the work on the first available machine.

Nimrod/G is a grid-aware version of Nimrod. It takes advantage of the features supported in the Globus toolkit such as the automatic discovery of allowed resources.

Furthermore, the concept of computational economy is introduced as part of the Nimrod/G scheduler. The architecture is extensible enough to use any other grid middleware services such as Legion, Condor, and NetSolve.

8.4.3 Java

Java is a high-level, object-oriented, general-purpose programming language with a number of features that make the language quite popular for distributed computing on global heterogeneous networks. Java source code is compiled into bytecode, which can then be executed by a Java interpreter. Compiled Java code can run on most computers because Java interpreters and runtime environments, known as Java Virtual Machines, exist for most operating systems. The definition of Java makes the compiled Java code be interpreted identically on any computer and unable to penetrate the operating environment. Therefore, Java codes are highly portable and safe, and hence well suited for code sharing. It is easy and safe to use in your distributed application remote Java code. Strong support for object-oriented, safe, and portable programming makes Java a unique software tool.

8.4.4 GridRPC

Although grid computing is regarded as a viable next-generation computing infrastructure, its widespread adoption is still hindered by several factors, one of which is the question, "How do we program on the grid (in an easy manner)?"

Currently, the most popular middleware infrastructure, the Globus toolkit, by and large provides basic, low-level services, such as security/authentication, job launching, directory service, and so on. Although such services are an absolute necessity especially provided as a common platform and abstractions across different machines in the grid for interoperability purposes (as such it could be said that Globus is a GridOS), there still tends to exist a large gap between the Globus services and the programming-level abstractions we are commonly used to. This is synonymous to the early days of parallel programming, where the programming tools and abstractions available to the programmers were low-level libraries such as (low-level) message-passing and/or thread libraries. In a metaphoric sense, programming directly on top of only Globus I/O can be regarded as performing parallel programming using only the Linux API on a Beowulf cluster.

By all means, there have been various attempts to provide a programming model and a corresponding system or a language appropriate for the grid. Many such efforts have been collected and cataloged by the Advanced Programming Models Research Group of the Global Grid Forum (Lee *et al.*, 2001). One particular programming model that has proven to be viable is an RPC mechanism tailored for the grid, or "GridRPC."

Although at a very high-level view, the programming model provided by GridRPC is that of standard RPC plus asynchronous coarse-grained parallel tasking, in practice there are a variety of features that will largely hide the dynamicity, insecurity, and instability of the grid from the programmers. These are namely

- ability to cope with medium to coarse-grained calls, with call durations ranging from >1 second to <1 week,
- various styles of asynchronous, task-parallel programming on the grid, with thousands of scalable concurrent calls,
- "dynamic" RPC, for example, dynamic resource discovery and scheduling,
- scientific data types and Interface Description Language (IDL), for example, large matrices and files as arguments, call-by-reference, and shared memory matrix arguments with sections/strides as part of a "scientific IDL,"
- grid-level dependability and security, for example, grid security with Grid Security Infrastructure (GSI) and automated fault tolerance with checkpoint/rollback and/or retries,
- simple client-side programming and management, that is, no client-side IDL management and very little state left on the client,
- server-side-only management of IDLs, RPC stubs, "gridified" executables, job monitoring, control, and so on, and

- very (bandwidth) efficient—does not send entire matrix when strides and array-sections are specified.

As such, GridRPC not only enables individual applications to be distributed but it can also serve as the basis for even higher-level software substrates such as distributed, scientific components on the grid. Moreover, recent work (Shirasuna *et al.*, 2002) has shown that GridRPC could be effectively built upon future grid software based on Web Services such as Open Grid Services Architecture (OGSA) (Foster *et al.*, 2002). Some representative GridRPC systems are NetSolve (Casanova and Dongarra, 1996), and Ninf (Nakada, Sato, and Sekiguchi, 1999). Historically, both projects started about the same time, and in fact both systems facilitate similar sets of features as described above. On the other hand, because of differences in the protocols and the APIs as well as their functionalities, the interoperability between the two systems has been poor at best. There had been crude attempts at achieving interoperability between the two systems using protocol translation via proxy-like adapters (Lee *et al.*, 2001), but for various technical reasons full support of mutual features proved to be difficult.

This experience motivated the need for a more unified effort by both parties to understand the requirements of the GridRPC API, protocols, and features and come to a common ground for potential standardization. In fact, as the grid became widespread, the need for a unified standard GridRPC became quite apparent, in the same manner as MPI standardization, based on past experiences with different message-passing systems, catapulted the adoption of portable parallel programming on large-scale MPPs and clusters.

PART IV

APPLICATIONS

In Chapter 7, we have noted that the design of heterogeneous parallel algorithms significantly outdistances their implementation in the form of portable and efficient applications. Most of the successful applications for large-scale heterogeneous systems, such as seti@home, use a trivial model of parallelism, where the whole problem is partitioned into a huge number of fully independent tasks that can be processed in parallel. The design and implementation of tightly coupled high-performance computing applications for heterogeneous platforms is definitely an underdeveloped area. At the same time, first such applications, based on nontrivial models and algorithms, have started appearing. In this part, we present some recent results in this area. Chapter 9 introduces Heterogeneous PBLAS, a set of parallel linear algebra subprograms for heterogeneous computational clusters. Parallel processing of remotely sensed hyperspectral images on heterogeneous clusters is presented in Chapter 10. Both applications are implemented using HeteroMPI, the extension of MPI for heterogeneous parallel computing introduced in Chapter 8. An astrophysical application that simulates the evolution of clusters of galaxies in the universe on a heterogeneous computational grid is described in Chapter 11. Its implementation in GridSolve and SmartGridSolve are discussed and compared.

High-Performance Heterogeneous Computing, by Alexey L. Lastovetsky and Jack J. Dongarra
Copyright © 2009 John Wiley & Sons, Inc.

CHAPTER 9

Numerical Linear Algebra Software for Heterogeneous Clusters

In this chapter, we outline a package called Heterogeneous Parallel Basic Linear Algebra Subprograms (HeteroPBLAS) (Reddy, Lastovetsky, and Alonso, 2008), which is built on top of PBLAS (Choi *et al.*, 1996b) and provides optimized PBLAS for heterogeneous computational clusters. Its first research implementation (HeteroScaLAPACK, 2008) is available. HeteroPBLAS is developed in the framework of the ongoing work on heterogeneous ScaLA-PACK (HeteroScaLAPACK), a parallel linear algebra package for heterogeneous computational clusters.

9.1 HeteroPBLAS: INTRODUCTION AND USER INTERFACE

PBLAS is a parallel set of basic linear algebra subprograms (BLAS) (Dongarra *et al.*, 1990) that perform message passing and whose interface is similar to the BLAS. The design goal of PBLAS was to provide specifications of distributed kernels, which would simplify and encourage the development of high-performance and portable parallel numerical software, as well as provide manufacturers with a small set of routines to be optimized. These subprograms were used to develop parallel libraries such as the ScaLAPACK (Choi *et al.*, 1996a), which is a well-known standard package providing high-performance linear algebra routines for (homogeneous) distributed memory message passing MIMD computers supporting MPI and/or PVM.

As has been noted in Chapters 7 and 8, there may be two main approaches to the design and implementation of scientific software for heterogeneous clusters. The first approach is to develop brand-new software that implements the dedicated heterogeneous parallel algorithms and uses the traditional one-process-per-processor configuration of the parallel application. The second approach is to use the traditional homogeneous algorithms and a nontraditional multiple-processes-per-processor configuration of the parallel application in order to balance the load of the heterogeneous processors and achieve higher performance compared with the one-process-per-processor configuration. While not intended for achieving the top performance via the optimal distribution of computations and communications, this approach is easier to accomplish. It allows for the complete reuse of high-quality scientific software, developed for homogeneous distributed memory systems, in heterogeneous environments with minimal development efforts and good speedup. The main task that should be solved is finding the optimal configuration of the parallel application.

The design of HeteroPBLAS, which provides optimized PBLAS for heterogeneous computational clusters, adopts the multiprocessing approach and thus reuses the PBLAS software completely. The library automates the tedious and error-prone tasks of determining accurate platform parameters, such as speeds of the processors, latencies, and bandwidths of the communication links connecting different pairs of processors, and optimal algorithmic parameters, such as the number of processes, number of processors, number of processes per processor involved in the execution of the parallel algorithm, and mapping of the processes to the executing nodes of the heterogeneous cluster. HeteroMPI (Lastovetsky and Reddy, 2006) is the instrumental library used to implement HeteroPBLAS.

The main routine is the context creation function, which provides a context for the execution of the PBLAS routine. There is a context creation function for each and every PBLAS routine. This function frees the application programmer from having to specify the process grid arrangement to be used in the execution of the PBLAS routine. It tries to determine the optimal process grid arrangement.

All the routines have names of the form **hscal_pxyyzzz_ctxt**. The second letter, **x**, indicates the data type as follows:

X	MEANING
s	single precision real data
d	double precision real data
c	single precision complex data
z	double precision complex data

Thus **hscal_pxtrsm_ctxt** refers to any or all of the routines **hscal_pctrsm_ctxt**, **hscal_pdtrsm_ctxt**, **hscal_pstrsm_ctxt**, and **hscal_pztrsm_ctxt**.

The next two letters, **yy**, indicate the type of matrix (or of the most significant matrix): **ge**—general, **sy**—symmetric, **he**—hermitian, **tr**—triangular.

TABLE 9.1   HeteroBLAS Context Creation Routines

Level 1 PBLAS	Level 2 PBLAS	Level 3 PBLAS
hscal_pxswap_ctxt	hscal_pxgemv_ctxt	hscal_pxgemm_ctxt
hscal_pxscal_ctxt	hscal_pxhemv_ctxt	hscal_pxsymm_ctxt
hscal_pxcopy_ctxt	hscal_pxsymv_ctxt	hscal_pxhemm_ctxt
hscal_pxaxpy_ctxt	hscal_pxtrmv_ctxt	hscal_pxsyrk_ctxt
hscal_pxdot_ctxt	hscal_pxtrsv_ctxt	hscal_pxherk_ctxt
hscal_pxdotu_ctxt	hscal_pxger_ctxt	hscal_pxsyr2k_ctxt
hscal_pxdotc_ctxt	hscal_pxgeru_ctxt	hscal_pxher2k_ctxt
hscal_pxnrm2_ctxt	hscal_pxgerc_ctxt	hscal_pxtran_ctxt
hscal_pxasum_ctxt	hscal_pxher_ctxt	hscal_pxtranu_ctxt
hscal_pxamax_ctxt	hscal_pxher2_ctxt	hscal_pxtranc_ctxt
	hscal_pxsyr_ctxt	hscal_pxtrmm_ctxt
	hscal_pxsyr2_ctxt	hscal_pxtrsm_ctxt
		hscal_pxgeadd_ctxt
		hscal_pxtradd_ctxt

The last three letters, **zzz**, indicate the computation performed. Thus **hscal_pcgeadd_ctxt** indicates a context routine for the PBLAS routine **pcgeadd**, which adds two general matrices containing elements of type single precision complex data. The names of the context creation routines are shown in Table 9.1.

For example, the context creation function for the PDGEMM routine has an interface, as shown below:

```
int hscal_pdgemm_ctxt(char* transa, char* transb,
    int * m, int * n, int * k, double * alpha, int * ia, int * ja,
    int * desca, int * ib, int * jb, int * descb, double * beta,
    int * ic, int * jc, int * descc, int * ictxt)
```

This function call returns a handle to a group of MPI processes in ictxt and a return value of **HSCAL_SUCCESS** on successful execution. It differs from the PDGEMM call in the following ways:

• It returns a context but does not actually execute the PDGEMM routine
• The matrices **A**, **B**, and **C** containing the data are not passed as arguments
• It has an extra return argument, **ictxt**, which contains the handle to a group of MPI processes that is subsequently used in the actual execution of the PDGEMM routine
• A return value of **HSCAL_SUCCESS** indicating successful execution, or otherwise an appropriate error code

- The context element in the descriptor arrays **desca**, **descb**, and **descc** need not be filled

hscal_pdgemm_ctxt is a collective operation and must be called by all the processes running in the HeteroPBLAS application. The context contains a handle to a HeteroMPI group of MPI processes, which tries to execute the PBLAS routine faster than any other group. This context can be reused in multiple calls of the same routine or any other routine that uses a similar parallel algorithm as that by PDGEMM. During the creation of the HeteroMPI group of MPI processes, the HeteroPBLAS runtime system detects the optimal process arrangement and solves the problem of selecting the optimal set of processes running on different computers of the heterogeneous network. The solution to the problem is based on the following:

- The performance model of the PBLAS routine. This is in the form of a set of functions generated by a compiler from the description of the performance model of the PBLAS routine.
- The performance model of the executing network of computers, which reflects the state of this network just before the execution of the PBLAS routine.

The performance model of the heterogeneous network of computers is summarized as follows:

- The performance of each processor is characterized by the execution time of the same serial code
  - The serial code is provided by the application programmer.
  - It is supposed that the code is representative of the computations performed during the execution of the application.
  - The code is performed at run time in the points of the application specified by the application programmer. Thus, the performance model of the processors provides a current estimation of their speed demonstrated on the code representative of the particular application.
- The communication model (Lastovetsky, 2002) is seen as a hierarchy of communication layers. Each layer is characterized by its latency and bandwidth. Unlike the performance model of processors, the communication model is static. Its parameters are obtained once upon the initialization of the environment and do not change.

The mapping algorithms used to solve the problem of selecting processes are detailed in Lastovetsky (2002) and Lastovetsky and Reddy (2006).

The context, returned by the function described above, is passed to the Basic Linear Algebra Communication Subprograms (BLACS) (Dongarra and Whaley, 1995) routine `blacs_gridinfo` to obtain the row and column index in the process grid of the calling process and the optimal process grid arrangement. HeteroPBLAS also provides the following operation to obtain the estimated execution time (in seconds) of the PBLAS routine using the optimal process grid arrangement:

```
double hscal_timeof(const int * ictxt)
```

This is only the estimated execution time since the PBLAS routine is not actually executed on the underlying hardware. These two routines are serial and can be called by any process that is participating in the context. The function **hscal_in_ctxt** is used to determine the membership of a process in a context.

In addition to the context management routines, auxiliary routines are provided for each PBLAS routine, which determine the total number of computations (arithmetical operations) performed by each process and the total number of communications in bytes between a pair of processes involved in the execution of the homogeneous PBLAS routine. An auxiliary routine is also provided for the serial BLAS equivalent of each PBLAS routine, which determines the total number of arithmetical operations involved in its execution. These routines arc serial and can be called by any process. They do not actually execute the corresponding PBLAS/BLAS routine; they just calculate the total number of computations and communications involved.

The reader is referred to the HeteroPBLAS programmer's manual for more details of the HeteroPBLAS user interface (HeteroScaLAPACK, 2008). To summarize the essential differences between calling a homogeneous PBLAS routine and a heterogeneous PBLAS routine, consider the four basic steps involved in calling a homogeneous PDGEMM PBLAS routine as shown in Figure 9.1:

1. Initialize the process grid using **blacs_gridinit**.
2. Distribute the matrices on the process grid. Each global matrix that is to be distributed across the proccss grid is assigned an array descriptor using the ScaLAPACK TOOLS routine descinit. A mapping of the global matrix onto the process grid is accomplished using the user-defined routine **pdmatgen**.
3. Call the PBLAS routine **pdgemm**.
4. Release the process grid via a call to blacs_gridexit. When all the computations have been completed, the program is exited with a call to **blacs_exit**.

Figure 9.2 shows the essential steps involved in calling the heterogeneous PDGEMM PBLAS routine:

1. Initialize the heterogeneous PBLAS run time using the operation

```
int hscal_init(int * argc, int *** argv)
```

```
    int main(int argc, char **argv) {
        int nprow, npcol, pdgemmctxt, myrow, mycol, c__0 = 0, c__1 = -1;
/* Problem parameters */
        char *TRANSA, *TRANSB;
        int  *M, *N, *K, *IA, *JA, *DESCA, *IB, *JB, *DESCB, *IC, *JC,
            *DESCC;
        double *ALPHA, *A, *B, *BETA, *C;
/* Initialize the process grid */
        blacs_get__(&c__1, &c__0, &pdgemmctxt);
        blacs_gridinit__(&pdgemmctxt, "r", nprow, npcol);
        blacs_gridinfo__(&pdgemmctxt, &nprow, &npcol, &myrow, &mycol);
/* Initialize the array descriptors for the matrices A, B and C */
        descinit_(DESCA, …, &pdgemmctxt);   /* for Matrix A */
        descinit_(DESCB, …, &pdgemmctxt);   /* for Matrix B */
        descinit_(DESCC, …, &pdgemmctxt);   /* for Matrix C */
/* Distribute matrices on the process grid using user-defined pdmatgen */
        pdmatgen_(&pdgemmctxt, …); /* for Matrix A */
        pdmatgen_(&pdgemmctxt, …); /* for Matrix B */
        pdmatgen_(&pdgemmctxt, …); /* for Matrix C */
/* Call the PBLAS 'pdgemm' routine */
        pdgemm_(TRANSA, TRANSB, M, N, K, ALPHA, A, IA, JA, DESCA, B, IB,
                JB, DESCB, BETA, C, IC, JC, DESCC);
/* Release the process grid and Free the BLACS context */
        blacs_gridexit__(&pdgemmctxt);
/* Exit the BLACS */
        blacs_exit__(&c__0);
    }
```

Figure 9.1. Basic steps involved in calling the homogeneous PBLAS routine **PDGEMM**.

where **argc** and **argv** are the same as the arguments passed to main. This routine must be called before any other HeteroPBLAS context management routine and must be called once. It must be called by all the processes running in the HeteroPBLAS application.

2. Get the heterogeneous PDGEMM routine context using the routine **hscal_pdgemm_ctxt**. The function call **hscal_in_ctxt** returns a value of 1 for the processes chosen to execute the PDGEMM routine, or otherwise 0.

3. Execute the Steps 2 and 3 involved in calling a homogeneous PBLAS routine.

4. Release the context using the context destructor operation **int** hscal_ free_ctxt(**int** * ctxt).

```
    int main(int argc, char **argv) {
        int nprow, npcol, pdgemmctxt, myrow, mycol, c__0 = 0;
/* Problem parameters */
        char *TRANSA, *TRANSB;
        int  *M, *N, *K, *IA, *JA, *DESCA, *IB, *JB, *DESCB, *IC, *JC,
            *DESCC;
        double *ALPHA, *A, *B, *BETA, *C;
/* Initialize the heterogeneous ScaLAPACK runtime */
        hscal_init(&argc, &argv);
/* Initialize the array descriptors for the matrices A, B and C
    No need to specify the context argument */
        descinit_(DESCA, …, NULL);  /* for Matrix A */
        descinit_(DESCB, …, NULL);  /* for Matrix B */
        descinit_(DESCC, …, NULL);  /* for Matrix C */
/* Get the heterogeneous PDGEMM context */
        hscal_pdgemm_ctxt(TRANSA, TRANSB, M, N, K, ALPHA, IA, JA, DESCA,
                        IB, JB, DESCB, BETA, IC, JC, DESCC, &pdgemmctxt);
        if (!hscal_in_ctxt(&pdgemmctxt)) {
            hscal_finalize(c__0);
        }
/* Retrieve the process grid information */
        blacs_gridinfo__(&pdgemmctxt, &nprow, &npcol, &myrow, &mycol);
/* Initialize the array descriptors for the matrices A, B and C */
        descinit_(DESCA, …, &pdgemmctxt);  /* for Matrix A */
        descinit_(DESCB, …, &pdgemmctxt);  /* for Matrix B */
        descinit_(DESCC, …, &pdgemmctxt);  /* for Matrix C */
/* Distribute matrices on the process grid using user-defined pdmatgen */
        pdmatgen_(&pdgemmctxt, …); /* for Matrix A */
        pdmatgen_(&pdgemmctxt, …); /* for Matrix B */
        pdmatgen_(&pdgemmctxt, …); /* for Matrix C */
/* Call the PBLAS 'pdgemm' routine */
        pdgemm_(TRANSA, TRANSB, M, N, K, ALPHA, A, IA, JA, DESCA, B, IB,
                JB, DESCB, BETA, C, IC, JC, DESCC);
/* Release the heterogeneous PDGEMM context */
        hscal_free_ctxt(&pdgemmctxt);
/* Finalize the Heterogeneous ScaLAPACK runtime */
        hscal_finalize(c__0);
    }
```

Figure 9.2. Essential steps involved in calling the heterogeneous PBLAS routine **PDGEMM**.

5. When all the computations have been completed, the program is exited with a call to **hscal_finalize**, which finalizes the heterogeneous PBLAS run time.

It is relatively straightforward for the application programmers to wrap Steps 2–4 in a single function call, which would form the heterogeneous counterpart of the homogeneous PDGEMM PBLAS routine. It can also be seen that the application programmers need not specify the process grid arrangement for the execution of the PBLAS routine as it is automatically determined. Apart from this, the only other major rewriting effort required is the redistribution of matrix data from the process grid arrangement used in the homogeneous PBLAS program to the process grid arrangement automatically determined by the heterogeneous PBLAS program. The matrix redistribution/copy routines (Dongarra *et al.*, 1995; Prylli and Tourancheau, 1996) provided by the ScaLAPACK package for each data type can be used to achieve this redistribution. These routines provide a truly general copy from any block cyclically distributed (sub)matrix to any other block cyclically distributed (sub)matrix.

9.2 HeteroPBLAS: SOFTWARE DESIGN

The software hierarchy of the HeteroPBLAS package is shown in Figure 9.3. The package can be downloaded from http://hcl.ucd.ie/project/Hetero ScaLAPACK. The building blocks are HeteroMPI, BLACS, PBLAS, and BLAS. The HeteroPBLAS context creation routines call the interface functions of HeteroMPI, which invoke the HeteroMPI run time. The HeteroPBLAS auxiliary functions of PBLAS, BLACS, and BLAS call the instrumented PBLAS, BLACS, and BLAS code shown in the software hierarchy diagram as IPBLAS, IBLACS, and IBLAS, respectively. The instrumented code reuses the existing code base completely. The only modifications are as follows: (a) replacement of the serial BLAS computation routines and the BLACS communication routines by calls to functions determining the number of arithmetical operations performed by each process and number of communications in bytes performed by a pair of processes, respectively, and (b) wrapping the parallel regions of the code in mpC **par** loops. An optimized set of BLACS for heterogeneous clusters and a well-defined interface of corresponding auxiliary functions will be provided in future releases of the software.

The first step in the implementation of the context creation routine for a PBLAS routine is the description of its performance model using a performance model definition language (PMDL). The performance model allows an application programmer to specify his or her high-level knowledge of the application that can assist in finding the most efficient implementation on heterogeneous clusters. This model allows the specification of all the main features of the underlying parallel algorithm that have an essential impact on

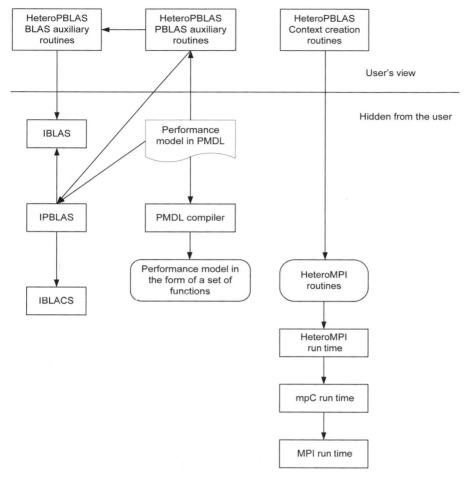

Figure 9.3. Heterogeneous PBLAS software hierarchy.

application execution performance on heterogeneous clusters. These features are as follows:

- The total number of processes executing the algorithm
- The total volume of computations to be performed by each of the processes in the group during the execution of the algorithm
    ∘ The volume is specified in the form of a formula including the parameters of the model
    ∘ The volume of computation is measured in computation units provided by the application programmer (the very code that has been used to characterize the performance of processors of the executing heterogeneous cluster)

- The total volume of data to be transferred between each pair of processes in the group during the execution of the algorithm
- The order of execution of the computations and communications by the parallel processes in the group, that is, how exactly the processes interact during the execution of the algorithm (which computations are performed in parallel, which are serialized, which computations and communication overlap, etc.)

The PMDL uses most of the features in the specification of network types of the mpC language (see Chapters 7 and 8). The mpC compiler compiles the description of this performance model to generate a set of functions that makes up the algorithm-specific part of the mpC runtime system. These functions are called by the mapping algorithms of mpC run time to estimate the execution time of the parallel algorithm. This happens during the creation of the context (the steps follow below).

The description of performance models of all the PBLAS routines has been the most intricate effort in this project. The key design issues were (a) accuracy to facilitate accurate prediction of the execution time of the PBLAS routine, (b) efficiency to execute the performance model in reasonable execution time, (c) reusability, as these performance models are to be used as building blocks for the performance models of ScaLAPACK routines, and (d) preservability, to preserve the key design features of the underlying PBLAS package.

The performance model definition of the PDGEMM PBLAS routine shown in Figure 9.4 is used to demonstrate the complexity of the effort of writing a performance model. It describes the simplest case of parallel matrix-matrix multiplication of two dense square matrices A and B of size $\mathbf{n} \times \mathbf{n}$. The reader is referred to Lastovetsky (2002, 2003) for more details of the main constructs, namely **coord**, **parent**, **node**, **link**, and **scheme**, used in a description of a performance model. This definition is an extensively stripped down version of the actual definition, which can be studied from the package. The data distribution blocking factor $\mathbf{b}$ is assumed to be equal to the algorithmic blocking factor. The performance model definition also assumes that the matrices are divided such that $(\mathbf{n}\% \ (\mathbf{b} \times \mathbf{p}))$ and $(\mathbf{n}\% \ (\mathbf{b} \times \mathbf{q}))$ (see explanation of variables below) are both equal to zero.

Line 1 is a header of the performance model declaration. It introduces the name of the performance model **pdgemm** parameterized with the scalar integer parameters $\mathbf{n}$, $\mathbf{b}$, $\mathbf{t}$, $\mathbf{p}$, and $\mathbf{q}$. Parameter $\mathbf{n}$ is the size of square matrices A, B, and C. Parameter $\mathbf{b}$ is the size of the data distribution blocking factor. Parameter t is used for the benchmark code, which is assumed to multiply two $\mathbf{t} \times \mathbf{b}$ and $\mathbf{b} \times \mathbf{t}$ matrices. Parameters $\mathbf{p}$ and $\mathbf{q}$ are output parameters representing the number of processes along the row and the column in the process grid arrangement.

Line 3 is a *coordinate declaration* declaring the 2D coordinate system to which the processor nodes of the network are related. Line 4 is a *node declaration*. It associates the abstract processors with this coordinate system to form

```
/* 1 */  algorithm pdgemm(int n, int b, int t, int p, int q)
/* 2 */  {
/* 3 */    coord I=p, J=q;
/* 4 */    node {I>=0 && J>=0: bench*((n/(b*p))*(n/(b*q))*(n*b)/(t*t));};
/* 5 */    link (K=p, L=q)
/* 6 */    {
/* 7 */       I>=0 && J>=0 && I!=K :
/* 8 */          length*((n/(b*p))*(n/(b*q))*(b*b)*sizeof(double))
/* 9 */                  [I, J]->[K, J];
/* 10 */      I>=0 && J>=0 && J!=L:
/* 11 */         length*((n/(b*p))*(n/(b*q))*(b*b)*sizeof(double))
/* 12 */                 [I, J]->[I, L];
/* 13 */   };
/* 14 */   parent[0,0];
/* 15 */   scheme
/* 16 */   {
/* 17 */     int i, j, k;
/* 18 */     for(k = 0; k < n; k+=b)
/* 19 */     {
/* 20 */       par(i = 0; i < p; i++)
/* 21 */         par(j = 0; j < q; j++)
/* 22 */           if (j != ((k/b)%q))
/* 23 */             (100.0/(n/(b*q))) %% [i,((k/b)%q)]->[i,j];
/* 24 */       par(i = 0; i < p; i++)
/* 25 */         par(j = 0; j < q; j++)
/* 26 */           if (i != ((k/b)%p))
/* 27 */             (100.0/(n/(b*p))) %% [((k/b)%p),j]->[i,j];
/* 28 */       par(i = 0; i < p; i++)
/* 29 */         par(j = 0; j < q; j++)
/* 30 */           ((100.0×b)/n) %% [i,j];
/* 31 */     }
/* 32 */   };
/* 33 */ };
```

Figure 9.4. Description of the performance model of the PDGEMM routine in the mpC's performance model definition language (PMDL).

a **p** × **q** grid. It specifies the (absolute) volume of computations to be performed by each of the processors. The statement **bench** just specifies that as a unit of measurement, the volume of computation performed by some benchmark code will be used. It is presumed that the benchmark code, which is used for estimating the speed of physical processors, multiplies two dense **t** × **b** and **b** × **t** matrices. The Line 4 of node declaration specifies that the volume of computations to be performed by the abstract processor with coordinates

(I,J) is **((n/(b × p)) × (n/(b × q)) × (n × b/t × t))** times bigger than the volume of computations performed by the benchmark code.

Lines 5–13 are *link declarations*. These specify the links between the abstract processors, the pattern of communication among the abstract processors, and the total volume of data to be transferred between each pair of abstract processors during the execution of the algorithm. Lines 7–9 of the link declaration describe vertical communications related to matrix A. Obviously, abstract processors from the same column of the processor grid do not send each other elements of matrix A. Only abstract processors from the same row of the processor grid send each other elements of matrix A. Abstract processor P_{IJ} will send **(n/(b × p)) × (n/(b × q))** number of **b × b** blocks of matrix A to processor P_{KJ}. The volume of data in one **b × b** block is given by **(b × b) × sizeof(double)** and so the total volume of data transferred from processor P_{IJ} to processor P_{KJ} will be **(n/(b × p)) × (n/(b × q)) × b × b × sizeof(double)**.

Lines 10–13 of the link declaration describe horizontal communications related to matrix B. Obviously, only abstract processors from the same column of the processor grid send each other elements of matrix B. In particular, processor P_{IJ} will send all its **b × b** blocks of matrix B to all other processors from column J of the processor grid. Abstract processor P_{IJ} will send **(n/(b × p)) × (n/(b × q))** number of **b × b** blocks of matrix B to processor P_{IL}. The volume of data in one **b × b** block is given by **(b × b) × sizeof(double)** and so the total volume of data transferred from processor P_{IJ} to processor P_{IL} will be given by **(n/(b × p)) × (n/ (b × q)) × b × b × sizeof(double)**.

Line 15 introduces the *scheme declaration*. The **scheme** block describes exactly how abstract processors interact during the execution of the algorithm. The scheme block is composed mainly of two types of units. They are computation and communication units. Each computation unit is of the form **e%%[i]** specifying that e percent of the total volume of computations is performed by the abstract processor with the coordinates **(i)**. Each communication unit is of the form **e%%[i]→[j]**, specifying the transfer of data from the abstract processor with coordinates **i** to the abstract processor with coordinates **j**. There are two types of algorithmic patterns in the scheme declaration that are sequential and parallel. The parallel algorithmic patterns are specified by the keyword **par**, and they describe the parallel execution of some actions (mixtures of computations and communications). The scheme declaration describes **(n/b)** successive steps of the algorithm. At each step **k**,

- Lines 20–23 describe vertical communications related to matrix A. **(100.0 × (n/b × q))** percent of data that should in total be sent from processor P_{IJ} to processor P_{KJ} will be sent at the step. The **par** algorithmic patterns imply that during the execution of this communication, data transfer between different pairs of processors is carried out in parallel.
- Lines 24–27 describe horizontal communications related to matrix B. **(100.0 × (n/b × p))** percent of data that should in total be sent from processor P_{IJ} to processor P_{IL} will be sent at the step.

- Lines 28–30 describe computations. Each abstract processor updates each its **b × b** block of matrix **C**, with one block from the pivot column and one block from the pivot row. At each of **(n/b)** steps of the algorithm, the processor will perform **(100 × b/n)** percent of the volume of computations it performs during the execution of the algorithm. The third nested **par** statement in the main **for** loop of the scheme declaration just specifies this fact. The **par** algorithmic patterns are used here to specify that all abstract processors perform their computations in parallel.

The simplest case of the PDGEMM PBLAS routine just described demonstrates the complexity of the task of writing a performance model. There are altogether 123 such performance model definitions covering all the PBLAS routines. They can be found in the HeteroPBLAS package in the directory /PBLAS/SRC. The performance model files start with prefix **pm_** followed by the name of the PBLAS routine and have a file extension mpc.

The execution of a HeteroPBLAS context creation routine consists of the following steps:

1. Updating the estimation of the speeds of the processors using the HeteroMPI routine **HMPI_Recon**. A benchmark code representing the core computations involved in the execution of the PBLAS routine is provided to this function call to accurately estimate the speeds of the processors. For example, in the case of the PDGEMM routine, the benchmark code provided is a local GEMM update of **m × b** and **b × n** matrices, where b is the data distribution blocking factor and **m** and **n**, are the local number of matrix rows and columns, respectively.

2. Finding the optimal values of the parameters of the parallel algorithm used in the PBLAS routine, such as the algorithmic blocking factor and the data distribution blocking factor, using the HeteroMPI routine **HMPI_Timeof**.

3. Creation of a HeteroMPI group of MPI processes using the HeteroMPI's group constructor routine **HMPI_Group_auto_create**. One of the inputs to this function call is the handle, which encapsulates all the features of the performance model in the form of a set of functions generated by the compiler from the description of the performance model of the PBLAS routine. During this function call, the HeteroMPI runtime system detects the optimal process arrangement and solves the problem of selecting the optimal set of processes running on different computers of the heterogeneous network. The selection process is described in detail in Lastovetsky (2002, 2003). It is based on the performance model of the PBLAS routine and the performance model of the executing heterogeneous cluster, which reflects the state of this cluster just before the execution of the PBLAS routine.

4. The handle to the HeteroMPI group is passed as input to the HeteroMPI routine **HMPI_Get_comm** to obtain the MPI communicator. This MPI

communicator is translated to a BLACS handle using the BLACS routine `Csys2blacs_handle`.

5. The BLACS handle is then passed to the BLACS routine `Cblacs_gridinit`, which creates the BLACS context. This context is returned in the output parameter.

The HeteroPBLAS program uses the multiprocessing approach, which allows more than one process involved in its execution to be run on each processor. The number of processes to run on each processor during the program start-up is determined automatically by the HeteroPBLAS command-line interface tools. During the creation of a HeteroMPI group in the context creation routine, the mapping of the parallel processes in the group is performed such that the number of processes running on each processor is as proportional to its speed as possible. In other words, while distributed evenly across parallel processes, data and computations are distributed unevenly over the processors of the heterogeneous network; this way each processor performs the volume of computations as proportional to its speed as possible. At the same time, the mapping algorithm invoked tries to arrange the processors along a 2D grid so as to optimally load balance the work of the processors.

9.3 EXPERIMENTS WITH HeteroPBLAS

Two sets of experiments with HeteroPBLAS are presented in this section. The first set of experiments is run on a homogeneous computing cluster "Grig" (https://www.cs.utk.edu/help/doku.php?id=clusters) consisting of 64 Linux nodes with two processors per node with Myrinet interconnect. The processor type is Intel EM64T. The software used is MPICH-1.2.7, ScaLAPACK-1.8.0, and Automatically Tuned Linear Algebra Software (ATLAS) (Whaley, Petitet, and Dongarra, 2001), which is an optimized BLAS library. Only 32 nodes (64 processors) are used in the experiments.

The speedup, which is shown in the figures, is calculated as the ratio of the execution time of the homogeneous PBLAS program and the execution time of the HeteroPBLAS program. Dense matrices of size $N \times N$ and vectors of size N were used in the experiments. The homogeneous PBLAS programs use the default parameters suggested by the recommendations from the ScaLA-PACK user's guide (Choi *et al.*, 1996a), which are as follows: (a) use the best BLAS and BLACS libraries available; (b) use a data distribution block size of 64; (c) use a square processor grid; and (d) execute no more than one process per processor. We chose two Level-3 routines, which are PDGEMM and PDTRSM, for demonstration because they exhibit two different algorithmic patterns. In the case of PDGEMM, the size of the problem solved at each step of its execution is constant, whereas in the execution of PDTRSM, the size of the problem decreases with each step.

The first set of experiments is composed of two parts. Figure 9.5(a)–(d) show the experimental results of the first part. Figure 9.5(a),(b) show the

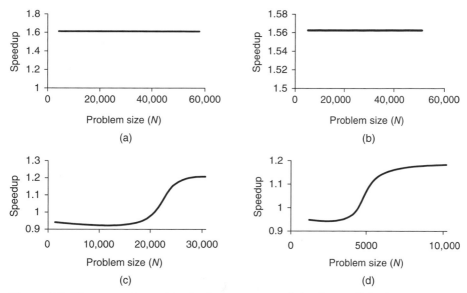

Figure 9.5. The network used is the homogeneous Grig cluster. N is the size of the vector/matrix. (a) Speedup of PDAXPY. (b) Speedup of PDGEMV. (c) Speedup of PDGEMM. (d) Speedup of PDTRSM.

experimental results from the execution of the PBLAS Level-1 routine PDAXPY and Level-2 routine PDGEMV on the homogeneous cluster. The homogeneous PBLAS programs use a 1×64 grid of processes (using a one-process-per-processor configuration).

Figure 9.5(c),(d) show the experimental results from the execution of the PBLAS Level-3 routines PDGEMM and PDTRSM, respectively. The homogeneous PBLAS program uses an 8×8 grid of processes (using a one-process-per-processor configuration).

In the second part, the optimal data distribution blocking factor and the optimal process grid arrangement, determined by the HeteroPBLAS program, were used in the execution of the corresponding homogeneous PBLAS program. From both parts, it was observed that there is no discernible overhead during the execution of HeteroPBLAS programs. The maximum overhead of about 7% incurred in the case of Level-3 routines occurs during the creation of the context. The execution times of HeteroPBLAS programs for Level-1 and Level-2 routines are the same if one process is executed per computer/node and not per processor. In the case of the first part, one can notice that the HeteroPBLAS programs perform better than the homogeneous PBLAS programs. This is because the homogeneous PBLAS programs use the default parameters (recommendations from the user's guide) but not the optimized parameters, whereas the HeteroPBLAS programs use accurate platform parameters and the optimal algorithmic parameters such as the optimal block factor and the optimal process arrangement. The parameters for

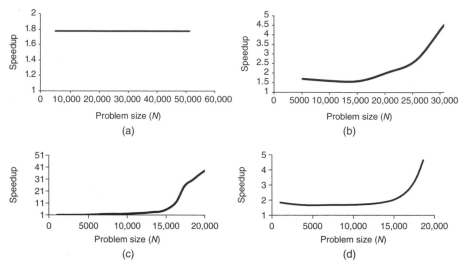

Figure 9.6. Experimental results on the heterogeneous cluster. N is the size of the vector/matrix. (a) Speedup of PDAXPY. (b) Speedup of PDGEMV. (c) Speedup of PDGEMM. (d) Speedup of PDTRSM.

the homogeneous PBLAS programs must be tweaked for a just comparison with the HeteroPBLAS programs, but this process is tedious and is automated by HeteroPBLAS, which is one of its advantages.

The second set of experiments is run on a small heterogeneous local network of sixteen different Linux workstations (hcl01–hcl16), whose specifications can be read at the URL http://hcl.ucd.ie/Hardware/Cluster+Specifications. As some of these workstations are dual-processor computers, 25 processors are used in the experiments. The network is based on 2-gigabit Ethernet with a switch enabling parallel communications between the computers. The software used is MPICH-1.2.5, ScaLAPACK-1.8.0, and ATLAS. The absolute speeds of the processors of the workstations, in megaflop/s, performing a local GEMM update of two matrices 3072×64 and 64×3072 are {8866, 7988, 8958, 8909, 9157, 9557, 8907, 8934, 2179, 5940, 3232, 7054, 6824, 3268, 3144, 3769}. Therefore, hcl06 has the fastest processor and hcl09 has the slowest processor. The heterogeneity of the network due to the heterogeneity of the processors is calculated as the ratio of the absolute speed of the fastest processor to the absolute speed of the slowest processor, which is 4.4.

Figure 9.6(a),(b) show the experimental results from the execution of the PBLAS Level-1 routine PDAXPY and Level-2 routine PDGEMV. The homogeneous PBLAS programs use a 1×25 grid of processes (using a one-process-per-processor configuration).

Figure 9.6(c),(d) show the experimental results from the execution of the PBLAS Level-3 routines PDGEMM and PDTRSM, respectively. The homogeneous PBLAS program uses a 5×5 grid of processes (using a one-process-per-processor configuration).

There are a few reasons behind the superlinear speedups achieved in the case of PDGEMM and eventually for very large problem sizes in the case of PDTRSM not shown in the figure. The first reason is the better load balance achieved through the proper allocation of the processes involved in the execution of the algorithm to the processors. During the creation of a HeteroMPI group of processes in the context creation routine, the mapping of the parallel processes in the group is performed such that the number of processes running on each processor is as proportional to its speed as possible. In other words, while distributed evenly across parallel processes, data and computations are distributed unevenly over the processors of the heterogeneous network; this way each processor performs the volume of computations as proportional to its speed as possible. In the case of execution of PDGEMM on the heterogeneous cluster, it can be seen that for problem sizes larger than 5120, more than 25 processes must be involved in the execution to achieve good load balance. Since only 25 processes are involved in the execution of the homogeneous PBLAS program, good load balance is not achieved. However, just running more than 25 processes in the execution of the program would not resolve the problem. This is because, in such a case, the optimal process arrangement and the efficient mapping of the process arrangement to the executing computers of the underlying network must also be determined. This is a complex task automated by HeteroMPI. The second reason is the optimal 2D grid arrangement of processes. During the creation of a HeteroMPI group of processes in the context creation routine, the function **HMPI_Group_auto_create** estimates the time of execution of the algorithm for each process arrangement evaluated. For each such estimation, it invokes the mapping algorithm, which tries to arrange the processes along a 2D grid so as to optimally load balance the work of the processors. It returns the process arrangement that results in the least estimated time of execution of the algorithm.

CHAPTER 10

Parallel Processing of Remotely Sensed Hyperspectral Images on Heterogeneous Clusters

In this chapter, we present research (Valencia *et al.*, 2008) conducted in the Neural Networks and Signal Processing Group at the University of Extremadura (Spain) in collaboration with the University College Dublin (UCD) Heterogeneous Computing Laboratory (HCL) (Ireland). The application described in the chapter is an example of a high-performance computing application that cannot be accommodated by traditional high-performance computer systems. The typical scenarios of the use of this application assume real-time processing of incoming images. One example is the processing of satellite images to monitor the real-time development of the situation on Earth (such as forest fires, floodings, air/water contaminations). In addition, the application is often interactive, for example, allowing the user to zoom the picture or change the monitoring properties. These types of scenarios are not suitable for the batch mode of execution, operated by traditional high-performance computer systems. Local clusters of workstations are a natural platform for applications requiring full control of the user over its execution.

10.1 HYPERSPECTRAL IMAGING: INTRODUCTION AND PARALLEL TECHNIQUES

Hyperspectral imaging identifies materials and objects in the air, land, and water on the basis of the unique reflectance patterns that result from the interaction of solar energy with the molecular structure of the material (Chang, 2003). Most applications of this technology require timely responses for swift decisions that depend on the high computing performance of algorithm analysis. Examples include target detection for military and defense/security deployment, urban planning and management, risk/hazard prevention and response (including wildland fire tracking), biological threat detection, and monitoring

---

High-Performance Heterogeneous Computing, by Alexey L. Lastovetsky and Jack J. Dongarra
Copyright © 2009 John Wiley & Sons, Inc.

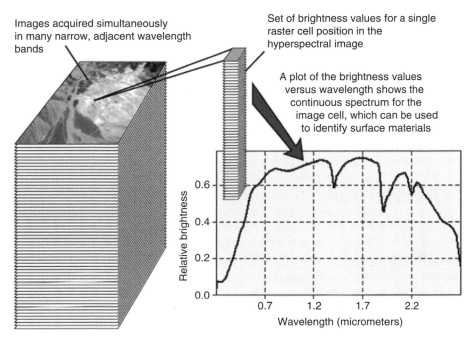

Images acquired simultaneously in many narrow, adjacent wavelength bands

Set of brightness values for a single raster cell position in the hyperspectral image

A plot of the brightness values versus wavelength shows the continuous spectrum for the image cell, which can be used to identify surface materials

Figure 10.1. The concept of hyperspectral imaging using the NASA Jet Propulsion Laboratory's AVIRIS system.

of oil spills and other types of chemical contamination. The concept of hyperspectral imaging was introduced when the Jet Propulsion Laboratory of the National Aeronautics and Space Administration (NASA) developed the Airborne Visible-Infrared Imaging Spectrometer (AVIRIS) system, which covers the wavelength region from 0.4 to 2.5 μm using 224 spectral channels (Fig. 10.1). This imager is able to continuously produce snapshot image cubes of tens, or even hundreds, of kilometers long, each of them with hundreds of megabytes (MB) in size; this explosion in the amount of collected information has rapidly introduced new processing challenges (Plaza *et al.*, 2006).

Despite the growing interest in hyperspectral imaging, only a few research efforts devoted to the design of parallel implementations currently exist in the open literature. It should be noted that some available parallel techniques are subject to nondisclosure restrictions, mainly due to their use in military and defense applications. However, with the recent explosion in the amount of hyperspectral imagery, parallel processing has now become a requirement in most remote sensing applications.

The utilization of parallel systems hyperspectral imaging applications has become more and more widespread in recent years. The idea of using commercial off the shelf (COTS) computer equipment, clustered together to work as a computational team (Brightwell *et al.*, 2000), was first explored to address the extremely high computational requirements introduced by Earth observation applications. This strategy, often referred to as Beowulf-class cluster computing, has already offered access to greatly increased computational power, but at a low cost (commensurate with falling commercial PC costs), in a number of remote sensing applications (Kalluri *et al.*, 2001; Wang *et al.*, 2002; Le Moigne, Campbell, and Cromp, 2002; Plaza and Chang, 2007). In particular, NASA is actively supporting massively parallel clusters for remote sensing studies, including those involving hyperspectral imagery. An example is Thunderhead, a 512-processor homogeneous Beowulf cluster at NASA's Goddard Space Flight Center in Maryland (see http://newton.gsfc.nasa.gov/thunderhead for details). Another example is the Columbia supercomputer at NASA Ames Research Center, a 10,240-CPU Silicon Graphics International (SGI) Altix supercomputer, with Intel Itanium-2 processors, 20 terabytes of total memory, and heterogeneous interconnects, including an InfiniBand network and 10-gigabit Ethernet.

Several hyperspectral imaging algorithms have been implemented in the system described above using the MPI as a standard development tool. Examples include the distributed spectral-screening principal component transform (S-PCT) algorithm (Achalakul and Taylor, 2003), which makes use of the principal component transform (PCT) to summarize and decorrelate the images by reducing redundancy and packing the residual information into a small set of images, termed *principal components*. The algorithm uses a standard master–slave decomposition technique, where the master coordinates the actions of the workers, gathers the partial results from them, and provides the final result. Another example of Beowulf cluster-based parallel algorithm in the literature is D-ISODATA (Dhodhi *et al.*, 1999), designed as the first parallel approach able to deal with the entire high-dimensional volume directly, thereby preserving all the spectral information in the data. It should be noted that the ISODATA classification procedure is widely regarded as a benchmark for most unsupervised classification algorithms (Richards and Jia, 2005).

A shortcoming of both S-PCT and D-ISODATA is that these algorithms rely on using the spectral information alone, without taking into account the spatial arrangement of pixels. Quite opposite, the hierarchical image segmentation algorithm (HSEG) (Tilton, 2001) has been recently proposed as a hybrid method that is able to use the spatial and the spectral information in the analysis of multichannel images. To counteract the extremely high computational complexity of the algorithm, a computationally efficient recursive approximation of HSEG (called RHSEG) was first developed and later transformed into an efficient MPI-based implementation by regularly allocating processing tasks among available CPUs (Tilton, 2007). Most recently, a morphological approach for the classification of hyperspectral images has been developed. The algorithm, called automated morphological classification (AMC), takes into account both the spatial and the spectral information in the analysis in combined fashion, as opposed to HSEG, which first uses spectral information to produce an initial segmentation and then refines the segmentation using spatial context. An MPI-based parallel version of the AMC has been developed and tested on NASA's Thunderhead cluster, showing parallel performance results superior to those achieved by other parallel hyperspectral algorithms in the literature (Plaza *et al.*, 2006).

Although most dedicated parallel machines for remote sensing data analysis employed by NASA and other institutions during the last decade have been chiefly homogeneous in nature (Dorband *et al.*, 2003), computing on heterogeneous networks of computers (HNOCs) has soon become a viable alternative to expensive parallel computing systems. These networks enable the use of existing resources and provide incremental scalability of hardware components. At the same time, HNOCs can achieve high communication speed at a low cost, using switch-based networks such as ATMs, as well as distributed service and support, especially for large file systems. Current remote sensing applications, constrained by the ever-growing dimensionality and size of the collected image data, can greatly benefit from this concept of distributed computing on HNOCs. Although the standard MPI has been widely used to implement parallel algorithms for HNOCs in the past, it does not provide specific means to address some additional challenges posed by these networks, including the distribution of computations and communications unevenly, taking into account the computing power of the heterogeneous processors and the bandwidth of the communication links. In this regard, HeteroMPI offers an excellent tool to develop parallel algorithms specifically adapted to heterogeneous platforms, and also to transform available parallel hyperspectral algorithms into efficient implementations for these systems. To achieve the latter goal, HeteroMPI only needs the programmer's description of the performance model of a parallel algorithm in generic fashion. This is a highly desirable feature in hyperspectral imaging applications, in which the main features of the underlying parallel algorithm have an essential impact on execution performance.

10.2   A PARALLEL ALGORITHM FOR ANALYSIS OF HYPERSPECTRAL IMAGES AND ITS IMPLEMENTATION FOR HETEROGENEOUS CLUSTERS

Morphological analysis has been recently introduced to analyze hyperspectral data sets (Soille, 2003; Plaza *et al.*, 2005). The morphological algorithm used in this work takes into account both the spatial and spectral information of the data in simultaneous fashion. Such spatial/spectral, hybrid techniques represent the most advanced generation of hyperspectral imaging algorithms currently available. The algorithm can be described as follows. Let f denote a hyperspectral data set defined on an L-dimensional (L-D) space, where N is the number of channels or spectral bands. The main idea of the algorithm is to impose an ordering relation in terms of spectral purity in the set of pixel vectors lying within a spatial search window or *structuring element* (SE) around each image pixel vector (Plaza *et al.*, 2005). To do so, a cumulative distance between one particular pixel $f(x,y)$, where $f(x,y)$ denotes an L-D vector at discrete spatial coordinates $(x,y) \in Z^2$, and all the pixel vectors in the spatial neighborhood given by a SE denoted by B (B-neighborhood) is defined as follows:

$$D_B[f(x, y)] = \sum_i \sum_j \text{SAM}[f(x, y), f(i, j)],$$

where (i, j) are the spatial coordinates in the B-neighborhood and SAM is the spectral angle mapper (Chang, 2003):

$$\text{SAM}(f(x, y), f(i, j)) = \cos^{-1}\left(\frac{f(x, y) \cdot f(i, j)}{\|f(x, y)\| \cdot \|f(i, j)\|} \right).$$

Based on this distance, the extended morphological erosion of f by B (Plaza et al., 2002) for each pixel in the input data scene is calculated as follows:

$$(f \ominus B)(x, y) = \arg\min_{(i,j)}\{D_B[f(x+i, y+j)]\},$$

where the **argmin** operator selects the pixel vector most highly similar, spectrally, to all the other pixels in the B-neighborhood. On the other hand, the extended morphological dilation of f by B (Plaza et al., 2002) is calculated as

$$(f \oplus B)(x, y) = \arg\max_{(i,j)}\{D_B[f(x+i, y+j)]\},$$

where the **argmax** operator selects the pixel vector that is most spectrally distinct to all the other pixels in the B-neighborhood. The inputs to the algorithm, called AMC, are a hyperspectral data cube f, a morphological SE with constant size of 3×3 pixels, B, a number of classes, c, and a number of iterations, $I_{\max}$. The output is a two-dimensional matrix that contains a classification label for each pixel vector $f(x, y)$ in the input image. The AMC algorithm can be summarized by the following steps:

1. Set $i = 1$ and initialize a morphological eccentricity index score $\text{MEI}(x,y) = 0$ for each pixel.
2. Move B through all the pixels of f, defining a local spatial search area around each $f(x,y)$, and calculate the maximum and minimum pixels at each B-neighborhood using dilation and erosion, respectively. Update the MEI at each pixel using the SAM between the maximum and the minimum.
3. Set $i = i + 1$. If $i = I_{\max}$, then go to step 4. Otherwise, replace f by its dilation using B, and go to Step 2.
4. Select the set of c pixel vectors in f with higher associated score in the resulting MEI image and estimate the subpixel abundance $\alpha_i(x,y)$ of those pixels at $f(x,y)$ using the standard linear mixture model described in Chang (2003).

5. Obtain a classification label for each pixel $f(x,y)$ by assigning it to the class with the highest subpixel fractional abundance score in that pixel. This is done by comparing all estimated abundance fractions $\{\alpha_1(x,y), \alpha_2(x,y), ..., \alpha_c(x,y)\}$ and finding the one with the maximum value, say $\alpha_{i*}(x, y)$, with $i* = \arg\left\{\max\limits_{1 \leq i \leq c}\{\alpha_i(x, y)\}\right\}$.

One of the main features of the algorithm above is the regularity in the computations. As shown in Plaza *et al.* (2006), its computational complexity is $O(p_f \times p_B \times I_{\max} \times N)$, where p_f is the number of pixels in f and p_B is the number of pixels in B. This results in high computational cost in real applications. However, an adequate parallelization strategy can greatly enhance the computational performance of the algorithm.

Two types of parallelism can be exploited in hyperspectral image analysis algorithms: spatial-domain parallelism and spectral-domain parallelism (Plaza *et al.*, 2006). Spatial-domain parallelism subdivides the image into multiple blocks made up of entire pixel vectors, and assigns one or more blocks to each processor. Spectral-domain parallelism subdivides the hyperspectral data into blocks made up of contiguous spectral bands (subvolumes), and assigns one or more subvolumes to each processor. The latter approach breaks the spectral identity of the data because each pixel vector is split among several processing units, and operations such as morphological erosion and dilation would need to originate from several processors, thus requiring intensive interprocessor communication. In this work, the spatial-domain parallelism is used in order to preserve the entire spectral information of each image pixel (Fig. 10.2). This

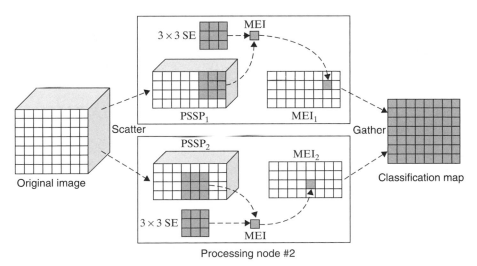

Figure 10.2. Example SE-based morphological computation performed using two processing units.

is a natural approach for low-level image processing, as many operations require the same function to be applied to a small set of elements around each data element present in the image data structure.

The parallel AMC algorithm uses a low-level image processing-oriented approach, in which each processor will be able to process a spatial/spectral data partition *locally*. A parallelizable spatial/spectral partition (PSSP) is defined as a hyperspectral data partition that can be processed independently at each processing node (Plaza *et al.*, 2006). Here, the concept of PSSP is used to define a virtual processor grid organization, in which processors apply the AMC algorithm locally to each partition, thus producing a set of *local* classification outputs that are then combined to form a *global* classification output. In order to adequately exploit the concept of PSSP, two important issues need to be taken into account:

1. An important issue in SE-based morphological image processing operations is that access to pixels outside the spatial domain of the input image is possible. This is particularly so when the SE is centered on a pixel located in the border of the original image. In sequential implementations, it is common practice to redirect such access according to a pre-defined border handling strategy. In our application, a border handling strategy is adopted when the location of the SE is such that some of the pixel positions in the SE are outside the input image domain (Fig. 10.3). In this situation, only those pixels inside the image domain are read for the MEI calculation. This strategy is equivalent to the common mirroring technique used in digital image processing applications, but slightly faster since fewer pixels are involved in the SE calculation.

2. Apart from the border handling strategy above, a communication overhead is introduced when the SE computation is split among several different processing nodes (Fig. 10.4). It should be noted that Figure 10.4 gives a simplified view. Depending on how many adjacent PSSPs are involved in the parallel computation of a SE, it may be necessary to introduce additional communication patterns. In this regard, it is

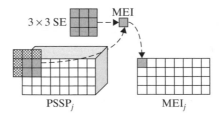

Figure 10.3. Border handling strategy implemented on a PSSP when pixels lying outside the input image domain are required for the SE-based morphological computation.

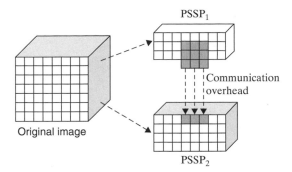

Figure 10.4. Communication overhead introduced for SE-based operation split among two adjacent processing nodes.

important to emphasize that the amount of redundant information introduced at each partition after the communication depends on the size of B, the SE used in the morphological operations.

The implemented versions of the AMC algorithm always use a constant 3×3-pixel SE through the different iterations. In other words, instead of increasing the size of the SE to consider a larger spatial neighborhood, the original image cube f or, equivalently, the local PSSP in parallel processing, is replaced by the resulting cube after applying a dilation operation using B (see Step 3 of the AMC algorithm). This allows us to perform multiscale analysis of the data without increasing significantly the communication overhead (Soille, 2003; Plaza *et al.*, 2005).

The presented parallel AMC algorithm is homogeneous, originally designed for the execution on homogeneous distributed memory systems. Correspondingly, its original MPI implementation assumes the one-process-per-processor configuration of the parallel application. The design of the parallel AMC application for HNOCs is based on the multiprocessing approach using the homogeneous AMC algorithm and the multiple-processes-per-processor configuration of the parallel application in order to balance the load of the heterogeneous processors. The heterogeneous AMC application automatically finds at run time the optimal mapping of its parallel processes to the heterogeneous processors of the executing HNOC. This design is implemented in HeteroMPI, and the major programming effort is the following description of the performance model of the parallel AMC algorithm in a generic parameterized form:

```
algorithm amc_perf (int m, int n, int se_size, int iter,
                    int p, int q, int partition_size[p*q])
{
    coord I=p, J=q;
```

```
    node { I>=0 && J>=0: bench*((partition_size[I*q+J]*iter);};
    parent[0,0];
}
```

where

- parameter m specifies the number samples of the data cube,
- parameter n specifies the number of lines,
- parameters se_size and iter, respectively, denote the size of the SE and the number of iterations executed by the algorithm,
- parameters p and q indicate the dimensions of the computational grid (in columns and rows, respectively), which are used to map the spatial coordinates of the individual processors within the processor grid layout, and
- finally, parameter partition_size is an array that indicates the size of the local PSSPs (calculated automatically using the relative estimated computing power of the heterogeneous processors using the benchmark function).

It should be noted that some of the definitions have been removed from the above code for simplicity. However, the most representative sections are included. Keyword **algorithm** begins the specification of the performance model, followed by its name and the list of parameters. The **coord** section defines the mapping of individual abstract processors performing the algorithm onto the grid layout using variables I and J. The **node** primitive defines the amount of computations that will be performed by each processor, which depends on its spatial coordinates in the grid as indicated by I and J and the computing power of the individual processors as indicated by partition_size, which is controlled by a benchmark function. Finally, the **parent** directive simply indicates the spatial localization of the master processor.

An important consideration in the performance model amc_perf described above is the nature of the benchmark function used as a baseline for the model definition. On the one hand, this function should be truly representative of the underlying application. On the other hand, the computations involved in such function should be small enough to give an accurate approximation of the processing power in a very short time (which, of course, depends on the particular application). In this work, the computation of the MEI index for a 3×3 SE (as described in Fig. 10.2) is adopted as the benchmark, which means that the benchmark function is Step 2 of the AMC algorithm described. The main reasons for this decision are as follows:

1. First and foremost, it should be noted that the AMC algorithm is based on repeatedly computing Step 2 (parameter I_{max} controls the total number

of iterations) and then assigns a classification label based on the estimated MEI score to each hyperspectral image pixel. Therefore, the use
of the core computations involved in Step 2 are truly representative of
the algorithm.

2. Second, the computation of the MEI index for a 3×3 SE prevents the
   inclusion into the performance model of border handling routines such
   as those depicted in Figures 10.3 and 10.4, which are only implemented
   for certain pixels, and thus are not fully representative of the algorithm's
   performance.

3. Third, it should be noted that the full computation of a 3×3 SE prevents
   the inclusion into the performance model of optimization aspects, such
   as the possible presence in the cache memory of pixels belonging to a
   certain SE neighborhood—centered, say, around a hyperspectral image
   pixel $f(x,y)$—and which would also be present in the SE neighborhoods
   centered around pixels that are spatially adjacent to $f(x,y)$ following
   eight-neighbor connectivity (Plaza *et al.*, 2006).

4. Finally, in order to properly model memory considerations associated to
   hyperspectral imaging applications, it is assumed in the computation of
   the benchmark function that the amount of data allocated to a single
   processor in the cluster is a full AVIRIS hyperspectral cube with 614×512
   pixels. The amount of data produced by the instrument in each pass is
   fixed (to 614×512 pixels with 224 spectral bands, each stored using 12
   bits). Since AVIRIS is the most advanced instrument of its kind, it has
   been adopted as a highly representative case study for the definition of
   the benchmark function. Therefore, this function assumes an unfavorable
   scenario in which each processor is forced to make use of reallocation/
   paging mechanisms due to cache misses. This approach allows us to
   realistically model the relative speed of heterogeneous processors by
   simply running a standardized core computation in hyperspectral image
   processing.

With the above considerations in mind, the performance model introduced
for AMC can be regarded as generic since it can be used to model any hyperspectral image processing algorithm that makes use of a sliding-window
approach to perform local computations in each pixel's neighborhood. In the
following subsection, we describe the communication pattern adopted for this
type of algorithm.

Once a heterogeneous set of data partitions has been obtained using the
performance model described in the previous subsection, a communication
framework among heterogeneous processors needs to be established. Figure
10.5 provides a graphical description of the communication framework adopted
in the application. As Figure 10.5(a) shows, the processors are arranged in a
virtual grid which, in the considered example, comprises 16 heterogeneous

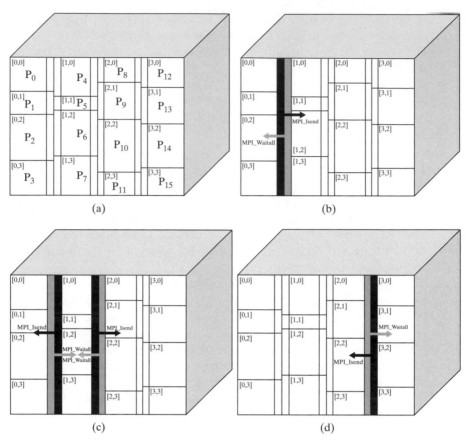

Figure 10.5. Communication framework for the parallel AMC algorithm. (a) Assignment of data partitions to a set of heterogeneous processors arranged in a 4×4 virtual processor grid; (b) Processors in leftmost column (column 0) first send their overlap borders to processors in column 1 and then wait for the overlap borders of processors in that column; (c) Processors in middle column (column 1) first send their overlap borders to processors in columns 0 and 2 and then wait for the overlap borders of processors in those columns; (d) Processors in rightmost column (column 3) first wait for the overlap borders of processors in column 2 and then send their overlap borders to processors in that column.

processors allocated into a 4×4 processor grid. The communication framework depicted in Figure 10.5 can be summarized by the following cases:

1. Processors located at the leftmost column of the grid. Processors located at the leftmost column first send all their overlap borders to the processors at the column located immediately to the right. Then, these

processors wait for the overlap borders that will be provided by the processors at the column immediately to the right (see Fig. 10.5(b)).

2. Processors located at an intermediate column of the grid. Processors located at an intermediate column first send all their overlap borders to the processors at the columns located immediately to the left and to the right. Then, these processors wait for the overlap borders that will be provided by the processors at the columns located immediately to the left and to the right (see Fig. 10.5(c)).

3. Processors located at the rightmost column of the grid. Processors located at the rightmost column first wait for the overlap borders that will be provided by the processors at the column immediately to the left. Then, these processors send all their overlap borders to the processors at the column located immediately to the left (see Fig. 10.5(d)).

The heterogeneity in communication patterns addressed above has been adopted on purpose in order to evaluate the best possible pattern to reduce the communication times. From Figure 10.5, it can be seen that an alternative communication pattern may consist of having processors located at even columns first send the overlap borders to the processors located at odd columns and then wait for the overlap borders provided by the processors at such columns, while the processors located at odd columns could first wait for the overlap borders provided by the processors located at even columns and then send the overlap borders to processors located at even columns. Specifically, the proposed communication pattern above has been adopted taking in mind the heterogeneous nature of the underlying hardware platform and the algorithm itself. The idea is that each processor communicates its part of the overlap border to the processors located at neighboring columns. There are several reasons for the above decision:

- First, the proposed communication framework simplifies the parallel algorithm design and alleviates the need to impose strong conditionals in the main loop of the parallel code in order to estimate the size of each particular communication for each particular processor. For instance, processor P_9 in Figure 10.5(a) would have to send its leftmost overlap border in chunks of different sizes to processors P_4, P_5, and P_6, respectively, and all these communications should be based on the processing power of each particular processor.

- Second, the proposed communication framework simplifies and enhances dynamic reconfiguration during execution, for example, by updating the processing power of each processor using the HMPI_Recon operation. This way, the amount of data to be computed and/or communicated at each heterogeneous partition can be dynamically adjusted.

- Finally, although other alternatives are indeed possible, the proposed approach favors the balance of communications and computations.

Once a performance model for the parallel AMC algorithm has been defined, implementation using HeteroMPI is quite straightforward, as shown by the main program below, which represents the most interesting fragment of the HeteroMPI code of the parallel implementation:

```
int main(int argc, char *argv[]){
  HMPI_Init(&argc,&argv);
  if(HMPI_Is_member(HMPI_COMM_WORLD_GROUP)){
    HMPI_Recon(benchmark, dims, 15, &output);
  }
  HMPI_Group_create(&gid, &MPC_NetType_amc_perf, modelp, num_param);
  if(HMPI_Is_free()){
    HMPI_Group_create(&gid, &MPC_NetType_hpamc_rend, NULL, 0);
  }
  if(HMPI_Is_free()){
    HMPI_Finalize(0);
  }
  if(HMPI_Is_member(&gid)){
    Tinit = MPI_Wtime();
    Communicator = *(MPI_Comm *)HMPI_Get_comm(&gid);
    if(&Communicator == NULL){
      HMPI_Finalize(0);
  }
    if(HMPI_Group_coordof(&gid,&dim,&coord) == HMPI_SUCCESS){
      HMPI_Group_performances(&gid, speeds);
      Read_image(name,image,lin,col,bands,data_type,init);
      for(i=imax; i>1; i=i--){
        AMC_algorithm(image,lin,col,bands,sizeofB,res);
        if(coord[0] == 0) { //First column in the virtual grid
          //MPI_Isend to send border to rightmost col
          //MPI_Waitall to receive border from rightmost col
        } else {
            if(coord[0] == p-1) { //Last col in the grid
              //MPI_Waitall to receive border from left col
              //MPI_Isend to send border to left col
            } else { //Any other case
                //MPI_Isend to send border to left col
                //MPI_Isend to send border to right col
                //MPI_Waitall to receive border from left col
                //MPI_Waitall to receive border from right col}
          }
          if (HMPI_Is_member(&gid)){
            free(image);}
            HMPI_Group_free(&gid);
            HMPI_Finalize(0);}
```

```
            }
         }
       }

   }
   }
   }
```

As shown by the piece of code above, the HeteroMPI runtime system is initialized using operation **HMPI_Init**. Then, operation **HMPI_Recon** updates the estimation of the performance of the processors. This is followed by the creation of a group of processes using operation **HMPI_Group_create**. The members of this group then execute the parallel algorithm. At this point, control is handed over to MPI. HeteroMPI and MPI are interconnected by the operation **HMPI_Get_comm**, which returns an MPI communicator with the communication group of MPI processes defined by `gid`. This is a local operation not requiring interprocess communication. The communicator is used to call standard MPI communication routines such as **MPI_Isend** and **MPI_Waitall**, following the communication pattern described in Figure 10.5. This is followed by freeing the group using operation **HMPI_Group_free** and the finalization of the HeteroMPI runtime system using operation **HMPI_Finalize**.

To conclude this section, it should be emphasized that HeteroMPI allows us to map our parallel application on a heterogeneous environment in accordance with the computational resources available from every single node. As a result, the amount of work in the AMC algorithm is distributed unequally among heterogeneous processors to balance the load. In other words, a HeteroMPI application is like any other MPI application and can be deployed to run in any environment where MPI applications are used (HeteroMPI applications can be run in environments where batch queuing and resource management systems are used). However, HeteroMPI uses its own measurements and performance models of the underlying system for running parallel applications efficiently. In this regard, it is important to note that the benchmark function used to measure the processing power of the processors in **HMPI_Recon** is essential, mainly because a poor estimation of the power and memory capacity of processors may result in load balancing problems (Plaza *et al.*, 2007). The effectiveness of the HeteroMPI implementation is addressed via experiments in the following section.

10.3 EXPERIMENTS WITH THE HETEROGENEOUS HYPERSPECTRAL IMAGING APPLICATION

Two heterogeneous clusters have been used for the experimental assessment of the HeteroMPI application. Table 10.1 shows the specifications of

TABLE 10.1 Specifications of Heterogeneous Processors in the HCL-1 Heterogeneous Cluster

Processor number	Name (processors)	Architecture description	CPU (MHz)	Memory (MB)	Cache (KB)	Relative speed
0, 1	Pg1cluster01(2)	Linux				
2, 3	Pg1cluster02(2)	2.4.18-10smp				
4, 5	Pg1cluster03(2)	Intel®	1977	1024	512	70
6, 7	Pg1cluster04(2)	Xeon™				
8	csultra01(1)					
9	csultra02(1)					
10	csultra03(1)	SunOS 5.8				
11	csultra05(1)	sun4u sparc	440	512	2048	30
12	csultra06(1)	SUNW,				
13	csultra07(1)	Ultra-5_10				
14	csultra08(1)					

processors in a heterogeneous cluster composed of 11 Linux/SunOS worksta-tions (15 processors) at the UCD HCL. From now on, we will refer to this platform as HCL-1.

The processors in Table 10.1 are interconnected via 100-megabit Ethernet communication network with a switch enabling parallel communications among the processors. Although this is a simple configuration, it is also a quite typical and realistic one as well. For illustrative purposes, Table 10.1 also reports the relative speeds of the heterogeneous processors in the cluster.

Another heterogeneous cluster, designated as HCL-2, was also used in the experiments (Table 10.2). It is made up of 16 nodes from Dell, IBM, and HP, with Celeron, Pentium 4, Xeon, and AMD processors ranging in speeds from 1.8 to 3.6 GHz. Accordingly, architectures and parameters such as cache and main memory all vary. Two machines have Small Computer System Interface (SCSI) hard drives, while the rest have Serial Advanced Technology Attach-ment (SATA). Operating systems used are Fedora Core 4 (11 nodes) and Debian (5). The network hardware consists of two Cisco 24 + 4-port gigabit switches. Each node has two gigabit Ethernet ports and the bandwidth of each port can be configured to meet any value between 8 KB/s and 1 GB/s (see http://hcl.ucd.ie/Hardware for additional details). Table 10.2 also reports the relative speed of each processor measured with the benchmark function (which took only 0.036 seconds to be executed in all cases). Figure 10.6(a) shows the Indian Pines AVIRIS hyperspectral data set considered in the experiments. The scene was collected by the AVIRIS sensor and is character-ized by very high spectral resolution (224 narrow spectral bands in the range 0.4–2.5 μm) and moderate spatial resolution (614 samples, 512 lines, and 20-m pixels). It was gathered over the Indian Pines test site in Northwestern Indiana, a mixed agricultural/forested area, early in the growing season. As shown by Figure 10.6(a), the data set represents a very challenging classification problem.

TABLE 10.2 Specifications of Heterogeneous Processors in the HCL-2 Heterogeneous Cluster

Processor number	Model description	Processor description	Operating system	CPU. (GHz)	Memory (MB)	Cache (KB)	HDD 1	HDD 2	Relative speed
0, 1	Dell Poweredge SC1425	Intel Xeon	Fedora Core 4	3.6	256	2048	240 GB SCSI	80 GB SCSI	7.93
2–7	Dell Poweredge 750	Intel Xeon	Fedora Core 4	3.4	1024	1024	80 GB SATA	N/A	7.20
8	IBM E-server 326	AMD Opteron	Debian	1.8	1024	1024	80 GB SATA	N/A	2.75
9	IBM E-server 326	AMD Opteron	Fedora Core 4	1.8	1024	1024	80 GB SATA	N/A	2.75
10	IBM X-Series 306	Intel Pentium 4	Debian	3.2	512	1024	80 GB SATA	N/A	6.13
11	HP Proliant DL 320 G3	Intel Pentium 4	Fedora Core 4	3.4	512	1024	80 GB SATA	N/A	6.93
12	HP Proliant DL 320 G3	Intel Celeron	Fedora Core 4	2.9	1024	256	80 GB SATA	N/A	3.40
13	HP Proliant DL 140 G2	Intel Xeon	Debian	3.4	1024	1024	80 GB SATA	N/A	7.73
14	HP Proliant DL 140 G2	Intel Xeon	Debian	2.8	1024	1024	80 GB SATA	N/A	3.26
15	HP Proliant DL 140 G2	Intel Xeon	Debian	3.6	1024	2048	80 GB SATA	N/A	8.60

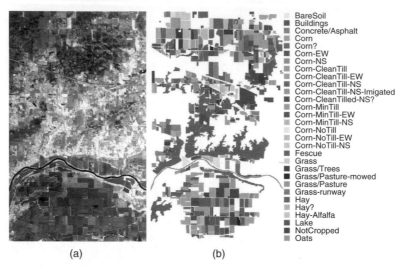

BareSoil
Buildings
Concrete/Asphalt
Corn
Corn?
Corn-EW
Corn-NS
Corn-CleanTill
Corn-CleanTill-EW
Corn-CleanTill-NS
Corn-CleanTill-NS-Imigated
Corn-CleanTilled-NS?
Corn-MinTill
Corn-MinTill-EW
Corn-MinTill-NS
Corn-NoTill
Corn-NoTill-EW
Corn-NoTill-NS
Fescue
Grass
Grass/Trees
Grass/Pasture-mowed
Grass/Pasture
Grass-runway
Hay
Hay?
Hay-Alfalfa
Lake
NotCropped
Oats

(a)   (b)

Figure 10.6. (a) Spectral band at 587 nm wavelength of an AVIRIS scene comprising agricultural and forest features at Indian Pines, Indiana. (b) Ground truth map with 30 mutually exclusive classes. (See color insert.)

The primary crops of the area, mainly corn and soybeans, were very early in their growth cycle with only about 5% canopy cover. Discriminating among the major crops under this circumstances can be very difficult, a fact that has made this scene a universal and extensively used benchmark to validate the classification accuracy of hyperspectral imaging algorithms. Fortunately, extensive ground truth (reference) information is available for the area. Figure 10.6(b) shows a ground truth map, given in the form of a class assignment for each labeled pixel with 30 mutually exclusive ground truth classes.

The parallel AMC algorithm was applied to the AVIRIS Indian Pines scene in Figure 10.6 using a fixed, 3×3-pixel SE and seven different values for parameter I_{max}, which defines the number of iterations executed by the algorithm (ranging from 1 to 7 in the experiments). Table 10.3 shows the classification accuracies (in percentage of correctly classified pixels) obtained using the seven considered numbers of iterations, along with the single-processor execution times (in minutes) measured in a Linux workstation with an Intel Xeon processor at 2 GHz, 1 GB of RAM and 512 KB of cache.

As shown in Table 10.3, the AMC algorithm was able to achieve very high classification accuracies, especially for $I_{max} = 7$ (above 90%), but the measured processing times were extremely high and are generally unacceptable in remote sensing applications, in which a response in (near) real-time is often required.

Table 10.4 shows the execution times (in seconds) of the HeteroMPI application in each of the processors of the heterogeneous cluster HCL-1. As shown in Table 10.4, the application was able to adapt efficiently to the heterogeneous computing environment where it was run. In particular, one can see that it was

TABLE 10.3   Classification Accuracies and Single-Processor Times for the AMC Algorithm

Iterations	1	2	3	4	5	6	7
Accuracy (%)	75.23	78.43	81.94	83.99	87.95	88.79	90.02
Time (minutes)	9.54	19.56	27.82	37.06	46.91	54.68	64.79

TABLE 10.4   Execution Times (in Seconds) of the HeteroMPI Application in Each of the Heterogeneous Processors of HCL-1 for Different Numbers of Iterations

Iterations	1	2	3	4	5	6	7
0	46.86	91.25	140.69	186.46	226.06	285.51	337.49
1	47.05	90.74	141.49	183.66	228.06	288.77	328.88
2	47.32	92.15	138.23	187.38	227.75	287.96	325.31
3	47.09	92.96	134.46	180.55	226.68	274.10	317.73
4	50.01	95.57	149.55	199.20	237.06	300.94	340.53
5	50.59	94.95	148.70	197.76	235.17	309.22	345.14
6	48.32	99.48	139.15	188.48	246.55	291.75	329.67
7	48.26	91.82	143.86	191.09	246.61	294.96	333.94
8	48.90	101.28	141.44	188.25	250.61	290.83	322.06
9	50.48	98.63	152.04	200.33	238.35	304.19	358.36
10	51.07	98.48	154.39	197.50	238.12	308.83	358.06
11	46.43	92.69	139.80	180.44	227.03	274.77	321.50
12	47.12	93.24	141.40	183.85	229.87	282.43	328.16
13	46.54	92.35	137.60	184.44	231.65	288.52	315.20
14	46.85	94.47	137.70	186.32	235.26	288.67	326.25

always about 11 times faster than the equivalent sequential application executed on a Linux workstation, which is almost identical to the **csultra** nodes in the considered heterogeneous cluster (see Table 10.1).

Most importantly, it was experimentally tested that the mean processing times in the eight Pg1cluster processors were almost identical to the mean processing times in the seven **csultra** nodes (for all considered problem sizes, i.e., number of iterations, ranging from $I_{max} - 1$ to $I_{max} = 7$). This fact reveals that the slight differences in the execution times reported in Table 10.4 are due to the intrinsic characteristics of the parallel problem and not to platform heterogeneity, which is accurately modeled by HeteroMPI.

In order to measure load balance, Table 10.5 shows the imbalance scores achieved by this application on the HCL-1 cluster. The imbalance is defined as $D = R_{max} / R_{min}$, where R_{max} and R_{min} are the maximum and minimum processor run times, respectively. Therefore, perfect balance is achieved when $D = 1$. It should be noted that the load balancing rates in Table 10.5 are even better than those reported in Plaza *et al.* (2006) for standard, spectral-based hyperspectral analysis algorithms executed in *homogeneous* computing platforms.

TABLE 10.5   Load Balancing Rates for the HeteroMPI Application Executed on HCL-1 with Different Numbers of Iterations

Iterations	1	2	3	4	5	6	7
R_{max}	46.43	90.74	134.46	180.44	226.06	309.22	358.36
R_{min}	51.07	101.28	154.39	200.33	250.61	274.10	315.20
D	1.09	1.11	1.14	1.11	1.10	1.12	1.13

TABLE 10.6   Processing Times (in Seconds) Measured at Each Processor of the HCL-2 Cluster for an Execution of the HeteroMPI Application with $I_{max} = 1$ and Different Numbers of Spectral Bands in the Considered AVIRIS Hyperspectral Scene

Processor	\multicolumn{4}{Number of spectral bands in the hyperspectral image}			
	120	140	160	180
0	14.02	16.73	19.09	21.45
1	14.02	16.74	19.09	21.46
2	13.98	16.67	19.03	21.39
3	14.03	16.74	19.11	21.47
4	13.98	16.69	19.04	21.41
5	14.01	16.72	19.10	21.46
6	13.99	16.70	19.05	21.41
7	14.03	16.74	19.11	21.47
8	13.99	16.72	19.08	21.42
9	13.97	16.67	19.02	21.39
10	14.00	16.70	19.07	21.44
11	13.95	16.65	19.00	21.37
12	12.72	16.71	19.06	21.40
13	12.71	16.68	19.04	21.42
14	12.72	16.70	19.07	21.44
15	12.71	16.68	19.05	21.40

The HeteroMPI application has been also run on the HCL-2 heterogeneous clusters, which provides a more heterogeneous environment than HCL-1 for the experiments. Table 10.6 reports the execution times (including both computations and communications) measured at each heterogeneous processor of the HCL-2 cluster after running the application with $I_{max} = 1$ and considering an increasing number of spectral bands for the 350×350-pixel scene (ranging from 120 bands to the maximum number of available bands in the scene, i.e., 180). In this example, the minimum possible number of algorithm iterations have been considered in order to reduce the ratio of computations to communications as much as possible, and thus be able to evaluate the impact of the communication pattern adopted for the algorithm.

TABLE 10.7 Processing Times (in Seconds) Measured at Each Processor of the HCL-2 Cluster for an Execution of the HeteroMPI Application with Different Numbers of Iterations (I_{max}) and the Full Spectral Information Available (180 Spectral Bands) in the Considered AVIRIS Hyperspectral Scene

Processor	Number of iterations					
	2	3	4	5	6	7
0	42.53	63.98	84.84	107.74	130.67	145.63
1	42.59	63.88	84.80	107.68	130.71	145.64
2	42.58	63.83	84.99	107.67	130.65	145.65
3	42.56	63.77	84.74	106.42	130.72	145.64
4	42.56	62.86	84.80	107.68	130.72	145.56
5	42.49	63.84	84.85	107.74	130.59	145.58
6	42.61	63.81	84.77	107.73	130.66	144.39
7	42.60	63.97	84.95	107.74	130.67	145.56
8	42.54	63.81	83.88	107.67	130.65	145.60
9	42.52	63.82	84.79	107.70	128.88	145.52
10	42.60	63.80	84.78	107.69	130.71	145.63
11	42.53	63.84	84.84	107.71	130.64	145.61
12	42.61	63.80	84.77	107.66	130.64	145.59
13	42.52	63.88	84.77	107.69	130.63	145.59
14	42.59	63.83	84.78	107.63	130.66	145.58
15	42.59	63.88	84.95	107.73	130.70	145.58

It should also be noted that the processing of hyperspectral images using, for the AMC algorithm and $I_{max} = 1$, only 120 out of 180 spectral bands represents a moderately interesting case study in hyperspectral imaging since the AMC algorithm has been shown to provide better classification results as the number of algorithm iterations is increased (see Table 10.3). In real applications, it is often desirable to use the full spectral information available in the hyperspectral data in order to be able to separate the classes more effectively, thus improving the final classification results. Table 10.7 reports the processing times (measured in seconds) at each processor of the HCL-2 cluster using $1 < I_{max} \leq 7$ iterations and all available spectral bands (180) in the considered AVIRIS Indian Pines scene. As shown in Table 10.7, the processing times reported for the 16 processors are well balanced in all cases, as was also observed in the experiments in the HCL-1 cluster (see Tables 10.4 and 10.5).

10.4 CONCLUSION

The heterogeneous hyperspectral imaging application presented in this chapter employs a very simple design and a very straightforward HeteroMPI implementation. This application can be improved in many ways. For example, the finding of the optimal values of the algorithmic parameters of the parallel

AMC algorithm could be included in the application. Another improvement could relax the assumption that each heterogeneous processor has a memory capacity sufficient to work with the entire hyperspectral data set without paging. While this is considered a reasonable assumption in most hyperspectral imaging scenarios (Plaza *et al.*, 2006), the experiments with some practically important problem sizes and realistic heterogeneous clusters have shown that not taking the possible paging into account can significantly increase the imbalance of the processor load for this application (Valencia *et al.*, 2008). Nonetheless, despite the simplicity of the application, the presented experimental results suggest that the implemented HeteroMPI-based approach is effective in terms of workload distribution, load-balancing rates, required interprocessor communications, and execution times. The case study reveals that the existing heterogeneous parallel computing technologies can be effectively used for designing and adapting existing high-performance hyperspectral imaging applications (mostly developed in the context of homogeneous computing platforms) to fully heterogeneous computing environments, which are currently the tool of choice in many remote sensing and Earth exploration missions. Combining this readily available computational power with the latest-generation sensor and parallel processing technology may introduce substantial changes in the systems currently used by NASA and other agencies for exploiting the sheer volume of the Earth and planetary remotely sensed data collected on a daily basis.

CHAPTER 11

Simulation of the Evolution of Clusters of Galaxies on Heterogeneous Computational Grids

A typical numerical simulation needs a lot of computational power and memory footprint to solve a physical problem with high accuracy. A single hardware platform that has enough computational power and memory to handle problems of high complexity is not easy to access. Grid computing provides an easy way to gather computational resources, whether local or geographically separated, that can be pooled together to solve large problems. GridRPC (Seymour *et al.*, 2002) is a standard Application Programming Interface (API) promoted by the Open Grid Forum that allows the user to smoothly design an application to interface with a grid environment. Currently, a number of grid middleware systems are GridRPC compliant, including GridSolve (YarKhan *et al.*, 2006), Ninf-G (Tanaka *et al.*, 2003), and the Distributed Interactive Engineering Toolbox (DIET) (Caron and Desprez, 2006). These systems are designed to achieve high performance in the execution of scientific applications by using a Grid environment.

A GridRPC middleware works by individually mapping the application's tasks to appropriate servers in the Grid and by communicating the data between the servers and the client computer. In the remote execution of a task, all its input data has to be communicated to the chosen server, and all the output data has to be communicated from it. Therefore, each remote task will cause some amount of data communication. Scientific applications that obviously benefit from the use of GridRPC consist of computationally intensive tasks consuming and producing relatively small amount of data. While best suited to run in a Grid environment, these applications are not representative of many real-life scientific applications. Unfortunately, they are typically chosen, or artificially created, to test and show the performance of GridRPC middleware systems.

We believe that to justify the use of GridRPC for a wide range of scientific applications, one should not use an extremely suitable application as a

High-Performance Heterogeneous Computing, by Alexey L. Lastovetsky and Jack J. Dongarra Copyright © 2009 John Wiley & Sons, Inc.

benchmark but rather a real-life application that shows the eventual limits and benefits of the GridRPC middleware system. Therefore, in this chapter, we present an application whose tasks have much more balanced a ratio between computation and communication, which is not biased in favor of computation. This application is Hydropad, an astrophysical application that simulates the evolution of clusters of galaxies in the universe. The Hydropad requires high-processing resources because it has to simulate an area comparable with the dimension of the universe and simultaneously try to achieve a high-enough resolution to show how the stars developed. In Section 11.2, we explain how the Hydropad can benefit from Grid enabling and execution on heterogeneous computational Grids and outline its GridRPC-based implementation. This is followed by experimental results obtained for the GridSolve version of the Hydropad, demonstrating that in many realistic situations, this GridRPC-based implementation will outperform the original sequential Hydropad. In Section 11.3, we briefly introduce SmartGridSolve (Brady, Guidolin, and Lastovetsky, 2008), a new middleware that extends the execution model of the GridRPC to overcome its limitations. This section also demonstrates that the SmartGridSolve can significantly improve the performance of the Hydropad, even in situations where GridSolve fails to do it.

11.1   HYDROPAD: A SIMULATOR OF GALAXIES' EVOLUTION

The Hydropad (Gheller, Pantano, and Moscardini, 1998) is a cosmological application that simulates the evolution of clusters of galaxies in the universe. The cosmological model on which this application is based has the assumption that the universe is composed of two different kinds of matter. The first is baryonic matter, which is directly observed and forms all bright objects. The second is dark matter, which is theorized to account for most of the gravitational mass in the universe. The evolution of this system can only be described by treating both components at the same time and by looking at all of their internal processes while their mutual interaction is regulated by a gravitational component (Hockney and Eastwood, 1981). Figure 11.1 shows an example of a typical output generated by the Hydropad.

The dark matter computation can be simulated using N-body methods (Hockney and Eastwood, 1981). These methods utilize the interactions between a large number of collision-less particles, N_p. These particles, subjected to gravitational forces, can simulate the process of the formation of galaxies. The accuracy of this simulation depends on the quantity of particles used. Hydropad utilizes a particle-mesh (PM) N-body algorithm, which has a linear computational cost, $O(N_p)$. In the first part, this method transforms the particles, through an interpolation, into a grid of density values. Afterward, the gravitational potential is calculated from this density grid. In the last part, the particles are moved depending on the gravitational forces of the cell where they were located.

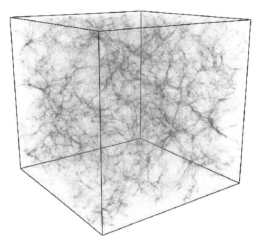

Figure 11.1. Example of a Hydropad output. (See color insert.)

The baryonic matter computation utilizes a piecewise parabolic-method (PPM) hydrodynamic algorithm (Colella and Woodward, 1984). This is a higher-order method for solving partial differential equations. The PPM reproduces the formation of pressure forces and the heating and cooling processes generated by the baryonic component during the formation of galaxies. For each time step of the evolution, the fluid quantities of the baryonic matter are estimated over the cells of the grid by using the gravitational potential. The density of this matter is then retrieved and used to calculate the gravitational forces for the next time step. The accuracy of this method depends on the number of cells of the grid used, N_g, and its computational cost is linear $O(N_g)$. The application computes the gravitational forces, needed in the two previous algorithms, by using the fast Fourier transform (FFT) method to solve the Poisson equation. This method has a computational cost of $O(N_g \log N_g)$. All the data used by the different components in the Hydropad are stored and manipulated in three-dimensional gridlike structures. In the application, the uniformity of these base structures permits easy interaction between the different methods.

Figure 11.2 shows the workflow of the Hydropad application. It is composed of two parts: the initialization of the data and the main computation. The main computation of the application consists of a number of iterations that simulate the discrete time steps used to represent the evolution of the universe, from the Big Bang to the present time. This part consists of three tasks: the gravitational task (FFT method), the dark matter task (PM method), and the baryonic matter task (PPM method). For every time step in the evolution of the universe, the gravitational task generates the gravitational field using the density of the two matters calculated at the previous time step. Hence, the dark and baryonic matter tasks use the newly produced gravitational forces

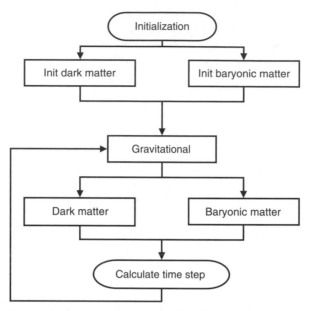

Figure 11.2. The workflow of the Hydropad application.

to calculate the movement of the matter that happens during this time step. Then the new density is generated and the lapse of time in the next time step is calculated from it. As shown in Figure 11.2, the dark matter task and the baryonic matter task are independent of each other.

The initialization part is also divided into two independent tasks. The main characteristic of dark matter initialization is that the output data is generated by the external application **grafic**, a module of the package Cosmological Initial Conditions and Microwave Anisotropy Codes (COSMICS) (Bertschinger, 1995). **Grafic**, given the initial parameters as an input, generates the position and velocity of the particles that will be used in the N-body method. The output data is stored in two files that has to be read by the application during the initialization part. Like the main application, **grafic** has a high memory footprint.

An important characteristic of the Hydropad is the difference in computational and memory loads of its tasks. Despite the linearity of both algorithms, the computational load of the baryonic matter component is far greater than that of the dark matter one, $C_{bm} \gg C_{dm}$, when the number of particles is equal to the number of cells in the grid, $N_p = N_g$. Furthermore, the quantity of data used by the dark matter computation is greater than that used by the baryonic matter one, $D_{dm} \gg D_{bm}$.

As previously indicated, the Hydropad utilizes three-dimensional grid structures to represent data. In the application code, these grids are represented as vectors. In the case of the dark matter component, the application stores the position and velocity in three vectors for each particle, one for each dimension. The size of these vectors depends on the number of particles, N_p, chosen to run in the simulation. For the gravitational and baryonic components, the different physical variables, such as force or pressure, are stored in vectors, with the size depending on the given number of grid cells, N_g. In a typical simulation, the number of particles is of the order of billions, while the number of cells in a grid can be over 1024 for each grid side. Given that for the values of $N_g = 128^3$ and $N_p = 10^6$, the total amount of memory used in the application is roughly 500 MB, one can see that the memory demand to run a typical simulation will be very high.

11.2 ENABLING HYDROPAD FOR GRID COMPUTING

GridRPC provides a simple remote procedure call (RPC) to execute, synchronously or asynchronously, a task in a Grid environment. GridRPC differs from the traditional RPC method since the programmer does not need to specify the server to execute the task. When the Grid-enabled application runs, each GridRPC call results in the middleware mapping the call to a remote server, and then the middleware is responsible for the execution of that task on the mapped server. As a result, each task is mapped separately and independently of other tasks of the application. Another important aspect of GridRPC is its communication model. For each task, the GridRPC middleware sends all the input data from the client machine to the remote server. Then, after the remote task has finished its execution, the middleware retrieves the output data back to the client machine. Therefore, remote execution of each task results in significant amount of data communicated between the client machine and the servers.

The Hydropad is not the ideal application for execution in a Grid environment because of the relatively low complexity of its tasks (log-linear at maximum) and the large amount of input and output data moved between tasks. Nevertheless, even such application can benefit from implementation in GridRPC.

The performance-related benefits include the potential for faster solution of a problem of a given size and solution of problems of larger sizes.

Faster Solution of a Given Problem. The Grid-enabled Hydropad has the potential to perform the simulations of the same given size faster than the original Hydropad on the client machine. There are two main reasons for this:

- The Hydropad application includes two independent tasks, the baryonic matter task and the dark matter task, that can be executed in parallel. The nonblocking GridRPC task call allows us to implement their parallel execution on remote servers of the Grid environment. This parallelization will decrease the computation time of the application.

• If the Grid environment contains machines more powerful than the client machine, then remote execution of the tasks of this application on these machines will also decrease the computation time of the application.

However, the decrease of the computation time does not come for free. The application will pay the communication cost due to the remote execution of the tasks. If communication links connecting the client machine and the remote servers are relatively slow, then the acceleration of computations will be compensated by the communication cost, resulting in the total execution time of the application being higher than in the case of its sequential execution on the client machine. For example, experiments with Hydropad in Section 11.2.2 show that with a 100 Mbit/s connection between the client machine and the servers, the Grid-enabled Hydropad is slower than the original serial one for simulations of smaller sizes. At the same time, for a 1 Gbit/s connection, the Grid-enabled Hydropad is always faster than its sequential counterpart. Thus, in many realistic Grid environments, the Grid-enabled Hydropad can outperform its original sequential version.

Solution of Larger Problems. The Grid-enabled Hydropad has the potential to perform larger simulations resulting in their higher accuracy. Indeed, the baryonic and dark matter tasks allocate temporary memory during their execution. Remote execution of these tasks will decrease the amount of memory used on the client machine as the temporary memory is now allocated on the remote machines. Therefore, within the same memory limitations on the client machine (say, the amount of memory that can be used by the application without heavy paging), the Grid-enabled Hydropad will allow for larger simulations.

The use of GridRPC for scientific applications does not only bring performance-related advantages. Other benefits related to the level of control over the application or development paradigm may be more difficult to notice but are equally important.

More Control over the Application. The Hydropad potentially can be executed not only in a Grid environment but also in a high-performance computer (HPC) system. Unfortunately, in an HPC system, where applications are executed in a batch mode, the user will not have much control over the execution. The Grid-enabled Hydropad allows the user to have high control over its execution because, although the tasks are being computed on remote servers, the main component of the application is running on the client machine. This can be important for many types of applications. The following are some examples:

• Applications that need a direct interaction with the data produced. For example, the user could visualize directly on the client machine the evolution of the universe while the Hydropad is running on the Grid. Furthermore, while the user is checking the simulation evolution, he could decide on the fly to change some parameters of the simulation or restart the application. This is possible since in the Grid-enabled Hydropad, the main data and the main execution are on the client machine.

- Applications that have a task that is inherently remote. For example, in the case of Hydropad, if **grafic** cannot be executed on the client machine because it needs a specific hardware, the user will have to generate the initial data on the remote server and then manually retrieve it. The use of GridRPC can simplify this situation by allowing a special task to interface with **grafic** directly on the remote server. This task can communicate immediately the initial data generated by **grafic** to the application.

An Easy and Powerful Development Paradigm. A numerical method, to be executed remotely, has to avoid internal state changes just as a function with isolated computation and no global variable does. This method of development creates tasks that have a specific interface for input/output values. Therefore, the GridRPC tasks can be easily reused in other Grid applications because their execution with the same input always produces the same output. This situation can reduce the programming effort on developing a Grid application. For example, programmers can use already existing tasks that they would not have the time or skill to write. Additionally, if the application needs to use tasks that are inherently remote because they are made of a proprietary code or bound to a specific hardware, such as **grafic** in the previous example, programmers can easily include them in the application.

11.2.1 GridRPC Implementation of the Hydropad

Hydropad was originally a sequential Fortran code (Gheller, Pantano, and Moscardini, 1998) that was upgraded (Guidolin and Lastovetsky, 2008) to take advantage of the GridRPC API and to work with the GridSolve middleware. The original code of the main Hydropad loop, written in the C language, looks as follows:

```
t_sim = 0;
while(t_sim < t_univ) {
  grav(phi, phiold, rhoddm, rhobm,…);
  if(t_sim==0)
    initvel(phi, …);
  dark(xdm, vdm, …, veldm);
  bary(nes, phi, …, velbm);
  timestep(veldm, velbm, …, t_step);
  t_sim += t_step;
}
```

Three functions, **grav**, **dark**, and **bary**, are called in this loop to perform the three main tasks of the application. In addition, at the first iteration of this loop, a special task, **initvel**, is called to initialize the velocities of the particles. The dark and baryonic matter tasks compute the general velocities of the respective matters. At each iteration, these velocities are used by a local function, **timestep**, to calculate the next time step of the simulation. The simulation will continue until this time becomes equal to the present time of the universe, $t_{sim} = t_{univ}$.

The GridRPC implementation of the Hydropad application uses the APIs **grpc_call** and **grpc_call_async** to execute a blocking and an asynchronous remote call of the Fortran functions, respectively. The first argument of both APIs is the handler of the task executed and the second is the session ID of the remote call, while the following arguments are the parameters of the task. Furthermore, the code uses the method **grpc_wait** to block the execution until the chosen, previously issued, asynchronous request has been completed. When the program runs, the GridSolve middleware maps each **grpc_call** and **grpc_call_async** function singularly to a remote server. Then, the middleware communicates the input data from the client computer to the chosen server and then executes the task remotely. At the end of the task execution, the output data is communicated back to the client. In the blocking call method, the client cannot continue the execution until the task is finished and all the outputs have been returned. Instead, in the asynchronous method, the client does not wait for the task to finish and proceeds immediately to execute the next code. The output of the remote task is retrieved when the respective wait call function is executed.

The following is the GridRPC implementation of the main loop of the Hydropad that simulates the evolution of universe:

```
t_sim = 0;
while(t_sim < t_univ) {
  grpc_call( grav_hndl, phiold,…);
  if(t_sim==0)
    grpc_call(initvel_hndl, phi, …);
  grpc_call_async(dark_hndl, &sid_dark, x1,…);
  grpc_call_async(bary_hndl, &sid_bary, nes,…);
  grpc_wait(sid_dark); /* wait for non blocking calls */
  grpc_wait(sid_bary); /* to finish */
  timestep(t_step, …);
  t_sim += t_step;
}
```

At each iteration of the loop, the first **grpc_call** results in the gravitational task being mapped and then executed. When this task is completed, the client proceeds to the next call, which is a nonblocking call of the dark matter task. This call returns after the task is mapped and its execution is initiated. Then, the baryonic matter call is executed in the same way. Therefore, the baryonic and dark matter tasks are executed in parallel. After this, the client waits for the outputs of both these parallel tasks using the **grpc_wait** calls.

11.2.2 Experiments with the GridSolve-Enabled Hydropad

In this section, the execution times and memory footprints of the GridSolve implementation of the Hydropad are compared against its sequential execution on the client machine. The hardware configuration used in the experiments consists of three machines: a client and two remote servers, S1 and S2. The two servers are heterogeneous; however, they have similar performance, 498 and 531 megaflops, respectively, and they have an equal amount of main memory, 1 GB each. The client machine is a computer with low hardware specifications, 256 MB of memory and 248 megaflops of performance, which is not suitable to perform large simulation. The bandwidth of the communication link between the two servers is 1 Gbit/s. The client-to-servers connection varies, depending on the experimental setup. We use two setups, client machine C1 with a 1 Gbit/s connection and client machine C2 with a 100 Mbit/s connection. These hardware configurations represent a situation when a user having a relatively weak computer can access more powerful machines. For each conducted simulation, Table 11.1 shows the initial problem parameters and the corresponding data sizes (the total memory used during the execution of the Hydropad on a single machine).

Table 11.2 shows the average execution time of simulation of one evolution step achieved by the local computation on the client machine and by the GridSolve version of the Hydropad. The experiments used C1 as the client machine. This machine has a fast network link to the servers S1 and S2. This table also presents the scale of paging that occurs in the client machine during the executions. One can see that for the local computation, the paging occurs when the problem size is equal or greater than the main memory, 256 MB. At the same time, for the GridSolve version, the paging begins later when the

TABLE 11.1   Input Values and Problem Sizes for the Hydropad Experiments

Problem ID	N_p	N_g	Data size (MB)
P1	120^3	60^3	73
P2	140^3	80^3	142
P3	160^3	80^3	176
P4	140^3	100^3	242
P5	160^3	100^3	270
P6	180^3	100^3	313
P7	200^3	100^3	340
P8	220^3	120^3	552
P9	240^3	120^3	624

TABLE 11.2   Results of Experiments Using Client C1 with 1 Gbit/s Connection to Servers

	Local		GridSolve		
Problem ID	Time step (seconds)	Paging	Time step (seconds)	Paging	Speedup
P1	14.09	No	7.20	No	1.96
P2	29.95	No	15.51	No	1.93
P3	35.29	No	16.48	No	2.14
P4	55.13	Light	29.11	No	2.14
P5	61.63	Light	29.07	No	2.12
P6	83.66	Yes	36.74	Light	2.28
P7	128.55	Yes	48.06	Yes	2.67
P8	227.89	Heavy	77.91	Heavy	2.92
P9	280.07	Heavy	91.75	Heavy	3.06

problem size is around 310 MB. The GridRPC implementation can save memory (thanks to the temporary data allocated remotely in the tasks), and hence increase the problem size that will not cause the paging.

In the sequential local execution, the paging is taking place during a task computation, while for the GridSolve version the paging occurs during a remote task data communication. Hence, for the Grid-enabled Hydropad, the paging on the client machine does not negatively affect the execution time of the experiments. The results in Table 11.2 show that the speedup obtained by GridSolve is around 2 until the client machine starts paging, then the local computation receives a heavy penalty from the paging. Figure 11.3 shows the execution times of the evolution step for the local computation and for the GridSolve version of the Hydropad.

Table 11.3 shows the results obtained by the GridSolve version when the client machine used, C2, has a slow client-to-server connection, 100 Mbit/s. The GridSolve version is slower than the local computation when the client machine is not paging. This is happening since there is a large amount of data communication between tasks. So, for this configuration, the time spent by communicating the data compensates the time gained due to computing tasks remotely. However, as the problem size gets larger and the client machine starts paging, the GridSolve version is getting faster than the local computation, even in the case of slow communication between the client and server machines.

11.3 SMARTGRIDSOLVE AND HYDROPAD

In this section, we briefly introduce SmartGridSolve (Brady, Guidolin, and Lastovetsky, 2008), whose early version was implemented as SmartNetSolve

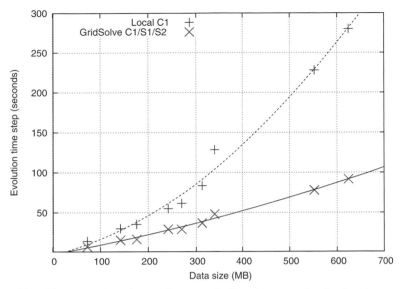

Figure 11.3. The execution times of one evolution time step by the local sequential simulation and by the GridSolve simulation, with client C1 having 1 Gbit/s connection to servers S1 and S2.

TABLE 11.3   Results of Experiments Using Client C2 with 100 Mbit/s Connection to the Servers

	Local		GridSolve		
Problem ID	Time step (seconds)	Paging	Time step (seconds)	Paging	Speedup
P1	14.09	No	18.01	No	0.78
P2	29.95	No	35.02	No	0.86
P3	35.29	No	43.09	No	0.82
P4	55.13	Light	55.66	No	0.97
P5	61.63	Light	58.17	No	1.06
P6	83.66	Yes	72.50	Light	1.15
P7	128.55	Yes	80.05	Yes	1.61
P8	227.89	Heavy	133.47	Heavy	1.71
P9	280.07	Heavy	155.36	Heavy	1.81

(Brady, Konstantinov, and Lastovetsky, 2006). SmartGridSolve is an extension of GridSolve that has been designed to bypass the limitations of the GridRPC model of execution. The GridRPC implementation of the Hydropad has some advantages over the sequential local computation; however, it is evident that the model of execution utilized by the GridRPC is not optimal. In a GridRPC system, all tasks are mapped individually. The mapper will always choose the fastest available server at the instant a task is called, regardless of the computational size of the task and regardless of whether the task is to be executed sequentially or in parallel.

A drawback of this behavior is highlighted by the Hydropad application. The parallel tasks in the Hydropad are not computationally balanced. The baryonic matter task is computationally far larger than the dark matter one, $C_{bm} \gg C_{dm}$. When a GridRPC system goes to map these two tasks, it does so without the knowledge that they are part of a group to be executed in parallel. Its only goal is to minimize the execution time of an individual task as it is called by the application. If the smaller dark matter task is called first, it will be mapped to the fastest available server. With the fastest server occupied, the larger baryonic task will then be mapped to a slower server, and the overall execution time of the group of tasks will be nonoptimal.

Another constraint of the GridRPC model that influences the performance of the Hydropad or any other application is that all the data computed remotely and communicated between remote tasks has to pass through the client machine. Servers computing tasks with data dependencies on each other cannot communicate with each other directly. The application programmer can try to avoid this issue by implementing data caching in the tasks. However, it requires the programmer to make heavy modification to the tasks, and this is a clear drawback. It also means that remote tasks passing data to each other must all run on the same server where the data they need is cached.

SmartGridSolve addresses all these issues. It expands the single task map and client–server model of the GridRPC by implementing the mapping of groups of tasks, the automatic data caching on servers, and the server-to-server communication. Collective mapping of groups of tasks, using a fully connected network, allows the SmartGridSolve to find an optimal mapping solution for an application that fully exploits a Grid environment. Furthermore, the direct server-to-server communication and automatic data caching that the Smart-GridSolve implements minimize the amount of memory used on the client and the volume of communication necessary between the client and the server. Data objects can reside only on the servers where they are needed, and they can be moved directly between servers without having to pass through the client. The main goal of the SmartGridSolve is to provide these functionalities to the user in a practical and simple way. To achieve this, it requires only minor changes and additions to the APIs of the GridRPC. The application programmer can gain from the improved performance using the SmartGridSolve by making only minor modifications to any application that is already GridRPC enabled.

11.3.1   SmartGridSolve Implementation of the Hydropad

The following code shows the modifications required to use the new Smart-GridSolve features in the Hydropad:

```
t_sim = 0;
while(t_sim < t_univ) {
  gs_smart_map("ex_map") {
    grpc_call( grav_hndl, phiold,…);
    if(t_sim==0)
      grpc_call(initvel_hndl, phi, …);
    grpc_call_async(dark_hndl, &sid_dark, x1,…);
    grpc_call_async(bary_hndl, &sid_bary, nes,…);
    grpc_wait(sid_dark); /* wait for non blocking calls */
    grpc_wait(sid_bary); /* to finish */
    if(gs_smart_local_region() {
      timestep(t_step, …);
      t_sim += t_step;
    }
  }
}
```

One can see that the difference between the examples is the minor additions of: the **gs_smart_map** block and the **gs_smart_local_region** condition. These belong to the SmartGridSolve API.

The code enclosed in the **gs_smart_map** block will be iterated through twice. On the first iteration, each **grpc_call** and **grpc_call_async** is discovered but not executed. At the beginning of the second iteration, when all the tasks within the scope of the block have been discovered, a task graph for them is generated. The discovered tasks are then executed remotely using this task graph to aid their mapping. The **gs_smart_local_region** function, in conjunction with a conditional statement, is used by the application programmer to indicate when a local computation is executed. At run time on the first discovery iteration, the code within this conditional statement is not executed. This is to mimic the behavior that the remote calls have on the discovering iteration. On the second iteration, the code inside the statement is executed normally.

The mapping in this SmartGridSolve code is performed at every iteration of the main loop; this can generate a good mapping solution if the Grid environment is not a stable one. For example, where there are other applications' tasks running on the Grid servers. If the Grid environment is dedicated, where only one application executes at a time, a better mapping solution may be generated if the area to map contains more tasks, that is, two or more loop cycles. A simple solution could be including an inner loop within the **gs_smart_map** code block. The application programmer could increase the number of tasks mapped together by increasing the number of iterations of the inner loop.

11.3.2 Experiments with the SmartGridSolve-Enabled Hydropad

In this section, the results obtained for the SmartGridSolve version of the Hydropad are compared with those for the GridSolve and local versions

TABLE 11.4 Results of Experiments Using Client C2 with 100 Mbit/s Connection to the Servers

Problem ID	Local		GridSolve			SmartGridSolve			
	Time step (seconds)	Paging	Time step (seconds)	Paging	Speedup over Local	Time step (seconds)	Paging	Speedup over Local	Speedup over GridSolve
P1	14.09	No	18.01	No	0.78	7.9	No	1.78	2.28
P2	29.95	No	35.02	No	0.86	15.68	No	1.91	2.75
P3	35.29	No	43.09	No	0.82	17.36	No	2.03	2.48
P4	55.13	Light	55.66	No	0.97	28.56	No	1.93	1.98
P5	61.63	Light	58.17	No	1.06	28.77	No	2.14	2.02
P6	83.66	Yes	72.50	Light	1.15	30.09	No	2.78	2.41
P7	128.55	Yes	80.05	Yes	1.61	31.63	Light	4.06	2.53
P8	227.89	Heavy	133.47	Heavy	1.71	52.30	Light	4.36	2.55
P9	280.07	Heavy	155.36	Heavy	1.81	55.47	Light	5.06	2.80

TABLE 11.5 Results of Experiments Using Client C1 with 1 Gbit/s Connection to the Servers

Problem ID	Local		GridSolve				SmartGridSolve			
	Time step (seconds)	Paging	Time step (seconds)	Paging	Speedup over Local		Time step (seconds)	Paging	Speedup over Local	Speedup over GridSolve
P1	14.09	No	7.20	No	1.96		6.99	No	2.02	1.03
P2	29.95	No	15.51	No	1.93		14.69	No	2.04	1.06
P3	35.29	No	16.48	No	2.14		15.52	No	2.27	1.06
P4	55.13	Light	29.11	No	2.14		27.22	No	2.03	1.07
P5	61.63	Light	29.07	No	2.12		27.13	No	2.27	1.07
P6	83.66	Yes	36.74	Light	2.28		27.22	No	3.07	1.35
P7	128.55	Yes	48.06	Yes	2.67		29.13	Light	4.41	1.65
P8	227.89	Heavy	77.91	Heavy	2.92		49.21	Light	4.63	1.58
P9	280.07	Heavy	91.75	Heavy	3.06		50.82	Light	5.52	1.81

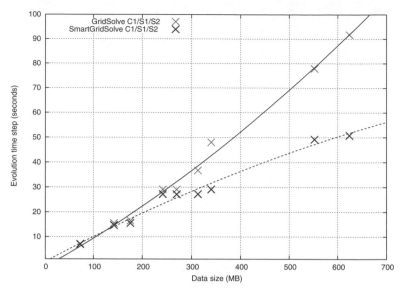

Figure 11.4. Execution times of the GridSolve and SmartGridSolve versions of the Hydropad.

(shown in Section 11.2.2). The problem sizes utilized in the experiments (Table 11.1) and the hardware configurations are the same as in previous experiments. As mentioned before, one of the primary improvements of the SmartGrid-Solve is its communication model, the use of which minimizes the amount of data movement between the client and servers. This advantage is most prominent when the client connection to the Grid environment is slow.

Table 11.4 shows the results of experiments using C2 as the client machine, which has a slow network connection of 100 Mbit/s, to servers S1 and S2. One can see that the SmartGridSolve version is much faster than the GridSolve and the sequential versions. The speedup over GridSolve is over 2 times, this is primarily due to the improved communication model of the SmartGridSolve.

Another important feature of the SmartGridSolve is the superior mapping system. Table 11.5 shows the results of experiments using C1 as the client machine. This machine has a faster network connection of 1 Gbit/s. The results show the performance gains obtained due to the improved mapping method. The advantage gained by using the communication model of the SmartGrid-Solve is minimized by the faster communication links (experiments with a single server were performed to confirm this). Despite the Hydropad having only two parallel tasks, the SmartGridSolve mapper can produce faster execution than the GridSolve one.

A secondary advantage of the direct server-to-server communication implemented by the SmartGridSolve is that the amount of memory used on the client machine will be lower than that for the GridSolve version. Therefore, the SmartGridSolve version of the Hydropad can execute larger problems without paging on the client machine. This can influence the execution time for lager problems as shown in Table 11.5. The speedup of SmartGridSolve over GridSolve, when the client machine pages, increases as the problem gets larger. This trend is also seen in Figure 11.4.

11.4 ACKNOWLEDGMENT

The sequential Hydropad was originally developed by Claudio Gheller. The Grid-enabled Hydropad is an application developed in the UCD Heterogeneous Computing Laboratory and is freely available at http://hcl.ucd.ie. The authors would like to thank Michele Guidolin for his contribution to the material presented in this chapter.

PART V

FUTURE TRENDS

CHAPTER 12

Future Trends in Computing

12.1 INTRODUCTION

In the last 50 years, the field of scientific computing has undergone rapid change—we have experienced a remarkable turnover of technologies, architectures, vendors, and usage of systems. Despite all these changes, the long-term evolution of performance seems to be steady and continuous, following Moore's law rather closely. In Figure 12.1, we plot the peak performance over the last five decades of computers that have been called "supercomputers." A broad definition for a supercomputer is that it is one of the fastest computers currently available. They are systems that provide significantly greater sustained performance than that available from mainstream computer systems. The value of supercomputers derives from the value of the problems they solve, not from the innovative technology they showcase. By performance we mean the rate of execution for floating-point operations. Here we chart kiloflop/s (thousands of floating-point operations per second), megaflop/s (millions of floating-point operations per second), gigaflop/s (billions of floating-point operations per second), teraflop/s (trillions of floating-point operations per second), and petaflop/s (1000 trillions of floating-point operations per second). This chart clearly shows how well Moore's law has held over almost the complete life span of modern computing—we see an increase in performance averaging two orders of magnitude every decade.

In the second half of the 1970s, the introduction of vector computer systems marked the beginning of modern supercomputing. A vector computer or vector processor is a machine designed to efficiently handle arithmetic operations on elements of arrays, called vectors. These systems offered a performance advantage of at least one order of magnitude over conventional systems of that time. Raw performance was the main, if not the only, selling point for supercomputers of this variety. However, in the first half of the 1980s, the integration of vector systems into conventional computing environments became more important. Only those manufacturers that provided standard programming environments, operating systems, and key applications were

---

High-Performance Heterogeneous Computing, by Alexey L. Lastovetsky and Jack J. Dongarra
Copyright © 2009 John Wiley & Sons, Inc.

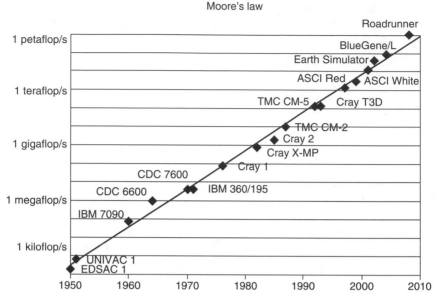

Figure 12.1. Moore's law and peak performance of various computers over time.

successful in securing industrial customers, who became essential for the manufacturers' survival in the marketplace. Performance was increased primarily by improved chip technologies and by producing shared memory multiprocessor systems, sometimes referred to as symmetric multiprocessors or SMPs. An SMP is a computer system that has two or more processors connected in the same cabinet, managed by one operating system, sharing the same memory, and having equal access to input/output (I/O) devices. Application programs may run on any or all processors in the system; assignment of tasks is decided by the operating system. One advantage of SMP systems is scalability; additional processors can be added as needed up to some limiting factor determined by the rate at which data can be sent to and from memory.

Fostered by several government programs, scalable parallel computing using distributed memory became the focus of interest at the end of the 1980s. A distributed memory computer system is one in which several interconnected computers share the computing tasks assigned to the system. Overcoming the hardware scalability limitations of shared memory was the main goal of these new systems. The increase in performance of standard microprocessors after the reduced instruction set computer (RISC) revolution, together with the cost advantage of large-scale parallelism, formed the basis for the "Attack of the Killer Micros." The transition from emitted coupled logic (ECL) to complementary metal-oxide semiconductor (CMOS) chip technology and the usage of "off the shelf" commodity microprocessors instead of custom processors for massively parallel processors (MPPs) was the consequence. The strict definition of MPP is a machine with many interconnected processors, where "many" is dependent on the state of the art. Currently, the majority of high-end machines have fewer than 256 processors, with the most on the order of 10,000 processors. A more practical definition of an MPP is a machine whose architecture is capable of having many processors—that is, it is scalable. In particular, machines with a distributed memory design (in comparison with shared memory designs) are usually synonymous with MPPs since they are not limited to a certain number of processors. In this sense, "many" is a number larger than the current largest number of processors in a shared memory machine.

12.2 COMPUTATIONAL RESOURCES

12.2.1 Complex and Heterogeneous Parallel Systems

Parallelism is a primary method for accelerating the total power that can be applied to any problem. That is, in addition to continuing to develop the performance of a technology, multiple copies are deployed, which provide some of the advantages of an improvement in raw performance, but not all. Of course, for the commercial side of the house, increased volume (aka commodity market) has its own reward. The SMP provided a straightforward environment for accessing moderate levels of parallelism. However, requirements for more memory (accuracy) and more speed (response time) drove systems beyond the point at which SMPs could maintain their flat memory architecture. Another simple model of computation is data parallelism, an intuitive programming standard for many physical problems defined on $R^3 \times t$. Systems and languages (e.g., CM-5, CM Fortran) that implemented this model were easily mastered by both computer and computational scientists.

Employing parallelism to solve large-scale problems is not without its price. While a flat memory address space, represented in hardware by SMPs and in software by data parallelism, is an appealing concept, the complexity of building parallel computers with thousands of processors to solve real-world problems requires a hierarchical approach—associating memory closely with CPUs. Consequently, the central problem faced by parallel codes is managing a complex memory hierarchy, ranging from local registers to far-distant processor memories. It is the communication of data and the coordination of processes within this hierarchy that represent the principal hurdles to effective, correct, and widespread acceptance of parallel computing. Thus, today's parallel computing environment has architectural complexity layered upon a multiplicity of processors. Scalability, the ability for hardware and software to maintain reasonable efficiency as the number of processors is increased, is the key metric.

The future will be more complex yet. Distinct computer systems will be networked together into the most powerful systems on the planet. The pieces of this composite whole will be distinct in hardware (e.g., CPUs), software (e.g., operating system [OS]), and operational policy (e.g., security). This future is most apparent when we consider geographically distributed computing on the computational grid. However, heterogeneity also has its advantages for concentrated computing within a single computer center. The fact is that there are fundamental difficulties inherent in the acquisition of large monolithic systems when the procurement lasts longer than the doubling time of the technology itself. Progress toward even more complexity in hardware platforms will paradoxically also drive broad uniformity in software environments and will drive the community toward recognition that the software framework, not the hardware, must define the computing environment. This increased complexity has at least one interesting side effect—superlinear speedup is possible on heterogeneous systems, provided the architectural diversity is sufficiently rich.

12.2.2   Intel-ization of the Processor Landscape

The High Performance Computing (HPC) community had already started to use commodity parts in large numbers in the 1990s. MPPs and constellations (constellations refer to a cluster of SMPs) typically use standard workstation microprocessors even when they may use custom interconnect systems. There was, however, one big exception; virtually, nobody used Intel microprocessors. Lack of performance and the limitations of a 32-bit processor design were the main reasons for this. This changed with the introduction of the Pentium III and, especially in 2001, with the Pentium IV, which featured greatly improved memory performance due to its front-side bus and full 64-bit floating-point support. The number of systems in the TOP500 with Intel processors exploded from only six in November 2000 to 375 in June 2008 (Fig. 12.2).

12.2.3   New Architectures on the Horizon

Interest in novel computer architectures has always been large in the HPC community, which comes as a little surprise, as this field was borne and continues to thrive on technological innovations. Some of the concerns of recent years were the ever-increasing space and power requirements of modern commodity-based supercomputers. In the BlueGene/L development, IBM addressed these issues by designing a very power- and space-efficient system. BlueGene/L does not use the latest commodity processors available but use computationally less powerful and much more power-efficient processor versions developed mainly not for the PC and workstation market but for embedded applications. Together with a drastic reduction of the available main memory, this leads to a very dense system. To achieve the targeted extreme performance level, an unprecedented number of these processors (up to 212,992) are combined using several specialized interconnects.

There was, and is, considerable doubt whether such a system would be able to deliver the promised performance and would be usable as a general-purpose system. First results of the current beta system are very encouraging

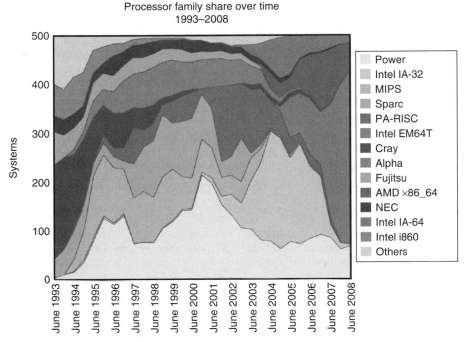

Figure 12.2. Main processor families seen in the TOP500. (See color insert.)

and the one-quarter size system of the future Lawrence Livermore National Laboratory (LLNL) in Livermore, California, system was able to claim the number one spot on the November 2004 TOP500 list.

12.3 APPLICATIONS

Computational physics applications have been the primary drivers in the development of parallel computing over the last 20 years. This set of problems has a number of common features, despite the substantial specific differences in problem domain:

- Applications were often defined by a set of partial differential equations (PDEs) on some subset of $R^3 \times t$.
- Multiphysics often took the form of distinct physical domains with different processes dominant in each.
- The life cycle of many applications was essentially contained within the computer room, building, or campus.

These characteristics focused attention on the discretizations of PDEs, the corresponding notion that resolution equals accuracy, and the solution of the linear and nonlinear equations generated by these discretizations. Data parallelism and domain decomposition provided an effective programming model and a ready source of parallelism. Multiphysics, for the most part, was also amenable to domain decomposition and could be accomplished by understanding and trading information about the fluxes between the physical domains. Finally, attention was focused on the parallel computer and on its speed and accuracy, and relatively little attention was paid to I/O beyond the confines of the computer room.

Data rather than computation will be the transformational element in many applications of the future. In fact, the existence of vast, new data sets has already transformed many applications, including marketing, bioscience, and earthquakes. I/O will be critical in accessing observational and experimental data for validation, in providing real-time surveillance for crisis and military applications, and in allowing an effective, trusted interface with the ultimate user of these simulations. Further afield still, the issues of data security, ownership, and privacy will raise significant technological, administrative, legal, and ethical questions.

12.4 SOFTWARE

The holy grail for software is *portable performance*. That is, software should be reusable across different platforms and provide significant performance, say, relative to peak speed, for the end user. Often, these two goals seem to be in opposition to each other. The classic programming environment is pictured in Figure 12.3.

Languages (e.g., Fortran, C) and libraries (e.g., MPI, Linpack) allow the programmer to access or expose parallelism in a variety of standard ways. By employing standards-based, optimized libraries, the programmer can sometimes achieve both portability and high performance. Tools allow the programmer to determine the correctness and performance of their code and, if falling short in some ways, suggest various remedies.

Software has always followed hardware. However, there is considerable pressure to reverse this relationship. First, large-scale application codes must be trivially or, at worst, easily portable across a variety of platforms. Second,

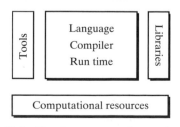

Figure 12.3. Classic programming environment.

the computing environment in the future will be significantly heterogeneous. These two issues require moving toward a software-centric worldview. Abstraction, away from the details of the hardware and system software, is necessary for ease of use, particularly for those not trained in the arcane ways of computer and computational science. Reusable libraries and components are necessary to leverage the time and talents of systems programmers and to provide performance across a wide variety of platforms. It is difficult to understand how competing armies of proprietary software will accomplish this.

12.5 SOME IMPORTANT CONCEPTS FOR THE FUTURE

12.5.1 Heterogeneous Hardware Environments

Hardware environments will be composed of multiple platforms that differ in performance, size, and vendor trademark. This is most easily envisioned in the context of distributed, grid computing, but is also under discussion in the concentrated (single site) computing arena. The primary difficulty will be increased complexity for both application and system software.

12.5.2 Software Architecture

Throughout the evolution of scientific computing, the computing environment has been defined by the hardware. There are indications that software—components and frameworks, problem solving environments, scripting languages, operating systems—will define the computing environment of the future. The primary difficulties will be validation in the face of increasing complexity and making certain that inertia does not retard the development of new capabilities, algorithms, techniques, and interfaces.

12.5.3 Open Source

Proprietary, vendor-specific software predominates high-end computing. However, the triad of programmer productivity, hardware heterogeneity, and system reliability will place significant pressure on this community to consider an open source infrastructure. However, this will not be without its difficulties and detractors due to such issues as development schedules, a viable economic model, and security.

12.5.4 New Applications

Computational physics has driven the development of parallel software, algorithms, and methods over the last two decades. However, new applications, many directly applicable to societal issues, will increasingly share the market space with traditional applications. Such meta-applications will require real-time data access, simulate processes described only by their phenomenology, and often be defined on graphs or have no natural structure at all. These applications will place a new focus on real-time I/O, trusted human interfaces, and ethical, legal, and jurisdictional issues.

12.5.5   Verification and Validation

The consequences of misuse or mistrust of socially relevant applications (e.g., safety and performance of nuclear weapons, global climate, critical infrastructure assurance) requires the development and deployment of formal, trusted systems—verification, validation, and quantification of uncertainty. This trust must extend to all aspects of the process: surveillance, experiment, theory, model, application code, software, hardware, and human interface. Among the difficulties are imposing formality on a complex, science-based process and accelerating acceptance of simulation-based decision-making tools.

12.5.6   Data

Access to data—observation, experiment, and real-time surveillance—is transforming entire disciplines (e.g., bioscience, geophysics, stockpile stewardship) and their projections onto computational science. This data will be of varying format, type, and quality, and the totality will be overwhelming to currently available I/O systems. In addition, socially relevant applications are making the validation of application codes critically important. The difficulties will be I/O from the following: real-time sources; data quality and assimilation; verification, security, and ownership of data; privacy; and man–machine interface.

12.6   2009 AND BEYOND

Four decades after the introduction of the Cray 1, the HPC market has changed its face quite a bit. It used to be a market for systems clearly different from any other computer systems. Today, the HPC market is no longer an isolated niche market for specialized systems. Vertically integrated companies produce systems of any size. The components used for these systems are the same, from an individual desktop PC up to the most powerful supercomputers. Similar software environments are available on all of these systems; this was the basis for the broad acceptance from industrial and commercial customers.

The increasing market share of industrial and commercial installations had several very critical implications for the HPC market. In the market for small-to medium-sized HPC systems, the manufacturers of supercomputers for numerical applications face strong competition from manufacturers selling their systems in the very lucrative commercial market. These systems tend to have better price/performance ratios due to the larger production numbers of systems accepted by commercial customers and the reduced design costs of medium-sized systems. The market for very high-end systems itself is relatively small and does not grow strongly, if at all. It cannot easily support specialized niche market manufacturers. This forces the remaining manufacturers to change the design for very high-end systems away from homogeneous large-scale systems and toward cluster concepts based on 'off the shelf' components.

"Cluster"-based architectures dominate as architectures in the TOP500. Nine years ago, in November 1999, we only had seven clusters in the TOP500, while in June 2008 the list showed 400 cluster systems. At the same time, the debate on whether we need new architectures for very high-end supercomputers has again increased in intensity.

Novel hybrid architectures are likely to appear in the TOP500 list. The number one machine today, the IBM Roadrunner, is just such a system. The Roadrunner is a heterogeneous design built from commodity parts. The system is composed of two processor chip architectures, the IBM PowerXCell and the AMD Opteron, which use Infiniband interconnect. The system can be characterized as an Opteron-based cluster with Cell accelerators. Each Opteron core has a Cell chip (composed of nine cores). The Cell chip has eight vector cores and a conventional PowerPC core. The vector cores provide the bulk of the computational performance.

Hybrid architectures and, in particular, standard CPU designs enhanced with specialized coprocessors such as Field Programmable Gate Arrays (FPGAs), Graphic Processing Units (GPUs), Cell, and so on are of continuously increasing interest in the HPC world. This, combined also with the ongoing changes in microprocessor architecture initiated by the introduction of new multicore and hybrid designs, will inevitably work a corresponding revolution in the practices and programming models of the scientific community. Many familiar and widely used algorithms and libraries will become obsolete and would have to be retaught and rewritten in order to fully exploit the power that the new generation of multicore and hybrid processors has to offer.

The state of the art in computational science applications requires increasingly diverse and complex algorithms and numerical solutions. Heterogeneous computing will continue to play an important role in computational science.

REFERENCES

Achalakul T and Taylor S. (2003). A distributed spectral-screening PCT algorithm. *Journal of Parallel and Distributed Computing* **63**(3):373–384.

Alexandrov A, Ionescu M, Schauser K, and Scheiman C. (1995). LogGP: Incorporating long messages into the LogP model. *Proceedings of the 7th Annual ACM Symposium on Parallel Algorithms and Architectures*, June 24–26, 1995, Santa Barbara, CA; ACM, New York, pp. 95–105.

Barbosa J, Tavares J, and Padilha A. (2000). Linear algebra algorithms in a heterogeneous cluster of personal computers. *Proceedings of the 9th Heterogeneous Computing Workshop (HCW 2000)*, May 1, 2000, Cancun, Mexico. IEEE Computer Society Press, pp. 147–159.

Bazterra V, Cuma M, Ferraro M, and Facelli J. (2005). A general framework to understand parallel performance in heterogeneous clusters: Analysis of a new adaptive parallel genetic algorithm. *Journal of Parallel and Distributed Computing* **65**(1):48–57.

Beaumont O, Boudet V, Petitet A, Rastello F, and Robert Y. (2001a). A proposal for a heterogeneous cluster ScaLAPACK (dense linear solvers). *IEEE Transactions on Computers* **50**(10):1052–1070.

Beaumont O, Boudet V, Rastello F, and Robert Y. (2001b). Matrix multiplication on heterogeneous platforms. *IEEE Transactions on Parallel and Distributed Systems* **12**(10):1033–1051.

Beaumont O, Boudet V, Rastello F, and Robert Y. (2001c). Heterogeneous matrix-matrix multiplication or partitioning a square into rectangles: NP-completeness and approximation algorithms. *Proceedings of the 9th Euromicro Workshop on Parallel and Distributed Processing (PDP 2001)*, February 7–9, 2001, Mantova, Italy, IEEE Computer Society, pp. 298–302.

Becker B and Lastovetsky A. (2006). Matrix multiplication on two interconnected processors. *Proceedings of the 8th IEEE International Conference on Cluster Computing (Cluster 2006)*, September 25–28, 2006, Barcelona, Spain; CD-ROM/Abstracts Proceedings, IEEE Computer Society.

Becker B and Lastovetsky A. (2007). Towards data partitioning for parallel computing on three interconnected clusters. *Proceedings of the 6th International Symposium on Parallel and Distributed Computing (ISPDC 2007)*, July 5–8, 2007, Hagenberg, Austria, IEEE Computer Society, pp. 285–292.

Bernaschi M and Iannello G. (1998). Collective communication operations: Experimental results vs. theory. *Concurrency: Practice and Experience* **10**(5):359–386.

Bertschinger E. (1995). COSMICS: Cosmological initial conditions and microwave anisotropy codes. *ArXiv Astrophysics e-prints*, http://arxiv.org/abs/astro-ph/9506070.

Boulet P, Dongarra J, Rastello F, Robert Y, and Vivien F. (1999). Algorithmic issues on heterogeneous computing platforms. *Parallel Processing Letters* **9**(2):197–213.

Brady T, Konstantinov E, and Lastovetsky A. (2006). SmartNetSolve: High level programming system for high performance grid computing. *Proceedings of the 20th International Parallel and Distributed Processing Symposium (IPDPS 2006)*, April 25–29, 2006, Rhodes, Greece; CD-ROM/Abstracts Proceedings, IEEE Computer Society.

Brady T, Guidolin M, and Lastovetsky A. (2008). Experiments with SmartGridSolve: Achieving higher performance by improving the GridRPC model. *Proceedings of the 9th IEEE/ACM International Conference on Grid Computing (Grid 2008)*, September 29–October 1, 2008, Tsukuba, Japan, IEEE Computer Society, pp. 49–56.

Brightwell R, Fisk L, Greenberg D, Hudson T, Levenhagen M, Maccabe A, and Riesen R. (2000). Massively parallel computing using commodity components. *Parallel Computing* **26**(2–3):243–266.

Buttari A, Dongarra J, Langou J, Langou J, Luszczek P, and Kurzak J. (2007). Mixed precision iterative refinement techniques for the solution of dense linear systems *International Journal of High Performance Computing Applications* **21**(4):457–466.

Canon L-C and Jeannot E. (2006). Wrekavoc: A tool for emulating heterogeneity. *Proceedings of the 20th International Parallel and Distributed Processing Symposium (IPDPS 2006)*, April 25–29, 2006, Rhodes, Greece; CD-ROM/Abstracts Proceedings, IEEE Computer Society.

Caron E and Desprez F. (2006). DIET: A scalable toolbox to build network enabled servers on the grid. *International Journal of High Performance Computing Applications* **20**(3):335–352.

Carriero N, Gelernter D, Mattson T, and Sherman A. (1994). The Linda alternative to message-passing systems. *Parallel Computing* **20**(4):633–655.

Casanova H. (2005). Network modeling issues for grid application scheduling. *International Journal of Foundations of Computer Science* **16**(2):145–162.

Casanova H and Dongarra J. (1996). NetSolve: A network server for solving computational science problems. *Proceedings of the 1996 ACM/IEEE Conference on Supercomputing*, November 17–22, 1996, Pittsburgh, PA; Washington, DC, CD-ROM/Abstracts Proceedings, IEEE Computer Society.

Chamberlain R, Chace D, and Patil A. (1998). How are we doing? An efficiency measure for shared, heterogeneous systems. *Proceedings of the ISCA 11th International Conference on Parallel and Distributed Computing Systems*, September 2–4, 1998, Chicago, IL, pp. 15–21.

Chang C-I. (2003). *Hyperspectral Imaging: Techniques for Spectral Detection and Classification*. New York: Kluwer.

Chen Y and Sun X-H. (2006). STAS: A scalability testing and analysis system. *Proceedings of the 2006 IEEE International Conference on Cluster Computing*, September 25–28, 2006, Barcelona, Spain; CD-ROM/Abstracts Proceedings, IEEE Computer Society.

Chetverushkin B, Churbanova N, Lastovetsky A, and Trapeznikova M. (1998). Parallel simulation of oil extraction on heterogeneous networks of computers. *Proceedings of the 1998 Conference on Simulation Methods and Applications (CSMA'98)*, November 1–3, 1998, Orlando, FL, Society for Computer Simulation, pp. 53–59.

Choi J, Dongarra J, Ostrouchov S, Petitet A, Walker D, and Whaley R. (1996a). The design and implementation of the ScaLAPACK LU, QR, and Cholesky factorization routines. *Scientific Programming* 5(3):173–184.

Choi J, Dongarra J, Ostrouchov S, Petitet A, Walker D, and Whaley R. (1996b). A proposal for a set of parallel basic linear algebra subprograms. *Proceedings of the Second International Workshop on Applied Parallel Computing, Computations in Physics, Chemistry and Engineering Science (PARA'95)*, August 21–24, 1995, Lyngby, Denmark; Berlin, Germany, Lecture Notes in Computer Science, vol. 1041, Springer, pp. 107–114.

ClearSpeed. (2008). http://www.clearspeed.com/.

Colella P and Woodward P. (1984). The piecewise parabolic method (PPM) for gas-dynamical simulations. *Journal of Computational Physics* 54(1):174–201.

Crandall P and Quinn M. (1995). Problem decomposition for non-uniformity and processor heterogencity. *Journal of the Brazilian Computer Society* 2(1):13–23.

Cuenca J, Giménez D, and Martinez J-P. (2005). Heuristics for work distribution of a homogeneous parallel dynamic programming scheme on heterogeneous systems. *Parallel Computing* 31(7):711–730.

Culler D, Karp R, Patterson D, Sahay A, Schauser KE, Santos E, Subramonian R, von Eicken T. (1993). LogP: Towards a realistic model of parallel computation. *Proceedings of the 4th ACM SIGPLAN Symposium on Principles and Practice of Parallel Programming*, May 19–22, 1993, San Diego, CA; ACM, New York, pp. 1–12.

Demmel J, Dongarra J, Parlett B, Kahan W, Gu M, Bindel D, Hida Y, Li X, Marques O, Riedy E, Vömel C, Langou J, Luszczek P, Kurzak J, Buttari A, Langou J, and Tomov S. (2007). For Prospectus for the Next LAPACK and ScaLAPACK Libraries. Department of Computer Science, University of Tennessee. *Tech. Rep. UT-CS-07-592*.

Deshpande A and Schultz M. (1992). Efficient parallel programming with Linda. *Proceedings of the 1992 ACM/IEEE Conference on Supercomputing*, November 16–20, 1992, Minneapolis, MN; Washington, DC, CD-ROM/Abstracts Proceedings, IEEE Computer Society, pp. 238–244.

Dhodhi M, Saghri J, Ahmad I, and Ul-Mustafa R. (1999), D-ISODATA: A distributed algorithm for unsupervised classification of remotely sensed data on network of workstations. *Journal of Parallel and Distributed Computing* 59(2):280–301.

Dongarra J and Whaley R. (1995). A User's Guide to the BLACS v1.0. Department of Computer Science, University of Tennessee. *Tech. Rep. UT-CS-95-281*.

Dongarra J, Croz J, Duff I, and Hammarling S. (1990). A set of level-3 basic linear algebra subprograms. *ACM Transactions on Mathematical Software* 16(1):1–17.

Dongarra J, van de Geijn R, and Walker D. (1994). Scalability issues affecting the design of a dense linear algebra library. *Journal of Parallel and Distributed Computing* 22(3):523–537.

Dongarra J, Prylli L, Randriamaro C, and Tourancheau B. (1995). Array Redistribution in ScaLAPACK Using PVM. Department of Computer Science, University of Tennessee. *Tech. Rep. UT-CS-95-310*.

Dorband J, Palencia J, and Ranawake U. (2003). Commodity computing clusters at goddard space flight center. *Journal of Space Communication* **1**(3):23–35.

Dovolnov E, Kalinov A, and Klimov S. (2003). Natural block data decomposition for heterogeneous clusters. *Proceedings of the 17th International Symposium on Parallel and Distributed Processing (IPDPS 2003)*, April 22–26, 2003, Nice, France; CD-ROM/Abstracts Proceedings, IEEE Computer Society.

Drozdowski M and Wolniewicz P. (2003). Out-of-core divisible load processing. *IEEE Transactions on Parallel and Distributed Systems* **14**(10):1048–1056.

Foster I. (2002). What is the grid: A three point checklist. *GridToday*, July 20, 2002, http://www.mcs.anl.gov/~itf/Articles/WhatIsTheGrid.pdf.

Foster I, Kesselman C, Nick J, and Tuecke S. (2002). *The physiology of the grid: An open grid services architecture for distributed systems integration.* http://www.globus.org/ogsa.

Fukushige T, Taiji M, Makino J, Ebisuzaki T, and Sugimoto D. (1996). A highly parallelized special-purpose computer for many-body simulations with an arbitrary central force: MD-GRAPE. *Astrophysical Journal* **468**: 51–61.

Gabriel E, Fagg G, Bosilca G, Angskun T, Dongarra J, Squyres J, Sahay V, Kambadur P, Barrett B, Lumsdaine A, Castain R, Daniel D, Graham R, and Woodall T. (2004). Open MPI: Goals, concept, and design of a next generation MPI implementation. In *Recent Advances in Parallel Virtual Machine and Message Passing Interface (Proceedings of EuroPVM/MPI 2004)*, Lecture Notes in Computer Science, vol. 3241, (eds. D Kranzlmüller, P Kacsuk, and J Dongarra) Berlin, Germany: Springer, pp. 97–104.

Garey M and Johnson D. (1979). *Computers and Intractability: A Guide to the Theory of NP-Completeness.* San Francisco, CA: Miller Freeman.

van de Geijn R and Watts J. (1997). SUMMA: Scalable universal matrix multiplication algorithm. *Concurrency: Practice and Experience* **9**(4):255–274.

Geist A, Beguelin A, Dongarra J, Jiang W, Manchek R, and Sunderam V. (1994). *PVM: Parallel Virtual Machine. A Users' Guide and Tutorial for Networked Parallel Computing.* Cambridge, MA: MIT Press.

Gheller C, Pantano O, and Moscardini L. (1998). A cosmological hydrodynamic code based on the piecewise parabolic method. *Royal Astronomical Society, Monthly Notices* **295**(3):519–533.

Globus. (2008). http://www.globus.org/.

Graham R, Shipman G, Barrett B, Castain R, Bosilca G, and Lumsdaine A. (2006). Open MPI: A high-performance, heterogeneous MPI. *Proceedings of the 8th IEEE International Conference on Cluster Computing (Cluster 2006)*, September 25–28, 2006, Barcelona, Spain; CD-ROM/Abstracts Proceedings, IEEE Computer Society.

Grama A, Gupta A, and Kumar V. (1993). Isoefficiency: Measuring the scalability of parallel algorithms and architectures. *IEEE Parallel & Distributed Technology* **1**(3):12–21.

GridToday. (2004). http://www.on-demandenterprise.com/features/grid_computing_--_hype_or_tripe__07-29-2008_08_06_35.html.

Gropp W, Lusk E, Ashton D, Balaji P, Buntinas D, Butler R, Chan A, Krishna J, Mercier G, Ross R, Thakur R, and Toonen B. (2007). *MPICH2 User's Guide.*

Version 1.0.6. Argonne, IL. Mathematics and Computer Science Division, Argonne National Laboratory.

Grove D and Coddington P. (2001). Precise MPI performance measurement using MPIBench. *Proceedings of HPC Asia*, September 24–28, 2001, Gold Coast, Queensland, Australia, pp. 24–28

Guidolin M and Lastovetsky A. (2008). Grid-Enabled Hydropad: A Scientific Application for Benchmarking GridRPC-based Programming Systems. School of Computer Science and Informatics, University College Dublin. *Tech. Rep. UCD-CSI-2008-10.*

Gupta R and Vadhiyar A. (2007). An efficient MPI_Allgather algorithm for grids. *Proceedings of the 16th International Symposium on High Performance Distributed Computing (HPDC-16)*, June 25–29, 2007, Monterey, CA, IEEE Computer Society, pp. 169–178.

Gustafson J, Montry G, and Benner R. (1988). Development of parallel methods for a 1024-processor hypercube. *SIAM Journal on Scientific and Statistical Computing* **9**(4):609–638.

HeteroScaLAPACK. (2008). Heterogeneous ScaLAPACK software (HeteroScaLAPACK). School of Computer Science and Informatics, University College Dublin. http://hcl.ucd.ie/project/HeteroScaLAPACK.

Higgins R and Lastovetsky A. (2005). Scheduling for heterogeneous networks of computers with persistent fluctuation of load. *Proceedings of the 13th International Conference on Parallel Computing (ParCo 2005)*, John von Neumann Institute for Computing Series, vol. 33, September 13–16, 2005, Malaga, Spain: Central Institute for Applied Mathematics, pp. 171–178.

High Performance Fortran Forum. (1997). *High Performance Fortran Language Specification (Version 2.0).* Houston, TX: High Performance Fortran Forum, Rice University.

Hockney R. (1994). The communication challenge for MPP: Intel Paragon and Meiko CS-2. *Parallel Computing* **20**(3):389–398.

Hockney R and Eastwood J. (1981). *Computer Simulation Using Particles.* New York: McGraw Hill.

Ibarra O and Kim C. (1977). Heuristic algorithms for scheduling independent tasks on nonidentical processors. *Journal of the ACM* **24**(2):280–289.

Intel. (2004). *Intel MPI Benchmarks. User Guide and Methodology Description.* Bruhl, Germany: Intel GmbH.

IEEE. (1985). *ANSI/IEEE Standard for Binary Floating Point Arithmetic: Std 754-1985.* New York: IEEE Press.

IEEE. (1987). *ANSI/IEEE Standard for Radix Independent Floating Point Arithmetic: Std 854-1987.* New York: IEEE Press.

IEEE. (1994). *IEEE Standard for Shared-Data Formats Optimized for Scalable Coherent Interface (SCI) Processors: Std 1596.5-1993.* New York: IEEE Press.

Gschwind M, Hofstee P, Flachs B, Hopkins M, Watanabe Y, Yamazaki T. (2006). Synergistic processing in Cell's multicore architecture. *IEEE Micro* **26**(2):10–24.

Kaddoura M, Ranka S, and Wang A. (1996). Array decompositions for nonuniform computational environments. *Journal of Parallel and Distributed Computing* **36**(2):91–105.

Kalinov A. (2006). Scalability of heterogeneous parallel systems. *Programming and Computer Software* **32**(1):1–7.

Kalinov A and Klimov S. (2005). Optimal mapping of a parallel application processes onto heterogeneous platform. *Proceedings of 19th International Parallel and Distributed Processing Symposium (IPDPS 2005)*, April 4–8, 2005, Denver, CO; CD-ROM/Abstracts Proceedings, IEEE Computer Society.

Kalinov A and Lastovetsky A. (1999a). Heterogeneous distribution of computations while solving linear algebra problems on networks of heterogeneous computers. *Proceedings of the 7th International Conference on High Performance Computing and Networking Europe (HPCN'99)*, Lecture Notes in Computer Science, vol. 1593, April 12–14, 1999, Amsterdam, The Netherlands; Berlin, Germany, Springer, pp. 191–200.

Kalinov A and Lastovetsky A. (1999b). mpC + ScaLAPACK = Efficient solving linear algebra problems on heterogeneous networks. *Proceedings of the 5th International Euro-Par Conference (Euro-Par'99)*, Lecture Notes in Computer Science, vol. 1685, August 31–September 3, 1999, Toulouse, France; Berlin, Germany, Springer, pp. 1024–1031.

Kalinov A and Lastovetsky A. (2001). Heterogeneous distribution of computations solving linear algebra problems on networks of heterogeneous computers. *Journal of Parallel and Distributed Computing* **61**(4):520–535.

Kalluri S, Zhang Z, JaJa J, Liang S, and Townshend J. (2001). Characterizing land surface anisotropy from AVHRR data at a global scale using high performance computing. *International Journal of Remote Sensing* **22**(11):2171–2191.

Karp A and Platt H. (1990). Measuring parallel processor performance. *Communications of the ACM* **22**(5):539–543.

Kielmann T, Bal H, and Verstoep K. (2000). Fast measurement of LogP parameters for message passing platforms. *Proceedings of IPDPS 2000 Workshops*, Lecture Notes in Computer Science, vol. 1800, May 1–5, 2000, Cancun, Mexico; Berlin, Germany, Springer, pp. 1176–1183.

Kishimoto Y and Ichikawa S. (2004). An execution-time estimation model for heterogeneous clusters. *Proceedings of 18th International Parallel and Distributed Processing Symposium (IPDPS 2004)*, April 26–30, 2004, Santa Fe, NM; CD-ROM/Abstracts Proceedings, IEEE Computer Society.

Kumar S, Chao H, Alamasi G, and Kale L. (2006). Achieving strong scaling with NAMD on Blue Gene/L. *Proceedings of the 20th International Parallel and Distributed Processing Symposium (IPDPS 2006)*, April 25–29, 2006, Rhodes, Greece; CD-ROM/Abstracts Proceedings, IEEE Computer Society.

Kumar V, Grama A, Gupta A, and Karypis G. (1994). *Introduction to Parallel Computing: Design and Analysis of Algorithms*. Redwood City, CA: Benjamin-Cummings and Addison-Wesley.

Kwok Y-K and Ahmad I. (1999). Static scheduling algorithms for allocating directed task graphs to multiprocessors. *ACM Computing Surveys* **31**(4):406–471.

Lastovetsky A. (2002). Adaptive parallel computing on heterogeneous networks with mpC. *Parallel Computing* **28**(10):1369–1407.

Lastovetsky A. (2003). *Parallel Computing on Heterogeneous Networks*. Hoboken, NJ: Wiley-Interscience.

Lastovetsky A. (2006). Scientific programming for heterogeneous systems—Bridging the gap between algorithms and applications. *Proceedings of the 5th International Symposium on Parallel Computing in Electrical Engineering (PARELEC 2006)*, September 13–17, 2006, Bialystok, Poland, IEEE Computer Society, pp. 3–8.

Lastovetsky A. (2007). On grid-based matrix partitioning for heterogeneous processors. *Proceedings of the 6th International Symposium on Parallel and Distributed Computing (ISPDC 2007)*, July 5–8, 2007, Hagenberg, Austria, IEEE Computer Society, pp. 383–390.

Lastovetsky A and O'Flynn M. (2007). A performance model of many-to-one collective communications for parallel computing. *Proceedings of the 21st International Parallel and Distributed Processing Symposium (IPDPS 2007)*, March 26–30, 2007, Long Beach, CA; CD-ROM/Abstracts Proceedings, IEEE Computer Society.

Lastovetsky A and Reddy R (2004a). Data partitioning with a realistic performance model of networks of heterogeneous computers. *Proceedings of the 18th International Parallel and Distributed Processing Symposium (IPDPS 2004)*, April 26–30, 2004, Santa Fe, NM; CD-ROM/Abstracts Proceedings, IEEE Computer Society.

Lastovetsky A and Reddy R. (2004b). On performance analysis of heterogeneous parallel algorithms. *Parallel Computing* **30**(11):1195–1216.

Lastovetsky A and Reddy R. (2005). Data partitioning for multiprocessors with memory heterogeneity and memory constraints. *Scientific Programming* **13**(2):93–112.

Lastovetsky A and Reddy R. (2006). HeteroMPI: Towards a message-passing library for heterogeneous networks of computers. *Journal of Parallel and Distributed Computing* **66**(2):197–220.

Lastovetsky A and Reddy R. (2007a). A novel algorithm of optimal matrix partitioning for parallel dense factorization on heterogeneous processors. *Proceedings of the 9th International Conference on Parallel Computing Technologies (PaCT-2007)*, Lecture Notes in Computer Science, vol. 4671, September 3–7, 2007, Pereslavl-Zalessky, Russia; Berlin, Germany, Springer, pp. 261–275.

Lastovetsky A and Reddy R. (2007b). Data partitioning with a functional performance model of heterogeneous processors. *International Journal of High Performance Computing Applications* **21**(1):76–90.

Lastovetsky A and Reddy R. (2007c). Data partitioning for dense factorization on computers with memory heterogeneity. *Parallel Computing* **33**(12):757–779.

Lastovetsky A and Rychkov V. (2007). Building the communication performance model of heterogeneous clusters based on a switched network. *Proceedings of the 2007 IEEE International Conference on Cluster Computing (Cluster 2007)*, September 17–20, 2007, Austin, TX, IEEE Computer Society, pp. 568–575.

Lastovetsky A and Twamley J. (2005). Towards a realistic performance model for networks of heterogeneous computers. In: *High Performance Computational Science and Engineering (Proceedings of IFIP TC5 Workshop, 2004 World Computer Congress)* (eds. MK Ng, A Doncescu, LT Yang, and T Leng). Berlin, Germany: Springer, pp. 39–58.

Lastovetsky A, Mkwawa I, and O'Flynn M. (2006). An accurate communication model of a heterogeneous cluster based on a switch-enabled Ethernet network. *Proceedings of the 12th International Conference on Parallel and Distributed Systems*

(ICPADS 2006), July 12–15, 2006, Minneapolis, MN, IEEE Computer Society, pp. 15–20.

Lastovetsky A, Reddy R, and Higgins R. (2006). Building the functional performance model of a processor. *Proceedings of the 21st Annual ACM Symposium on Applied Computing (SAC'06)*, April 23–27, 2006, Dijon, France, ACM Press, pp. 746–753.

Lastovetsky A, O'Flynn M, and Rychkov V. (2007). Optimization of collective communications in herompi. In *Recent Advances in Parallel Virtual Machine and Message Passing Interface (Proceedings of EuroPVM/MPI 2007)*, Lecture Notes in Computer Science, vol. 4757, (eds. F Cappello, T Herault, and J Dongarra). Berlin, Germany: Springer, pp. 135–143.

Lastovetsky A, O'Flynn M, and Rychkov V. (2008). MPIBlib: Benchmarking MPI communications for parallel computing on homogeneous and heterogeneous clusters. In *Recent Advances in Parallel Virtual Machine and Message Passing Interface (Proceedings of EuroPVM/MPI 2008)*, Lecture Notes in Computer Science, vol. 5205, (eds. A Lastovetsky, T Kechadi and J Dongarra) Berlin, Germany: Springer, pp. 227–238.

Le Moigne J, Campbell W, and Cromp R. (2002). An automated parallel image registration technique based on the correlation of wavelet features. *IEEE Transactions on Geoscience and Remote Sensing* **40**(8):1849–1864.

Lee C, Matsuoka S, Talia De, Sussman A, Mueller M, Allen G, and Saltz J. (2001). *A Grid Programming Primer*. Global Grid Forum. http://www.cct.lsu.edu/~gallen/Reports/GridProgrammingPrimer.pdf.

Mazzeo A, Mazzocca N, and Villano U. (1998). Efficiency measurements in heterogeneous distributed computing systems: from theory to practice. *Concurrency: Practice and Experience* **10**(4):285–313.

Message Passing Interface Forum. (1995). *MPI: A Message-passing Interface Standard, ver. 1.1*. University of Tennessee: Knoxville, TN.

MPI. (1994). MPI: A message-passing interface standard. *International Journal of Supercomputer Applications* **8**(3/4):159–416.

Nakada H, Sato M, and Sekiguchi S. (1999). Design and implementations of Ninf: Towards a global computing infrastructure. *Future Generation Computing Systems* **15**(5–6):649–658.

Ohtaki Y, Takahashi D, Boku T, and Sato M. (2004). Parallel implementation of Strassen's matrix multiplication algorithm for heterogeneous clusters. *Proceedings of the 18th International Parallel and Distributed Processing Symposium (IPDPS 2004)*, April 26–30, 2004, Santa Fe, NM; CD-ROM/Abstracts Proceedings, IEEE Computer Society.

Pastor L and Bosque J. (2001). An efficiency and scalability model for heterogeneous clusters. *Proceedings of the 2001 IEEE International Conference on Cluster Computing*, October 8–11, 2001, Newport Beach, CA: IEEE Computer Society, pp. 427–434.

Pjesivac-Grbovic J, Angskun T, Bosilca G, Fagg G, Gabriel E, and Dongarra J. (2007). Performance analysis of MPI collective operation. *Cluster Computing* **10**(2):127–143.

Plaza A. (2007). Parallel techniques for information extraction from hyperspectral imagery using heterogeneous networks of workstations. *Journal of Parallel and Distributed Computing* **68**(1):93–111.

Plaza A and Chang C-I. (eds.) (2007). *High-Performance Computing in Remote Sensing.* Boca Raton, FL: Chapman & Hall/CRC Press.

Plaza A, Martinez P, Plaza J, and Perez R. (2002). Spatial-spectral endmember extraction by multidimensional morphological operations. *IEEE Transactions on Geoscience and Remote Sensing* **40**(9):2025–2041.

Plaza A, Martinez P, Plaza J, and Perez R. (2005). Dimensionality reduction and classification of hyperspectral image data using sequences of extended morphological transformations. *IEEE Transactions on Geoscience and Remote Sensing* **43**(3): 466–479.

Plaza A, Plaza J, and Valencia D. (2006). AMEEPAR: Parallel morphological algorithm for hyperspectral image classification on heterogeneous networks of workstations. *Proceedings of the 6th International Conference on Computational Science (ICCS 2006)*, Lecture Notes in Computer Science, vol. 3993, May 28–31, 2006, Reading, UK; Berlin, Germany, Springer, pp. 24–31.

Plaza A, Valencia D, Plaza J, and Martinez P. (2006). Commodity cluster-based parallel processing of hyperspectral imagery. *Journal of Parallel and Distributed Computing* **66**(3):345–358.

Plaza A, Plaza J, and Valencia D. (2007). Impact of platform heterogeneity on the design of parallel algorithms for morphological processing of high-dimensional image data. *The Journal of Supercomputing* **40**(1):81–107.

Prylli L and Tourancheau B. (1996). Efficient block cyclic data redistribution. *Proceedings of the Second International Euro-Par Conference on Parallel Processing (EUROPAR'96)*, Lecture Notes in Computer Science, vol 1123, August 26–29, 1996, Lyon, France; Berlin, Germany, Springer, pp. 155–164.

Rabenseifner R. (1999). Automatic MPI counter profiling of all users: First results on a CRAY T3E 900-512. *Proceedings of the Message Passing Interface Developer's and User's Conference 1999 (MPIDC'99)*, September 26–29, 1999, Barcelona, Spain; Berlin, Germany, Springer, pp 77–85.

Reddy R and Lastovetsky A. (2006). HeteroMPI + ScaLAPACK: Towards a dense ScaLAPACK on heterogeneous networks of computers. *Proceedings of the 13th IEEE International Conference on High Performance Computing (HiPC 2006)*, Lecture Notes in Computer Science, vol. 4297, December 18–21, 2006, Bangalore, India, Springer, pp. 242–252.

Reddy R, Lastovetsky A, and Alonso P. (2008). Heterogeneous PBLAS: A Set of Parallel Basic Linear Algebra Subprograms for Heterogeneous Computational Clusters. School of Computer Science and Informatics, University College Dublin. *Tech. Rep. UCD-CSI-2008-2.*

Richards J and Jia X. (2005). *Remote Sensing Digital Image Analysis*, 4th ed. Berlin, Germany: Springer.

RIKEN. (2008). http://www.riken.go.jp/engn/index.html.

Rosenberry W, Kenney D, and Fisher G. (1992). *Understanding DCE.* Sebastopol, CA: O'Reilly.

ScaLAPACK. (1997). The ScaLAPACK project. http://www.netlib.org/scalapack/.

Seymour K, Nakada H, Matsuoka S, Dongarra J, Lee C, and Casanova H. (2002). Overview of GridRPC: A remote procedure call API for grid computing. *Proceedings of the Third International Workshop on Grid Computing (Grid 2002)*, Lecture

Notes in Computer Science, vol. 2536, November 18, 2002, Baltimore, MD; Berlin, Germany, Springer, pp. 274–278.

Shirasuna S, Nakada H, Matsuoka S, and Sekiguchi S. (2002). Evaluating Web services based implementations of GridRPC. *Proceedings of the 11th IEEE International Symposium on High Performance Distributed Computing (HPDC-11)*, July 24–26, 2002, Edinburgh, Scotland, IEEE Computer Society.

Smarr L and Catlett CE. (1992). Metacomputing. *Communications of the ACM* **35**(6):44–52.

Snir M, Otto S, Huss-Lederman S, Walker D, and Dongarra J. (1996). *MPI: The Complete Reference*. Cambridge, MA: MIT Press.

Soille P. (2003). *Morphological Image Analysis: Principles and Applications*, 2nd ed. Berlin, Germany: Springer.

Spring J, Spring N, and Wolski R. (2000). Predicting the CPU availability of time-shared Unix systems on the computational grid. *Cluster Computing* **3**(4):293–301.

Sterling T, Lusk E, and Gropp W. (2003). *Beowulf Cluster Computing with Linux*. Cambridge, MA: MIT Press.

Sulistio A, Yeo C, and Buyya R. (2004). A taxonomy of computer-based simulations and its mapping to parallel and distributed systems simulation tools. *Software: Practice and Experience* **34**(7):653–673.

Sun X-H and Rover D. (1994). Scalability of parallel algorithm-machine combinations. *IEEE Transactions on Parallel and Distributed Systems* **5**(6):599–613.

Sun X-H, Chen Y, and Wu M. (2005). Scalability of heterogeneous computing. *Proceedings of the 34th International Conference on Parallel Processing*, June 14–17, 2005, Oslo, Norway, IEEE Computer Society, pp. 557–564.

SunSoft. (1993). *The XDR Protocol Specification. Appendix A of "Network Interfaces Programmer's Guide."* SunSoft. http://docs.sun.com/app/docs/doc/801-6741/6i13kh8sg?a=view.

de Supinski B and Karonis N. (1999). Accurately measuring MPI broadcasts in a computational grid. *Proceedings of the Eighth International Symposium on High Performance Distributed Computing*, August 3–6, 1999, Redondo Beach, CA, pp. 29–37.

Tanaka Y, Nakada H, Sekiguchi S, Suzumura T, and Matsuoka S. (2003). Ninf-G: A reference implementation of RPC-based programming middleware for grid computing. *Journal of Grid Computing* **1**(1):41–51.

Thakur R, Rabenseifner R, and Gropp W. (2005). Optimization of collective communication operations in MPICH. *International Journal of High Performance Computing Applications* **19**(1):49–66.

Tilton J. (2001). Method for implementation of recursive hierarchical segmentation on parallel computers. US Patent Office, Washington, DC. Pending published application 09/839147.

Tilton J. (2007). Parallel implementation of the recursive approximation of an unsupervised hierarchical segmentation algorithm. In *High-Performance Computing in Remote Sensing* (eds. AJ Plaza and C-I Chang) Boca Raton, FL: Chapman & Hall/CRC Press, pp. 97–107.

Turcotte L. (1993). A Survey of Software Environments for Exploiting Networked Computing Resources. Engineering Research Center, Mississippi State University. *Tech. Rep. MSSU-EIRS-ERC-93-2.*

Unicore. (2008). http://unicore.sourceforge.net/.

Vadhiyar S, Fagg G, and Dongarra J. (2000). Automatically tuned collective communications. *Proceedings of the 2000 ACM/IEEE Conference on Supercomputing*, November 4–10, 2000, Dallas, TX, IEEE Computer Society.

Valencia D, Lastovetsky A, O'Flynn M, Plaza A, and Plaza J. (2008). Parallel processing of remotely sensed hyperspectral images on heterogeneous networks of workstations using HeteroMPI. *International Journal of High Performance Computing Applications* **22**(4):386–407.

Vetter J, Alam S, Dunigan T, Fahey M, Roth P, and Worley P. (2006). Early evaluation of the Cray XT3. *Proceedings of the 20th IEEE International Parallel and Distributed Processing Symposium (IPDPS 2006)*, April 25–29, 2006, Rhodes, Greece; CD-ROM/Abstracts Proceedings, IEEE Computer Society.

Wang P, Liu K, Cwik T, and Green R. (2002). MODTRAN on supercomputers and parallel computers. *Parallel Computing* **28**(1):53–64.

Whaley R, Petitet A, and Dongarra J. (2001). Automated empirical optimization of software and the ATLAS Project. *Parallel Computing* **27**(1–2):3–25.

Worsch T, Reussner R, and Augustin W. (2002). On Benchmarking Collective MPI Operations. In *Recent Advances in Parallel Virtual Machine and Message Passing Interface (Proceedings of EuroPVM/MPI 2002)*, Lecture Notes in Computer Science, vol. 2474, (eds. D Kranzlmüller, P Kacsuk, J Dongarra, and J Volkert) Berlin: Germany, pp. 271–279.

YarKhan A, Seymour K, Sagi K, Shi Z, and Dongarra J. (2006). Recent developments in GridSolve. *International Journal of High Performance Computing Applications* **20**(1):131–142.

Zhang X and Yan Y. (1995). Modeling and characterizing parallel computing performance on heterogeneous networks of workstations. *Proceedings of the Seventh IEEE Symposium in Parallel and Distributed Processing (SPDPS'95)*, October 25–28, 1995, San Antonio, TX, IEEE Computer Society, pp. 25–34.

Zhang X, Yan Y, and He K. (1994). Latency metric: An experimental method for measuring and evaluating program and architecture scalability. *Journal of Parallel and Distributed Computing* **22**(3):392–410.

Zorbas J, Reble D, and VanKooten R. (1989). Measuring the scalability of parallel computer systems. *Proceedings of the Supercomputing '89*, November 14–18, 1988, Orlando, FL, ACM Press, pp. 832–841.

APPENDICES

Appendix to Chapter 3

A.1 PROOF OF PROPOSITION 3.1

Consider an optimal allocation denoted by $o_1, \ldots, o_p$. Let j be such that $\forall i \in \{1, \ldots, p\}, \dfrac{o_j}{s_j} \ge \dfrac{o_i}{s_i}$. To prove the correctness of the algorithm, we prove the invariant (I): $\forall i \in \{1, \ldots, p\}, \dfrac{n_i}{s_i} \le \dfrac{o_j}{s_j}$. After the initialization, $n_i \le \dfrac{s_i}{\sum_{k=1}^{p} s_k} \times n$.

We have $n = \sum_{k=1}^{p} o_k \le \dfrac{o_j}{s_j} \times \sum_{k=1}^{p} s_k$. Hence, $\dfrac{n_i}{s_i} \le \dfrac{n}{\sum_{k=1}^{p} s_k} \le \dfrac{o_j}{s_j}$ and invariant

(I) holds. We use an induction to prove that invariant (I) holds after each increment. Suppose that, at a given step, some n_k will be incremented. Before that step, $\sum_{i=1}^{p} n_i < n$, hence, there exists $m \in \{1, \ldots, p\}$ such that $n_m < o_k$.

We have $\dfrac{n_m + 1}{s_m} \le \dfrac{o_m}{s_m} \le \dfrac{o_j}{s_j}$, and the choice of k implies that $\dfrac{n_k + 1}{s_k} \le \dfrac{n_m + 1}{s_m}$.

Invariant (I) does hold after the increment. Finally, the time needed to compute the n chunks with the allocation $(n_1, n_2, \ldots, n_p)$ is $\max_i \dfrac{n_i}{s_i}$, and our allocation is optimal. This proves Proposition 3.1.

A.2 PROOF OF PROPOSITION 3.5

If the algorithm assigns element a_k at each iteration, then the resulting allocation will be optimal by design. Indeed, in this case the distribution of elements over the processors will be produced by the heterogeneous set partitioning (HSP), and hence optimal for each subset $A^{(k)}$.

Consider the situation when the algorithm assigns a group of w ($w > 1$) elements beginning from the element a_k. In that case, the algorithm first produces a sequence of $(w + 1)$ distributions $\left(n_1^{(k)}, \ldots, n_p^{(k)}\right)$, $\left(n_1^{(k+1)}, \ldots, n_p^{(k+1)}\right)$, $\ldots, \left(n_1^{(k+w)}, \ldots, n_p^{(k+w)}\right)$ such that

- the distributions are optimal for subsets $A^{(k)}, A^{(k+1)}, \ldots, A^{(k+w)}$, respectively, and
- $\left(n_1^{(k)}, \ldots, n_p^{(k)}\right) > \left(n_1^{(k+i)}, \ldots, n_p^{(k+i)}\right)$ is only true for $i = w$ (by definition, $(a_1, \ldots, a_p) > (b_1, \ldots, b_p)$ if and only if $(\forall i)(a_i \geq b_i) \wedge (\exists i)(a_i > b_i)$.

Lemma 3.5.1. Let $(n_1, \ldots, n_p)$ and $(n_1', \ldots, n_p')$ be optimal distributions such that $n = \Sigma_{i=1}^{p} n_i > \Sigma_{i=1}^{p} n_i' = n'$, $(\exists i)(n_i < n_i')$ and $(\forall j)\left(\max_{i=1}^{p} \dfrac{n_i}{s_i} \leq \dfrac{n_j + 1}{s_j}\right)$. Then, $\max_{i=1}^{p} \dfrac{n_i}{s_i} = \max_{i=1}^{p} \dfrac{n_i'}{s_i}$.

Proof of Lemma 3.5.1. As $n \geq n'$ and $(n_1, \ldots, n_p)$ and $(n_1', \ldots, n_p')$ are both optimal distributions, then $\max_{i=1}^{p} \dfrac{n_i}{s_i} \geq \max_{i=1}^{p} \dfrac{n_i'}{s_i}$. On the other hand, there exists $j \in [1, p]$ such that $n_j < n_j'$, which implies $n_j + 1 \leq n_j'$. Therefore, $\max_{i=1}^{p} \dfrac{n_i'}{s_i} \geq \dfrac{n_j'}{s_j} \geq \dfrac{n_j + 1}{s_j}$. As we assumed that $(\forall j)\left(\max_{i=1}^{p} \dfrac{n_i}{s_i} \leq \dfrac{n_j + 1}{s_j}\right)$, then $\max_{i=1}^{p} \dfrac{n_i}{s_i} \leq \dfrac{n_j + 1}{s_j} \leq \dfrac{n_j'}{s_j} \leq \max_{i=1}^{p} \dfrac{n_i'}{s_i}$. Thus, from $\max_{i=1}^{p} \dfrac{n_i}{s_i} \geq \max_{i=1}^{p} \dfrac{n_i'}{s_i}$ and $\max_{i=1}^{p} \dfrac{n_i}{s_i} \leq \max_{i=1}^{p} \dfrac{n_i'}{s_i}$, we conclude that $\max_{i=1}^{p} \dfrac{n_i}{s_i} = \max_{i=1}^{p} \dfrac{n_i'}{s_i}$. *End of proof of Lemma 3.5.1.*

We can apply Lemma 3.5.1 to the pair $\left(n_1^{(k)}, \ldots, n_p^{(k)}\right)$ and $\left(n_1^{(k+l)}, \ldots, n_p^{(k+l)}\right)$ for any $l \in [1, w - 1]$. Indeed, $\Sigma_{i=1}^{p} n_i^{(k)} > \Sigma_{i=1}^{p} n_i^{(k+l)}$ and $(\exists i)\left(n_i^{(k)} < n_i^{(k+l)}\right)$. Finally, the HSP guarantees that $(\forall j)\left(\max_{i=1}^{p} \dfrac{n_i^{(k)}}{s_i} \leq \dfrac{n_j^{(k)} + 1}{s_j}\right)$ (see Boulet *et al.*, 1999; Beaumont *et al.*, 2001a). Therefore, $\max_{i=1}^{p} \dfrac{n_i^{(k)}}{s_i} = \max_{i=1}^{p} \dfrac{n_i^{(k+1)}}{s_i} = \ldots = \max_{i=1}^{p} \dfrac{n_i^{(k+w-1)}}{s_i}$. In particular, this means that for any $(m_1, \ldots, m_p)$ such that $\min_{j=k}^{k+w-1} n_i^{(j)} \leq m_i \leq \max_{j=k}^{k+w-1} n_i^{(j)}$ $(i = 1, \ldots, p)$, we will have $\max_{i=1}^{p} \dfrac{m_i}{s_i} = \max_{i=1}^{p} \dfrac{n_i^{(k)}}{s_i}$. The allocations made in the end by the Reverse algorithm for the elements $a_k, a_{k+1}, \ldots, a_{k+w-1}$ result in a new sequence of distributions for subsets $A^{(k)}, A^{(k+1)}, ..., A^{(k+w-1)}$ such that each next distribution differs from the previous one for exactly one processor. Each distribution $(m_1, \quad ..., \quad m_p)$ in this new sequence satisfies the inequality $\min_{j=k}^{k+w-1} n_i^{(j)} \le m_i \le \max_{j=k}^{k+w-1} n_i^{(j)}$ $(i = 1, ..., p)$. Therefore, they will all have the same cost $\max_{i=1}^{p} \dfrac{n_i^{(k)}}{s_i}$, which is the cost of the optimal distribution for these subsets found by the HSP. Hence, each distribution in this sequence will be optimal for the corresponding subset. This proves Proposition 3.5.

Appendix to Chapter 4

B.1 PROOF OF PROPOSITION 4.1

First, we formulate a few obvious properties of the functions $s_i(x)$.

Lemma 4.1. The functions $s_i(x)$ are bounded.

Lemma 4.2. Any straight line coming through the origin of the coordinate system intersects the graph of the function $s_i(x)$ in no more than one point.

Lemma 4.3. Let $x_i^{(M_k)}$ be the coordinate of the intersection point of $s_i(x)$ and a straight line M_k coming through the origin of the coordinate system ($k \in \{1,2\}$). Then $x_i^{(M_1)} \geq x_i^{(M_2)}$ if and only if $\angle(M_1,X) \leq \angle(M_2,X)$, where $\angle(M_k,X)$ denotes the angle between the line M_k and the x-axis.

Since $s_i(x)$ are continuous and bounded, the initial lines U and L always exist. Since there is no more than one point of intersection of the line L with each of $s_i(x)$, L will make a positive angle with the x-axis. Thus, both U and L will intersect each $s_i(x)$ exactly in one point. Let $x_i^{(U)}$ and $x_i^{(L)}$ be the coordinates of the intersection points of the U and L with $s_i(x)$ ($1 \leq i \leq p$), respectively. Then, by design, $\Sigma_{i=1}^{p} x_i^{(U)} \leq n \leq \Sigma_{i=1}^{p} x_i^{(L)}$. This invariant will hold after each iteration of the algorithm. Indeed, if line M bisects the angle between lines U and L, then $\angle(L,X) \leq \angle(M,X) \leq \angle(U,X)$. Hence, $\Sigma_{i=1}^{p} x_i^{(U)} \leq \Sigma_{i=1}^{p} x_i^{(M)} \leq \Sigma_{i=1}^{p} x_i^{(L)}$. If $\Sigma_{i=1}^{p} x_i^{(M)} \leq n$, then $\Sigma_{i=1}^{p} x_i^{(U)} \leq \Sigma_{i=1}^{p} x_i^{(M)} \leq n \leq \Sigma_{i=1}^{p} x_i^{(L)}$ and after Step 4 of the algorithm, $\Sigma_{i=1}^{p} x_i^{(U)} \leq n \leq \Sigma_{i=1}^{p} x_i^{(L)}$. If $\Sigma_{i=1}^{p} x_i^{(M)} \geq n$, then $\Sigma_{i=1}^{p} x_i^{(U)} \leq n \leq \Sigma_{i=1}^{p} x_i^{(M)} \leq \Sigma_{i=1}^{p} x_i^{(L)}$ and after Step 4 of the algorithm, $\Sigma_{i=1}^{p} x_i^{(U)} \leq n \leq \Sigma_{i=1}^{p} x_i^{(L)}$. Thus, after each iteration of the algorithm, the "ideal" optimal line O such that $\Sigma_{i=1}^{p} x_i^{(O)} = n$ will be lying between lines U and L. When the algorithm reaches Step 5, we have $x_i^{(L)} - x_i^{(U)} < 1$ for all $1 \leq i \leq p$,

High-Performance Heterogeneous Computing, by Alexey L. Lastovetsky and Jack J. Dongarra
Copyright © 2009 John Wiley & Sons, Inc.

which means that the interval $\left[x_i^{(L)}, x_i^{(U)}\right]$ contains, at most, one integer value. Therefore, either $n_i = \lfloor x_i^{(U)} \rfloor = \lfloor x_i^{(O)} \rfloor$ or $n_i = \lfloor x_i^{(U)} \rfloor = \lfloor x_i^{(O)} \rfloor - 1$. Proposition 4.1 is proved.

B.2 PROOF OF PROPOSITION 4.2

The execution time obtained with allocation $(n_1, n_2, \ldots, n_p)$ is given by $\max_i \dfrac{n_i}{s_i(n_i)}$. The geometrical interpretation of this formula is as follows. Let M_i be the straight line connecting the points $(0,0)$ and $(n_i, s_i(n_i))$. Then $\dfrac{n_i}{s_i(n_i)} = \cot \angle (M_i, X)$. Therefore, minimization of $\max_i \dfrac{n_i}{s_i(n_i)}$ is equivalent to maximization of $\min_i \angle (M_i, X)$. Let $\{S_1, S_2, \ldots\}$ be the set of all straight lines such that

- S_k connects $(0,0)$ and $(m, s_i(m))$ for some $i \in \{1, \ldots, p\}$ and some integer m, and
- S_k lies below M_i for any $i \in \{1, \ldots, p\}$.

Let $\{S_1, S_2, \ldots\}$ be ordered in the decreasing order of $\angle(S_k, X)$. The execution time of the allocation $(n_1, n_2, \ldots, n_p)$ is represented by line M_k such that $\angle(M_k, X) = \min_i \angle (M_i, X)$. Any increment of n_i means moving one more line from the set $\{S_1, S_2, \ldots\}$ into the set of lines representing the allocation. At each step of the increment, Algorithm 4.3 moves the line making the largest angle with the x-axis. This means that after each increment, the algorithm gives the optimal allocation $(n_1, n_2, \ldots, n_p)$ under the assumption that the total number of chunks, which should be allocated, is equal to $n_1 + n_2 + \ldots + n_p$ (any other increment gives a smaller angle, and hence, longer execution time). Therefore, after the last increment, the algorithm gives the optimal allocation $(n_1, n_2, \ldots, n_p)$ under the assumption that $n_1 + n_2 + \ldots + n_p = n$. Proposition 4.1 is proved.

B.3 PROOF OF PROPOSITION 4.3

First, we estimate the complexity of one iteration of Algorithm 4.2. At each iteration, we need to find the points of intersection of p graphs $y = s_1(x)$, $y = s_2(x), \ldots, y = s_p(x)$ and a straight line $y = a \times x$. In other words, at each iteration, we need to solve p equations of the form $a \times x = s_i(x)$. As we need the same constant number of operations to solve each equation, the complexity of this part of one iteration will be $O(p)$. The test for stopping (Step 2 of the algorithm) also takes a constant number of operations per function $s_i(x)$, making the complexity of this part of one iteration $O(p)$. Therefore, overall, the complexity of one iteration of Algorithm 4.2 will be $O(p)$.

Next, we estimate the number of iterations of this algorithm. To do it, we use the following lemma that states one important property of the initial lines U and L obtained at the Step 1 of Algorithm 4.2.

Lemma 4.4. Let the functions $s_i(x)$ $(1 \leq i \leq p)$ satisfy the conditions of Proposition 4.1, and the heterogeneity of processors $P_1, P_2, ..., P_p$ be bounded. Let O be the point $(0,0)$, A_i be the point of intersection of the initial line U and $s_i(x)$, and B_i be the point of intersection of the initial line L and $s_i(x)$. Then, there exist constants c_1 and c_2 such that $c_1 \leq \dfrac{OB_i}{OA_i} \leq c_2$ for any $i \in \{1,2, ...,p\}$.

Proof of Lemma 4.4. The full proof of Lemma 4.4 is technical and very lengthy. Here, we give a relatively compact proof of the lemma under the additional assumption that the functions $s_i(x)$ $(1 \leq i \leq p)$ are monotonically decreasing. First, we prove that there exist constants c_1 and c_2 such that $c_1 \leq \dfrac{OB}{OA} \leq c_2$, where A is the point of intersection of the initial line U and

$s_{\max}(x) = \max_i s_i(x)$, and B is the point of intersection of the initial line L and $s_{\max}(x)$ (see Fig. B.1). Since the heterogeneity of the processors $P_1, P_2, ..., P_p$ is

bounded, there exists a constant c such that $\max_{x \in R_+} \dfrac{s_{\max}(x)}{s_{\min}(x)} \leq c$. In particular,

this means that $\dfrac{BD}{FD} \leq c$ and $\dfrac{AC}{EC} \leq c$. Let us prove that $\dfrac{OB}{OA} \leq c$. We have

$OB = \sqrt{OD^2 + BD^2}$. Since $\dfrac{OD}{OC} = \dfrac{BD}{EC}$, we have $OD = \dfrac{BD}{EC} \times OC$. Since $s_{\min}(x)$

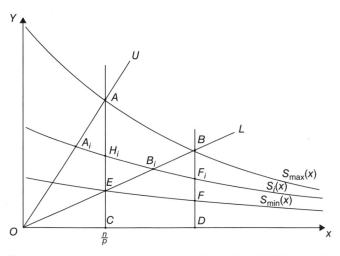

Figure B.1. The picture after of the initial step of Algorithm 4.2. Here, $s_{\max}(x) = \max_i s_i(x)$ and $s_{\min}(x) = \min_i s_i(x)$.

monotonically decreases on the interval $\left[\dfrac{n}{p}, \infty\right]$, $FD \leq EC$, and hence,

$\dfrac{BD}{EC} \leq \dfrac{BD}{FD} \leq c$. Thus, $OD \leq c \times OC$ and $BD \leq c \times EC$. Therefore,

$\sqrt{OD^2 + BD^2} \leq \sqrt{c^2 + OC^2 + c^2 \times EC^2} = c \times \sqrt{OC^2 + EC^2} = c \times OE$, and hence,

$\dfrac{OB}{OE} \leq c$. Since $OA \leq OE$, then $\dfrac{OB}{OA} \leq \dfrac{OB}{OE} \leq c$. Next, let us prove that $\dfrac{OB}{OA} \geq \dfrac{1}{c}$.

We have $OB \geq OE$ and $AC \leq c \times EC$. Therefore,

$\dfrac{OB}{OA} \geq \dfrac{OE}{OA} = \dfrac{\sqrt{OC^2 + EC^2}}{\sqrt{OC^2 + AC^2}} = \dfrac{OC \times \sqrt{1 + \left(\dfrac{EC}{OC}\right)^2}}{OC \times \sqrt{1 + c^2 \times \left(\dfrac{EC}{OC}\right)^2}} = \dfrac{1}{c} \times \sqrt{\dfrac{1 + \left(\dfrac{EC}{OC}\right)^2}{\dfrac{1}{c^2} + \left(\dfrac{EC}{OC}\right)^2}}$. Since

$c \geq 1$, then $\sqrt{\dfrac{1 + \left(\dfrac{EC}{OC}\right)^2}{\dfrac{1}{c^2} + \left(\dfrac{EC}{OC}\right)^2}} \geq 1$, and hence, $\dfrac{OB}{OA} \geq \dfrac{1}{c}$.

Now we are ready to prove Lemma 4.4. We have $\dfrac{OB_i}{OA_i} \leq \dfrac{OB}{OA_i} = \dfrac{1}{OA_i} \times OB$.

Since $s_i(x)$ is monotonically decreasing, then $\dfrac{OA}{OA_i} \leq \dfrac{AC}{CH_i}$. Since the

heterogeneity of the processors is bounded by the constant c, then $\dfrac{AC}{CH_i} \leq c$.

Hence, $\dfrac{1}{OA_i} \leq \dfrac{c}{OA}$. Therefore, $\dfrac{OB_i}{OA_i} \leq \dfrac{c}{OA} \times OB = c \times \dfrac{OB}{OA} \leq c^2$. Next, we have

$\dfrac{OB_i}{OA_i} \geq \dfrac{OB_i}{OA}$. Since $s_i(x)$ is monotonically decreasing, then $\dfrac{BD}{F_iD} \geq \dfrac{OB}{OB_i}$. Since

the heterogeneity of the processors is bounded by the constant c, then $\dfrac{BD}{F_iD} \leq c$.

Therefore, $OB_i \geq \dfrac{OB}{c}$. Thus, $\dfrac{OB_i}{OA_i} \geq \dfrac{OB_i}{OA} \geq \dfrac{OB}{c \times OA} \geq \dfrac{1}{c^2}$.

This proves Lemma 4.4.

Bisection of the angle $\angle A_iOB_i$ at the very first iteration will divide the segment A_iB_i of the graph of the function $s_i(x)$ in the proportion $\dfrac{Q_iB_i}{A_iQ_i} \approx \dfrac{OB_i}{OA_i}$

(see Fig. B.2). Correspondingly, $\dfrac{x_i^{(L)} - x_i^{(M)}}{x_i^{(M)} - x_i^{(U)}} \approx \dfrac{OB_i}{OA_i}$. Since $(b - a)$ approximates

the number of integers in the interval $[a, b]$, $\Delta_i = \min\left\{\dfrac{x_i^{(L)} - x_i^{(M)}}{x_i^{(L)} - x_i^{(U)}}, \dfrac{x_i^{(M)} - x_i^{(U)}}{x_i^{(L)} - x_i^{(U)}}\right\}$

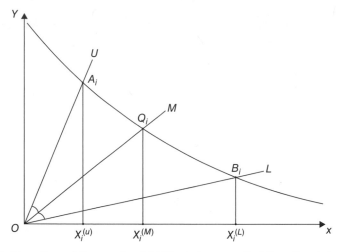

Figure B.2. Bisection of the angle $\angle A_i O B_i$ at the very first iteration into two equal angles. The segment $A_i B_i$ of the graph of the function $s_i(x)$ will be divided in the proportion $\dfrac{Q_i B_i}{A_i Q_i} \approx \dfrac{O B_i}{O A_i}$.

will approximate the lower bound on the fraction of the set $\{|x_i^{(U)}|, |x_i^{(U)}| + 1, \ldots, \lfloor x_i^{(L)} \rfloor\}$ of possible numbers of chunks to be allocated to the processor P_i, which is excluded from consideration after this bisection. Since $c_1 \le \dfrac{O B_i}{O A_i} \le c_2$, then $\Delta_i \ge \dfrac{c_1}{c_2 + 1} = \Delta$. Indeed, let $q_i = x_i^{(L)} - x_i^{(M)}$ and $r_i = x_i^{(M)} - x_i^{(U)}$. We have $c_1 \le \dfrac{q_i}{r_i} \le c_2$. Therefore, $c_1 \times r_i \le q_i \le c_2 \times r_i$ and

$(c_1 + 1) \times r_i \le q_i + r_i \le (c_2 + 1) \times r_i$. Hence, $\dfrac{q_i}{q_i + r_i} \ge \dfrac{c_1 \times r_i}{(c_2 + 1) \times r_i} = \dfrac{c_1}{c_2 + 1}$.

$\Delta_i \ge \dfrac{c_1}{c_2 + 1} = \Delta$ means that after this bisection, at least $\Delta \times 100\%$ of the possible solutions will be excluded from consideration for each processor P_i. The difference in length between $O B_i$ and $O A_i$ will be getting smaller and smaller with each next iteration. Therefore, no less than $\Delta \times 100\%$ of the possible solutions will be excluded from consideration after each iteration of Algorithm 4.2. The number of possible solutions in the initial set for each processor P_i is obviously less than n. The constant Δ does not depend on p or n (actually, this parameter just characterizes the heterogeneity of the set of processors). Therefore, the number of iterations k needed to arrive at the final solution can be found from the equation $(1 - \Delta)^k \times n = 1$, and we have

$k = \dfrac{1}{\log_2\left(\dfrac{1}{1-\Delta}\right)} \times \log_2 n$. Thus, overall, the complexity of Algorithm 4.2 will be

$O(p \times \log_2 n)$. Proposition 4.3 is proved.

B.4 FUNCTIONAL OPTIMIZATION PROBLEM WITH OPTIMAL SOLUTION, LOCALLY NONOPTIMAL

Consider a simple example with three processors $\{P_1, P_2, P_3\}$ distributing nine columns. Table B.1 shows the functional performance models of the processors $S = \{s_1(x,y), s_2(x,y), s_3(x,y)\}$, where $s_i(x,y)$ is the speed of the update of a $x \times y$ matrix by processor P_i.

Table B.2 shows the distribution of these nine columns, demonstrating that there may be no globally optimal allocation of columns that minimizes the execution time of all steps of the LU factorization.

The first column of Table B.2 represents the step k of the parallel LU factorization. The second column shows the global allocation of columns minimizing the total execution time of LU factorization. The third column shows the execution time of the step k of the LU factorization resulting from this allocation. The execution time $t_i^{(k)}$ for processor P_i needed to update a matrix of

size $(9-k) \times n_i^{(k)}$ is calculated as $\dfrac{V(9-k, n_i^{(k)})}{s_i(9-k, n_i^{(k)})} = \dfrac{(9-k) \times n_i^{(k)}}{s_i\left(9-k, n_i^{(k)}\right)}$, where $n_i^{(k)}$

TABLE B.1   Functional Model of Three Processors, P_1, P_2, P_3

Problem sizes (x,y)	$s_1(x,y)$	$s_2(x,y)$	$S_3(x,y)$
(1, 1), (1, 2), (1, 3), (1, 4), (1, 5), (1, 6), (1, 7), (1, 8)	6, 6, 6, 6, 6, 4, 4, 4	18, 18, 18, 18, 18, 18, 18, 2	18, 18, 18, 18, 18, 18, 18, 2
(2, 1), (2, 2), (2, 3), (2, 4), (2, 5), (2, 6), (2, 7), (2, 8)	6, 6, 6, 6, 5, 4, 3, 3	18, 18, 18, 18, 9, 8, 8, 2	18, 18, 18, 18, 15, 12, 8, 2
(3, 1), (3, 2), (3, 3), (3, 4), (3, 5), (3, 6), (3, 7), (3, 8)	6, 6, 6, 5, 4, 3, 3, 3	18, 18, 18, 9, 8, 8, 6, 2	18, 18, 18, 12, 8, 8, 8, 2
(4, 1), (4, 2), (4, 3), (4, 4), (4, 5), (4, 6), (4, 7), (4, 8)	6, 6, 5, 4, 3, 3, 3, 3	18, 18, 9, 9, 8, 6, 5, 2	18, 18, 12, 9, 8, 6, 6, 2
(5, 1), (5, 2), (5, 3), (5, 4), (5, 5), (5, 6), (5, 7), (5, 8)	6, 5, 4, 3, 3, 3, 2, 2	18, 9, 8, 8, 6, 5, 3, 1	18, 15, 8, 8, 6, 5, 5, 1
(6, 1), (6, 2), (6, 3), (6, 4), (6, 5), (6, 6), (6, 7), (6, 8)	4, 4, 3, 3, 3, 2, 1, 1	18, 8, 8, 6, 5, 3, 2, 1	18, 12, 8, 6, 5, 3, 3, 1
(7, 1), (7, 2), (7, 3), (7, 4), (7, 5), (7, 6), (7, 7), (7, 8)	4, 3, 3, 3, 2, 1, 1, 1	18, 8, 8, 6, 5, 3, 2, 1	18, 8, 8, 6, 5, 3, 2, 1
(8, 1), (8, 2), (8, 3), (8, 4), (8, 5), (8, 6), (8, 7), (8, 8)	4, 3, 3, 3, 2, 1, 1, 1	2, 2, 2, 2, 1, 1, 1, 1	2, 2, 2, 2, 1, 1, 1, 1

TABLE B.2 Distribution of Nine Column Panels over Three Processors, P_1, P_2, P_3

Step of LU factorization (k)	Global allocation of columns minimizing the overall execution time	Execution time of LU at step k	Local optimal distribution $\{n_1^{(k)}, n_2^{(k)}, n_3^{(k)}\}$ for problem size $(9-k, 9-k)$	Minimum possible execution time for problem size $(9-k, 9-k)$
1	$P_1P_1P_1P_1P_2P_3P_2P_3$	8	$\{4, 2, 2\}$	8
2	$P_1P_1P_1P_2P_3P_2P_3$	7	$\{2, 3, 2\}$	$\dfrac{14}{3}$
3	$P_1P_1P_2P_3\,P_2P_3$	3	$\{1, 2, 3\}$	$\dfrac{3}{2}$
4	$P_1P_2P_3P_2P_3$	$\dfrac{10}{9}$	$\{1, 2, 2\}$	$\dfrac{10}{9}$
5	$P_2P_3P_2P_3$	$\dfrac{4}{9}$	$\{0, 2, 2\}$	$\dfrac{4}{9}$
6	$P_3P_2P_3$	$\dfrac{1}{3}$	$\{0, 1, 2\}$	$\dfrac{1}{3}$
7	P_2P_3	$\dfrac{1}{9}$	$\{0, 1, 1\}$	$\dfrac{1}{9}$
8	P_3	$\dfrac{1}{18}$	$\{0, 0, 1\}$	$\dfrac{1}{18}$
Total execution time of LU factorization		20		

denotes the number of columns updated by the processor P_i (formula for the volume of computations explained below). The fourth column shows the distribution of columns, which results in the minimal execution time to solve the problem size $(9-k, 9-k)$ at step k of the LU factorization. This distribution is determined by considering all possible mappings and choosing the one that results in minimal execution time. The fifth column shows these minimal execution times for the problem size $(9-k, 9-k)$. For example, consider the step $k = 2$, the local optimal distribution resulting in the minimal execution time for the problem size $\{7, 7\}$ is $\{P_1\ P_1\ P_2\ P_2\ P_2\ P_3\ P_3\}$, the speeds given by the speed functions S shown in Table B.2 are $\{3, 8, 8\}$. So the number of columns assigned to processors $\{P_1, P_2, P_3\}$ are $\{2, 3, 2\}$, respectively. The execution times

are $\left\{\dfrac{7\times2}{3}, \dfrac{7\times3}{8}, \dfrac{7\times2}{8}\right\} = \left\{\dfrac{14}{3}, \dfrac{21}{8}, \dfrac{14}{8}\right\}$. The execution time to solve the

problem size $\{7, 7\}$ is the maximum of these execution times, $\dfrac{14}{3}$.

Consider again the step $k = 2$ shown in bold in the Table B.2. It can be seen that the global optimal allocation shown in the second column does not result in the minimal execution time for the problem size at this step, which is $\{7, 7\}$. The execution time of the LU factorization at this step based on the global optimal allocation is 7, whereas the minimal execution time given by the local optimal distribution for the problem size $\{7, 7\}$ at this step is $\dfrac{14}{3}$.

High-Performance Heterogeneous Computing, by Alexey L. Lastovetsky and Jack J. Dongarra
Copyright © 2009 John Wiley & Sons, Inc.